W9-API-453

Infertility

Renate D. Klein has a biology degree from Zurich University and degrees in Women's Studies from the University of California and London University. She is co-editor with Gloria Bowles of *Theories of Women's Studies* (Routledge, 1983) and Rita Arditti and Shelley Minden of *Test-Tube Women: What Future for Motherhood?* (Pandora Press, 1984) and co-author with Gena Corea et al. of *Man-Made Women* (Hutchinson, 1985). In 1986 she was awarded the Georgina Sweet Fellowship to research the experiences of women who drop out of test-tube baby programmes in Australia. She is currently a research fellow at Deakin University, Victoria, Australia, where she is continuing her research on the new reproductive technologies and genetic engineering. Renate Klein is a founding member of the Feminist International Network of Resistance to Reproductive and Genetic Engineering (FINRRAGE), an editor of *Reproductive and Genetic Engineering: Journal of International Feminist Analysis*, the *Athene Series*: an international collection of feminist books and the *Women's Studies International Forum*.

Infertility

Women speak out

ABOUT THEIR EXPERIENCES OF REPRODUCTIVE MEDICINE

WOMEN'S COLLEGE HOSPITAL

WOMEN'S HEALTH CENTRE

THE RESOURCE CENTRE

EDITED BY

RENATE D.KLEIN

PANDORA

PANDORA PRESS

London   Sydney   Wellington

WP
570
I77
1989
0000 1143

First published by Pandora Press, an imprint of the Trade
Division of Unwin Hyman, in 1989.

© Renate D. Klein, 1989, except for 'Transferring one
woman's pain to another is not the solution' which
is © Elizabeth Kane, 1989 and 'Battleground' which
is © Susan Eisenberg, 1986.

All rights reserved. No part of this publication may be reproduced,
stored in a retrieval system, or transmitted in any form or by any means,
electronic, mechanical, recording or otherwise, without the prior
permission of Unwin Hyman Limited.

PANDORA PRESS
Unwin Hyman Limited
15/17 Broadwick Street
London W1V 1FP

Unwin Hyman Inc
8 Winchester Place, Winchester, MA 01890

Allen & Unwin Australia Pty Ltd
P.O. Box 764, 8 Napier Street, North Sydney, NSW 2060

Allen & Unwin NZ Ltd (in association with the
Port Nicholson Press)
60 Cambridge Terrace, Wellington, New Zealand

British Library Cataloguing in Publication Data
Infertility: Women speak out about their
experiences of reproductive medicine
   1. Woman. Infertility
   I. Title   II. Klein, Renate D.
   618.1'78
   ISBN 0-04-440367-4

Phototypeset by Input Typesetting Ltd, London,
in 10/11 pt Plantin
Printed in Finland by WSOY

Back Cover photo: Ponch Hawkes

Contents

■

CONTENTS

For all the women
who say **NO** to
reproductive technology

ACKNOWLEDGEMENTS

.

Obviously, this book would not exist without the women who wrote the pieces – be it of their own experiences or of an interview with a woman who had undergone an infertility 'treatment' – so to you go my heartfelt thanks for all your hard work, patience in rewriting, and your commitment to telling the shocking stories. I also thank you for keeping faith in me that, one day, this book would be published – in the face of contributions that could not be written because it was too painful, cross-continent mail that must have been dropped in some ocean, somewhere in the world, and other delays. Specifically, I want to thank the forty women who contributed to my study on the impact of test-tube baby technology on their lives in Australia and whose words are dispersed throughout the book in special inserts. I want to acknowledge how much I learnt from meeting tough articulate women who survived the arrogance, pain and dehumanizing experience of reproductive technologies – and their executors – that, upon hearing them, made me feel sick and angry at the same time. I express my hope that many more will speak out about their experiences when they have read this book **and know that they are not alone, that it is not their fault** – and that they don't have to remain silent.

Then there are all the women from FINRRAGE who gave support in one way or another; among them in Australia Christine Ewing, Lariane Fonseca, Sarah Ferber and Christine Crowe; in England Debbie Steinberg (who has prepared the Glossary and Index with such care), Jalna Hanmer and Pat Spallone; in Sweden Cynthia de Wit; in Bangladesh Farida Akhter; in Israel Alison Solomon; in West Germany Maria Mies, Ute Winkler, Helga Satzinger, Barbara Orland; in France Françoise Laborie; in Ireland Rita Burtenshaw; in Denmark Lene Koch and in the

USA Rita Arditti, Shelley Minden and above all Gena Corea whose courageous groundbreaking work on the new reproductive technologies makes her 'the mother' of us all who are concerned about the impact of these technologies on women: to all of you goes a big 'thank you'.

I also thank the many women who in one way or another have helped with a name, a newspaper clipping, a discussion, a meal or a hug when I needed it; among them Diane Bell, Mona Howard, Susanne von Paczensky, Jeanette Winterson, Lynne Spender, Renate Sadrozinski, Hanni Wiederkehr, Gloria Bowles, Jocelynne Scutt, Maresi Nerad, Ros Lewis, Annette Burfoot, Louise Vandelac, Diana Russell, Vimal Balasubrahmanyan, Phyllis Hall, Helga Dierichs, Cheris Kramarae, Charlotte Bunch, Lynette Drumble, Ros de Lanerolle, Sneja Gunew, Ginny West-wood, Rose Mildenhall, Margret Krannich, Annette Goerlich, Manisha Gupte and Ailbhe Smyth. Dale Spender's support has been such a constant in my life for so many years that I couldn't imagine what it would be like if her many notes stopped coming through the mail. Christine Zmroczek's friendship is an ongoing pleasure and great delight even if at present, unfortunately, we couldn't be further apart, geographically speaking. And Janice Raymond's sharp mind and committed friendship have often helped me get clearer about what I really want to say. In addition I am grateful to Claire French, Melbourne, and Della Couling, London, for translating some of the German pieces. And I thank my parents, Finy and Hermann Klein, for their support and love.

Since one has to eat whilst compiling and editing books, my thanks go to the Australian Federation of University Women for awarding me the Georgina Sweet Fellowship to do research in Australia, particularly to Jenny Barker, and to the Women's Studies Program and Deakin University for appointing me as their Post-Doctoral Research Fellow from 1987 to 1989. My thanks also go to the secretaries at Deakin who patiently typed many pages of transcripts of interviews: Judy Barker, Nancy Stefanovic, Jane Veale, Bev Bartlett and Jan Wapling as well as Claire Warren and Chele Matthews in Melbourne who typed most of this manuscript.

Candida Lacey and Philippa Brewster of Pandora Press were wonderful: the instant support and enthusiasm they showed for this book meant a lot to me. Candida Lacey in particular deserves a medal for being *the* most efficient and helpful editor and I am deeply indebted to her for the patience with which she bore with 'Swissisms' and other idiosyncrasies in my writing. And I am grateful to Jill Holmden for her sensitive copy-editing and to Heather Kelly for her careful proofreading.

Finally, words cannot begin to express my gratitude and thanks to Robyn Rowland and Susan Hawthorne. Their friendship and love has been a constant source of support, energy and joy in my life over the past years. With Robyn I share the passionate commitment to ending all violence against women, including the damage done by reproductive technology and I thank her for the many hours she spent reading and commenting on this manuscript and for her encouragement of my work in general. I am looking forward to many more joint projects: hard work and good laughs – not forgetting the fiery dances afterwards! With Sue I share life with the Australian fauna – possums in the roof and blue tongue lizards in the garden – and an exciting supply of feminist novels and radical feminist theory (not to speak of the word processor). I thank her for being a sister spirit and for her wonderful kindness, generosity of the heart and the tremendous amount of encouragement (including substantial amounts of chocolate) which made me go on even when the task seemed endless. Her own writing is an inspiration and I thank her for the light she has brought into my life.

Melbourne, August 1988

THE MAKING OF THIS BOOK

.

RENATE KLEIN

Since the birth of the first child conceived *in vitro* (in the glass) outside a woman's body in 1978 – Louise Brown in England – reproductive medicine, and specifically the 'test-tube baby method', has been a highly publicized media topic in the western world.

Hailed as a 'miracle cure' for infertility and an end to the anguish of involuntary childlessness, the media has glamorized *in vitro* fertilization (IVF) and portrayed the doctors and scientists who promote it as benevolent 'lab-fathers' whose work is selfless devotion to people with a fertility problem. Stories about donating eggs and hiring so-called surrogate mothers, freezing eggs and embryos and setting up egg banks regularly appear in the press. We are also led to believe that experimentation on embryos, which can be done only by creating embryos after appropriating a woman's eggs from her ovaries and fertilizing them with sperm outside her body, promises enormous benefits to humankind.

In presenting new reproductive technology as an exciting 'scientific breakthrough' and 'technological progress', and IVF as a 'standard procedure', scientists, doctors and the media alike mislead the general public into believing that IVF is a successful technology. In reality it is a *failed* technology, with 'success rates' ranging internationally between only 5 and 10 per cent. In other words, out of 100 women who begin IVF, only five to ten will have a baby – and this often after repeated attempts. Such biased reporting also hides the fact that the IVF procedure contains dangerous health hazards for women: dangerous because the invasive technology, and especially the hormones administered to the women to 'superovulate' them (stimulating their ovaries so that they will produce more than one ripe egg per month), brings with it the risk of burst ovaries (as many as forty-seven eggs have been collected at one time), ovarian cysts, septicaemia, adhesions and a host of other so-called 'side effects'. The adverse reactions to these 'hormonal cocktails' range from migraine, dizziness, vision problems, weight gain and depression to breast cancer and ovarian cancer. Also, it is to be feared that children who are born to women subjected to these drugs – specifically, clomiphene citrate – might be affected in similar ways as children of women who took DES because of structural similarities in the chemistry of the two drugs. (Diethylstilbestrol was a drug given to 4–6 million pregnant women between the 1940s and the early 1970s to prevent miscarriage. It was never proven to be effective. Years later, many of the women who had taken the drug developed breast cancer. Moreover, a high number of their children now have fertility problems, specifically the women who have increased rates of spontaneous abortions, ectopic pregnancies, premature deliveries as well as cancers of the vagina and cervix.)

The public is not informed about what these technologies involve. *Even more importantly: the women who are considering undergoing IVF are not told what these 'miracle cures' entail*. Neither do we know what women feel, think and experience when they discover their own or their partner's fertility problem and decide to undergo medical investigation. This is an obvious discrepancy given the fact that it is on *women's bodies* that the doctors and scientists perform their experiments: women are being used as living test-sites for drugs and new techniques. Little is said about the often long and extremely painful journeys that lead women through a host of 'conventional' infertility treatments into IVF. And even less is known about the complex reasons why a considerable number of women with a fertility problem decide to use invasive medical procedures in an attempt to have their own child at any price – and why some don't.

Why children at any price? Is it – as many say – the individual passionate desire to care for and nurture children? The wish for intimacy? To become a 'proper' adult and assume responsibility? Is it to achieve a sense of identity and importance – to see it in a more political context – in a world in which, sadly, for many women, motherhood is the only 'power' they might obtain whilst, as *women*, we remain oppressed and powerless? How much of the pain of infertility is a result of the enormous *stigma* attached to the inability to give birth to one's own child? How often is pressure put on a woman to give her husband 'his' child? And how deeply ingrained is the assumption that *all* women have always wanted and needed to be mothers – in spite of the fact that poor women, women of 'undesirable' ethnicities and women in 'Third World' countries are kept from having children? In what ways does science exploit women's vulnerability when they feel that if they want to have a child, they cannot question any of the procedures offered but must comply with what they are told? Is this 'choice' or, rather, should we speak of *coercion*? And, most importantly, to what extent can reproductive medicine with its focus on the 'defective' parts of the woman ever be successful in relieving the sense of incompleteness which some infertile women experience?

It is questions like these that this book explores. As a feminist critic who together with many other women internationally has spent the last six years investigating the impact of these new technologies on women, I was often confronted with people who said, 'But women want it . . .' or even worse 'these women are neurotic, obsessed . . .' I felt that it was time that women described their *own* experiences of infertility and rejected the popular (patriarchal) belief that it was they who had *asked* for this kind of dehumanized technology, and that, somehow – to add insult to injury – because they were in the predicament of wanting a child for one reason or another, they had to be grateful that they were offered this technological 'fix'.

I set out to find women who would be willing to write about their feelings and experiences with reproductive medicine. This was no easy task. But through assistance from FINRRAGE (an international feminist network critical of these technologies) and my own research in Australia with forty women who had left IVF programmes without a child, I soon had many contacts. Without exception, women were willing to talk to me, and I spent many fascinating, if often emotionally difficult hours listening to their stories of the many paradoxes, dilemmas and contradictions they experienced with their fertility problem. The sense of desperation followed by hope – and then desperation again . . . and again, when the technologies did not deliver the promised goods, was overwhelming; as was their sense of de-stabilization when their lives were – and are – in limbo for years because, 'perhaps next month it will work'. Overwhelming too was *my* anger at hearing what the women were subjected to – all under the guise of 'helping' them to have a child. I became even more determined to make their experiences known to the general public.

This is what this book sets out to do. Writing from a variety of backgrounds and a range of countries, mainly in their own words, sometimes in interview form, the women in this book talk passionately about the impact of their fertility problem on their lives. They describe the medical procedures they underwent *and* the many 'failures' they experienced. Their stories are painfully honest, infuriating and deeply distressing. The myth of benevolent medicine is shattered and what emerges is overwhelming evidence of invasive technologies that often severely violate a woman's sense of dignity. Disturbingly, the women's experiences also reveal an enormous amount of medical malpractice: reproductive medicine appears to be built on the premise that in order to 'know' there must be female 'guinea pigs' . . . and that only after having 'statistical' proof of severe problems might a medical procedure be stopped or a drug withdrawn from the market. Equally disturbing are the many stories which make it clear that having once begun this process, many of the women feel trapped in the medical treadmill. 'Giving up: The choice that isn't' says Kirsten Kozolanka from Canada and I hope her reflections will make readers understand some of the painful dilemmas that make it so difficult for women to 'quit' once they have stepped through the specialist's door.

Part One is about women's experiences of conventional infertility treatment. For women, infertility frequently means years of hiding in shame, offering to divorce their partners, swallowing dangerous and debilitating hormone-like drugs, turning their sex life into a reproductive performance according to temperature charts and hormone levels and letting their work, relationship and sense of self be dominated by the demands of their gynaecologists. For some this experience ends with having a child; others decide to adopt. One Dutch woman speaks for many when she says, 'Infertility is a lingering process'. If we lived in a world in which infertility was not seen as a 'disease' that can be 'cured', these technologies would not be needed and women's suffering from technological accidents and experimental procedures could be avoided. As it is, pressures from society can turn a fertility problem into a curse which provokes feelings of guilt, anxiety, loss of self-esteem, severe depression, and above all the desperate belief that, 'I have to try one more time, one more procedure'.

Part Two looks at the IVF procedure. What becomes apparent is that IVF is a continuation of 'conventional' fertility treatments: there is a range of overlapping procedures and the 'trial and error' approach is continued. In the 'test-tube world', however, there is even more interest in advancing the 'frontiers' of science by experimenting on living women. IVF is less successful than 'conventional' infertility treatment and is an extremely taxing experience, both physiologically and psychologically, which may severely damage the women's health and well-being. Moreover, because many women see IVF as a last resort and repeat the procedure many times over many years, their despair when it does not work is even greater than when conventional infertility treatment fails them.

Part Three considers how fertile women are also exploited in the name of infertility. Introduced by Gena Corea, five women – so called ex-surrogate mothers, among them Elizabeth Kane who was the US's first 'surrogate' – speak out about their shocking experiences. Some were prescribed drugs so that they superovulated and produced their eggs more quickly and conveniently for the insemination doctors. This is just one indication of how the range and application of reproductive technologies is quickly extending to fertile women.

Part Four draws on the previous chapters and includes women's suggestions of how to deal constructively with infertility *without* using reproductive medicine. Talking from personal experience, Alison Solomon from Israel describes the severe crisis which an infertility problem can trigger and offers ideas on how to cope, survive – and thrive. Lindsey Napier, founder of *Concern*, a self-help group in Sydney, Australia, talks about ideas for an alternative vision of infertility as 'in-fertility': a state of being that has many facets. Specifically, she suggests that feminists –

without being patronizing or condescending – should develop support systems for women with a fertility problem in order to make it possible for them to resist the technologies. Traute Schönenberg and Ute Winkler from West Germany talk about their experiences of offering groups for women with a fertility problem at the Feminist Health Centre in Frankfurt and Ann Pappert from Canada proposes that infertile women should take an active role in feminist campaigns against the new reproductive technologies.

Part Five contextualises the women's experiences and assess the impact of reproductive technology and its twin, genetic engineering, on *all* women now and in the future. I present an overview of the latest international technological developments and focus specifically on what these technologies might come to mean for women in the so-called 'Third World'. The directions are unmistakable; the ongoing harmful experiments to develop new contraceptives that are being carried out on women's bodies in these countries prefigure what is to come. This is the other side of a brutal ideology which sees women as mere breeders who need to be controlled: not fertile enough in some countries, too fertile in others. I then conclude with a call for international resistance and a brief review of actions feminists in many countries have undertaken against these technologies over the last few years.

So the book ends on a positive note. All the women who speak out in these pages are survivors and I hope that their insights in recounting their experiences as well as envisaging new models of 'in-fertility' and of trying to lead their lives differently will be inspiring to other women and give them the courage and stamina to say **no** to technological intervention. If you have a fertility problem I hope that this book will help you to say 'No, I don't have to undergo any of this technological intervention', and thereby save yourself years of painful and most probably unsuccessful treatments. And if you have similar stories to tell about your *own* experiences with reproductive medicine, *do* speak out – let the world know what is happening to thousands of women worldwide under the guise of 'scientific progress'.

The increasing medicalization of reproduction via the new technologies will affect *all* women's control over their lives in the very near future and *resistance* is urgently needed. There is a great deal at stake for doctors, scientists and pharmaceutical companies who make their fortunes – and/or gain academic fame – from experimenting on women or, as in the case of surrogacy, selling women's bodies as incubators for the 'product', the child. 'In-fertility' as a complex and variable state of being which is not 'second-best' and which does not necessarily have to be 'overcome' by having one's own biological child, needs to be acknowledged by a larger part of society, including people with a fertility problem. Only then will women have a *real* choice to say 'No' to conventional fertility treatment as well as to IVF.

Reproductive medicine fails women. As one Australian woman said: 'The only ones it works for are the scientists and doctors – not us'. Women *do* have the power to withdraw our services and we should act on this.

PART ONE

.

Infertility Treatments

Our families – and particularly my in-laws – were shocked and, as they told me, disappointed not to have grand-children. Since I told them they've treated me very condescendingly . . . with a mixture of pity and contempt . . . somewhere along the lines that I was now a sick person who could not be taken seriously.

Increasingly, I felt displaced at family events. Everyone had children but us. Although I'd just been promoted I know Mum's eyes would have lighted up much more if I had announced 'I'm pregnant'.

Eventually I told more and more people that it was Tom's problem because *everybody* assumed it was my fault and I felt very pressured by their patronizing approach to me.

After the gynaecologist had spoken the verdict 'blocked tubes', I went straight to a birthday party for one of my best friends. I couldn't contain myself and broke the news to everyone. But I got quite annoyed with the responses. I'm sure they meant well but within minutes I was swamped with advice that ranged from 'see a herbalist' to 'try IVF' and from 'cold baths' to 'relax'. I got really angry when one of Alan's friends offered to 'fill in' – so that I could be shown how 'one really makes babies'. It was the first and last time I mentioned the infertility in public.

There's one lady at work who's got three kids and she just won't have the infertility. She said, 'Look, I've got a friend who had her first baby at forty, and you've still got four years to go, and you know, you're not to give up.' And I said, 'Yes, but I'm sick of it, you know, it's been thirteen years and I've had enough.' 'No,' she said, 'you can't give up. Not yet!'

GIVE ME CHILDREN, OR ELSE I DIE

.

KATHARINA STENS*
West Germany

'And when Rachel saw that she bare Jacob no children, Rachel envied her sister; and said unto Jacob, Give me children, or else I die.'

(Genesis 30:1)

'At least four,' I answered, laughing, at my lover's question about how many children I wanted. It was not until the following day that I could tell him that, since my stay as an exchange student in the USA five years earlier, I had not had my period. Gynaecologists assured me that organically there was nothing to prevent a pregnancy – these disturbances in the cycle mostly pass of their own accord.

Being a medical doctor myself, I am certainly a critical and troublesome patient; I ask questions and then persist with more. Looking back over the events I will tell now, I by no means consider myself a passive victim, but know that I *actively* subjected myself to this violation of my body. Nor do I wish to disparage reproductive medicine. Instead, this account is intended far more as a stimulus towards thinking about what technology does to us in a sphere as intimate as human procreation.

Over the years I became increasingly uneasy and repeatedly consulted gynaecologists. My head was X-rayed: no trace of a brain tumour. The hormone levels in the blood were tested: adequate basal quantities of sex hormones. The size and position

* This is a pseudonym. The author is a doctor.

of the ovaries and uterus were repeatedly examined and declared normal. I felt my absent periods as an existential deficiency, as proof that I was not a complete woman; it was an aching wound that I tried to conceal with all sorts of activities, in order to convince myself and others how wonderful I was: intelligent, witty, enterprising . . . What good to me was a gynaecologist's remark that I should be happy not to have periods, as they were only a nuisance (for him as a man?). Anyway, if I wanted to, he added, I could get pregnant any time, for modern gynaecology that would pose no problem.

In 1981, two years after these initial enquiries, we married: young, in love, naive, looking hopefully towards our future together. We never thought much about marriage, it just seemed an automatic consequence of our friendship. And we wanted children soon too! We didn't think much about that either . . .

I began looking for a woman doctor as I was furious with all those men who had been rummaging around my lower abdomen. Once there had even been two of them: a student in his final year was allowed to increase his experience using my body, without seeking my consent. I didn't think I could stand any more of this permanent humiliation, and hoped for more understanding and sympathy from a woman. It is more pleasant to be examined by a woman, without the presence of third parties. I can relax my abdominal walls better, when I'm lying half naked and shivering on the examination table, legs raised and spread out, infinitely vulnerable.

The new diagnostic procedure involved the measurement of hormone levels in the blood, and collection of urine every twenty-four hours. At first I resisted. I could not imagine how to deposit a two litre container unnoticed at work and keep carting it off to the toilet. The doctor told me I had to do it, otherwise I could forget the therapy. But these laborious examinations did not yield any new aspects. Both the old and new diagnosis said amenorrhoea caused by malfunction of the hypothalamus. By this time I knew the information in my gynaecology textbook by heart: a mostly functional, psychogenic-psychoreactive disorder.

I came across an article by a psychoanalyst who argued that an important part of infertility in women was often suppressed aggression, the result of poor mothering by a woman who did not allow her daughter any life of her own and therefore hindered her development as a fertile woman capable of sustaining relationships. In such cases the longed-for child becomes the carrier of all hopes, a substitute for one's own unfulfilled finding of self. According to the article, infertile women often have shaky self-confidence and a sense of inferiority as women. They have high expectations of every important person, whom they easily idealize and regard as omnipotent, and also a defensive readiness to reproach and be aggressive as well as a profound fear of getting close to anyone. But this purely intellectual view was unable to help me; on the contrary, it drove me even more deeply into despair. It was not difficult to recognize myself in this description, at least partially. But, I asked myself, might not these personality traits of infertile women described by the analyst not only be the cause, but also the result, of years of disappointment through the unfulfilled desire to have children? Many questions without answers.

His spermatogram was normal; the therapy on my body could begin. Every morning I measured my temperature before getting up, every day I had the feeling of failing as a woman. No temperature rise, no ovulation. 'It's only right and proper that a "defective" woman like you can't have a baby.' This thought settled in my mind.

Next I was swallowing tablets that stimulate ovulation. I tried to reduce the nausea by taking them in the evening. On each of the days during which ovulation might occur, before or during working hours I dashed to examinations; more probing of the ovaries through the abdominal walls; more cervical smears when the doctor considered it worthwhile. I slept with my husband every day if necessary, in spite of my night duty at the hospital, we went on until desire and sperm were exhausted.

I began to sense that this course of violently enforced action could not be the right way to conceive a child, but I did not want to leave anything untried. If I did, I thought, I would reproach myself later for having missed an opportunity. But when the doctor insisted on a diagnostic laparoscopy to check that the fallopian tubes were not blocked and wanted to send me to hospital as an in-patient for three days, I finally refused to co-operate.

I talked twice with a psychiatrist, the first doctor I felt able to trust. He advised psychoanalysis, recommending a woman analyst in the nearby city. After three discussions with me in the summer of 1983 she said that she would like to take over the therapy, but had no time free in the foreseeable future. I could apply again in one and a half years. Would I like to try with one of her colleagues? But he too had an equally long waiting list. So for the time being I could not expect much help from the psychotherapeutic side either.

I then went to see an infertility specialist. I found him more likeable than his predecessors, but he too concentrated only on the desolate state of my hormone balance, which he thought he would be able to clear up. He considered psychoanalysis totally superfluous and only when I insisted did he agree to a discussion with a psychologist, who sometimes worked with him. But the meeting with her was disappointing, we did not manage to really connect with one another, and I felt I was being fobbed off by meaningless phrases.

After renewed X-ray and laboratory tests I was now going to ultrasound examinations twice a week with a very full, painful bladder, as only in this way will the ovaries appear on the screen. 'Not really a problem,' I told myself, 'get up early in the morning, do not eat breakfast, but instead drink a litre of black tea . . .' First of all a cyst – a liquid-filled cavity – was discovered in my left ovary which, I was told, should be operated on and removed as quickly as possible. I resisted this and managed to postpone the operation time and time again. Repeated ultrasound examinations revealed that taking tablets had not caused any adequate growth of the follicles in the ovaries. I was told that now, more drastic measures needed to be taken.

Beforehand, however, it had to be proved that my fallopian tubes were not blocked. In contrast to his colleague, this gynaecologist did not insist on a laparoscopy, but was happy with an X-ray. In the leaflet on display in the waiting-room I read: 'For an X-ray examination of the uterine cavity and the fallopian tubes – a hysterosalpinogram – an X-ray "contrast meal" is injected without anaesthetic through the cervix. By means of several X-rays it can then be ascertained whether the uterine cavity has filled up and how far the X-ray "contrast meal" has flowed via the fallopian tubes into the abdominal cavity.'

This was the only information available. Totally unsuspecting, during the lunch break I made my way to one of the large X-ray practices in the city. Sitting on a sort of gynaecological examination couch, my lower body bared, I was greeted by the radiologist. A tearing pain went through me when he injected the 'contrast meal'. After the examination, blood was flowing from my vagina. Without a word, I received an intravenous penicillin injection and a prescription for penicillin tablets, which I was to take over the following days in order to prevent any infection of the lower abdominal region. When I left the practice, wobbly at the knees, I was quite decided not to do this. Two hours later, while I myself was examining a patient, I was suddenly gripped by a cramp in my lower abdomen such as I had never felt before. I spent the next few hours curled up on a couch in my boss's room. How I cycled home that evening still remains a mystery to me. I then swallowed the penicillin tablets with an air of desperation. Subsequently I learned in discussions with other women that the pain and cramps did not only occur in my case, but are typical. This X-ray examination, the result of which showed no abnormality, was the prelude to the events of the following weeks.

I was now supplied with the hormone from the brain essential for maturation of the egg cells, the so-called gonadotropin releasing hormone (GnRH), by means of a newly developed hormone pump. This device, the size of a cigarette packet, called a 'cyclomat', is carried out of sight under one's clothing on a narrow belt. Every ninety minutes it pumps a small amount of the missing hormone through a thin plastic tube directly into a vein in the upper arm. Putting the tube in place caused a lot of bleeding; the bandage had to be opened and adjusted. This was probably one of the causes of inflammation of the vein on my upper right arm.

Although I should have known better, at first I ignored the pain. One morning, when I was the only physician on duty in the practice, I was suddenly unable to move my arm because of the pain. I was also shivering and had a temperature. In between treating patients, I lay down for a few minutes on the examination couch, until a colleague took over at midday. I just about managed to drag myself to the gynaecologist. In his view there was nothing much wrong. He pulled the plastic tube out of the inflamed vein on my right arm and then inserted a new tube into a vein on my upper left arm. I did not take the anti-inflammation medicine he had given me as it only suppresses the body's own powers of resistance.

Back at home, I finally collapsed, and for five days I remained in bed with a high temperature and an inflamed vein. During this time I wrote the following:

> The 'pump' on my left arm; in my upper right arm a fat thrombophlebitis . . . I myself in doubt, if not even in despair, feeling infinitely helpless, out of control, worthless, for days always close to tears, often in tears, in fact, the tube in my left arm – how ludicrous. In me two 'loosened up ovaries', stimulated by the 'gonadotropin releasing hormone' – on the sonograph (?) they look like two Swiss cheeses. When is ovulation, when 'must' we sleep together – am I not deceiving myself if I believe one can conceive a child in this way???. . . . I have the feeling I am asking too much of him, pulling him down into my depths of despair. How much longer can he and will he go along with this?

The tube in my left arm led to 'only' a local inflammation without high temperature. I carried the pump for about twenty days, but contrary to the assurances of the manufacturers – 'Most patients completely forget after a short time that they are carrying a small device on their body' – I could not get used to this foreign object.

The expected success did not take place this time either; obstinate as I was, my body refused to co-operate – for which I am thankful today. As a souvenir of my life with the pump there remains a pencil-thick strand on my upper right arm – the residual state of the inflamed vein, in which blood will probably never flow again – and a new knowledge of reproductive medicine, which I later tried to express in a poem:

Sterility

the pump generates
the GnRH stimulates
the ovum ovulates

the mucous membrane menstruates
the body copulates
even if it conceives
who is in therapy here?

A renewed attempt with the hormone pump was totally out of the question for me. As a rule this treatment is only given up after several unsuccessful attempts. The gynaecologist next suggested treatment with human gonadotropin (a hormone from the pituitary gland). I could do the daily intramuscular injections myself, at home, although two to three times a week I had to collect urine specimens every twenty-four hours and go to the practice in the mornings for ultrasound examinations. The possible complications could not frighten me off. The complications included a danger of over-stimulation of the ovaries with cyst formation and a 25 per cent chance of multiple pregnancies, of which most are twins. This time my ovaries reacted at once to the treatment. In spite of low amounts of hormones, soon numerous cysts with diameters of up to several centimetres were discernible in the ultrasound. The oestrogen counts in the urine went soaring up. On my examination chart I read the remark: *CAVE!!!* (careful!!!); any further addition of hormones threatens to burst the ovaries. And so this attempt too had to be abandoned and a suspension of treatment imposed for several weeks during which time the cysts slowly receded. To my question about why my body reacted on one occasion too sluggishly, and on another too excessively, the gynaecologist could give no satisfactory answer. The inner environment of my ovaries is disturbed, he said, that is why no regular maturation of the ova can occur. Faced with these facts, he seemed to be just as helpless as I was.

If over the past months I had constantly doubted the technological manipulations of my body, the situation now seemed totally futile to me. Myself and a baby, a wish against all laws of nature. The sight of pregnant women and the presence of friends' small children became unbearable. A three-week holiday in sunny Greece brought hardly any relief. After returning to a cold Germany everything looked even more hopeless. More and more frequently I had days in which, out of sheer despair, I simply did not want to live any more.

And then, in December 1985, just after the beginning of

psychoanalysis it happened: a completely unexpected telephone call from the Youth Welfare Department, where for a long time we had been registered as wanting to adopt a child. On the third Advent day we were presented with a little girl, just four weeks old.

Since then over a year has passed. The baby with fat hamster cheeks has become an extremely lively little fidget, a happy child radiating *joie de vivre*, whom I never cease to wonder at. Since January 1986 I have been having my periods spontaneously, still irregularly, anxiously awaited every month, but mostly after ovulation. I know again how wonderful an orgasm can be. My attitude to wanting children has changed: not to make them, but to let them come. I am still young, not yet thirty, but even if I were not to get pregnant, I think I can accept my fate better.

NOWHERE FOR ME TO BE

.

MARGARET LEWIS*
Australia

Margaret Lewis is the pseudonym of an
Australian woman who lives in Sydney.

I've been chasing a baby since I was twenty-two. I'm now thirty-
five. I want to try to do more with my life other than focus on
whether or not I have a baby. This is very hard for me to say,
because although I think I've come to accept my infertility on an
intellectual level, it's been my experience that no matter how
much I prepare myself, when the thought of my infertility
suddenly comes up, there's still an emotional backlash, something
I'm completely unprepared for, and something I've got to work
through each time.

I used to assume that one day I would be a mother, a biological
mother. The only thing I thought when I was sixteen or seventeen
was of meeting somebody, getting married, buying a house, and
having a baby, or babies. That's how I saw my life. Today I
think differently . . . I question a lot more.

I didn't assume that every woman should be a mother. Later
on I realized that being a mother was something I really wanted

---

* This interview was conducted and edited by Christine Crowe. Infertility, although a 'hidden' condition, is at the same time, for many
women, often a condition which places them under considerable social
scrutiny. In this article one woman speaks of her experience of infertility;
how it has affected her sense of identity and her social relationships.
Christine Crowe wishes to thank 'Margaret Lewis' who wishes to be
anonymous, for her courage, insight and revelations.

to do. I had a lot of loving in me and it seemed to me that the only way to share it was by having a child. I do feel less feminine because I am not a mother. It's that very intimate caring, the looking after a more vulnerable person, that I miss. When you look beyond conceiving, which did occupy my thoughts for a very long time, it's the caring that's ultimately the most important for me. I really wanted that very intimate, very physical relationship with a baby or child.

It took a long time for me to realize, to accept, that I had a fertility problem. I kept getting different stories from different doctors. As far as I know, I have adhesions around my left ovary. These adhesions prevent the egg from getting out of the ovary and into the fallopian tube. According to the last report, the right ovary wasn't producing any eggs – even though I have taken fertility drugs such as Perganol and Clomid to stimulate this production. This is all I can tell you after quite a few years of investigations.

In the beginning I was told that my fertility problem was 'just a matter of time'. I saw one gynaecologist every month for two years. Every month he would do a 'dilation of the cervix' to stretch it. He would then say: 'Go home now and get pregnant' – and I never did become pregnant.

During this time I had to take my temperature every morning, for two years. I had to fill in a chart and bring it back to the doctor. I got upset about this procedure, especially when my period was due. At that stage I was desperately trying *not* to think about whether or not I was pregnant . . . and the very first thing I would have to do when I woke up in the morning was take my temperature. It set the tone of the day, and it was terrible. When you're trying to become pregnant, and you have to time things according to the day of the month, sex and lovemaking becomes a very dull and uninteresting routine. It's degrading . . . and sometimes it's just impossible to have sex according to a timetable. I know I'm not the only woman in this situation who has put circles around certain days of the month, indicating that they have had sex on those days, when it hasn't happened at all. I wanted to be a 'good' patient, and also, if we had not had sex for a week or so, I would put a circle anyway, just so the doctor would not wonder whether anything was wrong with the marriage.

I finally got to the point where I said to myself: 'There's just got to be more to my infertility treatment than this!' That's when I started going to see other doctors.

Over the years I've been told that my infertility was caused by various things. One gynaecologist said that I had fibroids on the outside of the uterus, and that these needed to be removed, so I had surgery to remove the fibroids. After a while it became obvious that there must be something else causing my fertility problem, so I consulted another doctor. According to this doctor, I had a retroverted uterus, and the only 'cure' was surgery. So I agreed to more surgery. I've had so many operations to 'fix' various parts of my body, so that I can have a baby. Each time I was told that *this* piece of surgery would cure the problem.

When you don't know your chances of becoming pregnant, when you are trying month after month, the hope that you will become pregnant is always there. It usually sets you up for a lot of pain too. I remember, for example, going to one doctor when my period was ten days late, I was elated, really high. He told me that I was pregnant. Well, by the time I'd driven home from his surgery, a journey which takes about one hour, I was bleeding. I had to pull over to the side of the road. That experience, to me, was one of the worst, because I'd built up hope for those ten days, and thought that the doctor had confirmed my hopes.

I just don't know whether all of the operations I've had have actually caused the adhesions. Some women suffer more than others from adhesions after surgery. I know that it's pointless to speculate at this stage, but I can't help but wonder.

After several years I ended up going to the fertility clinic at the hospital. It was there that I had my first laparoscopy. After the operation the doctor came into the room and spoke to the woman in the next bed, who had also undergone a laparoscopy on the same day. He gave her some very bad news, and I thought to myself: 'Thank goodness he's not going to come to me and tell me *that*!' Up until that point, I was getting some kind of treatment, being patted on the back, and told: 'Go home, you'll fall pregnant this month!' I had absolutely no idea that there was a real fertility problem – even though I had been trying to get pregnant for years. I just took the doctor's advice every time, went home, full of hope, and tried again to become pregnant.

The doctor told me that I had masses of adhesions on the ovary and that without more treatment I would have a very small chance of conceiving. It took him about six weeks to talk me into having more surgery. You see, after the laparoscopy, and hearing the news, I had thought to myself: 'That's it, that's enough, I'm finished with all this!' I was so sick and tired of having doctors tell me that I needed surgery to have various parts 'fixed'. I took them by their word, I took their advice because they were doctors, and they were supposed to know more than I did about these things. Well, in time, I did have another operation . . . because even at that stage I was still hoping that maybe this time it would work.

I really think that hope, in this case, is like a whirlpool. You're ready to try *one* more procedure, *one* more operation. It's very hard to stop. Infertility is such a hidden condition. It's so personal, so self-based. At that point, I think I could have been talked into agreeing to anything, into going anywhere, if it gave me one more chance.

When I was first told of my infertility, I cried. I just couldn't believe it. I suppose that for all those years I had been kidding myself. In my heart I knew there was a problem, but I didn't think it would be this bad, this final. Up until then I had been getting a lot of social pressure about not having children, but the hope that maybe *next* time, after the *next* treatment, I would become pregnant always acted as some kind of buffer between what other people said to me about not having children, and what I felt about myself.

I was really depressed. I was stunned . . . I couldn't think. Even now, although I think I have become a lot stronger, or a lot more accepting, it really depends on the day as to how I will react, what I will see when I go out, for example. In the beginning I saw pregnant women, baby shops and children everywhere! I thought the whole world was just loaded with baby shops! It was like a knife turning. If you want children you can't exist in this society, be infertile and be in your thirties, and not get a stab in the heart. You have to develop a good blunting system because there are so many social pressures on women and so many reminders.

Ultimately all the tests were taxing, and all the 'trying', all the timetables, put a strain on my marriage. Although my husband has been very supportive, and has never once blamed me, the 'sex according to a timetable' got to him more than it did to me. When we had to have sex on a particular day, around ovulation time for example, so that I could put a circle on my temperature chart, I would 'nag' him till we did. It sounds crazy now, but when I still had hope in the early years, I would do exactly as the doctors wanted. After a while, I just couldn't.

I felt so isolated sometimes, even though my husband was loving and caring. I felt sad, I felt really unhappy. You do grow apart, there is a distance between us. I fluctuated between seeing the problem as 'our' problem and 'my' problem. Even when I do see it as 'our' problem, I still feel responsible because it is *my* body which is not functioning as it should, or as I would like it to. I felt responsible, as if I had done something to cause the problem without my knowing it. Maybe I had not done something that I should have done. It's difficult for me to explain. Maybe I have had infections which have gone untreated. Maybe I have abused my body in the past. It's not something I've gone into with doctors because it's too late now.

I used to feel so guilty. He could have had a family by now, if he had married someone else. Sometimes I worry that I've let my husband down, that we can't extend our lives through a family, that he has no link to the future. These thoughts go through my head occasionally.

I used to blame my body. Now, there are days when I feel perfectly OK about my body. But this morning I feel absolutely terrible. I sometimes feel that my body has let me down, and I suppose it has, because it has stopped me from doing something I have wanted to do for a long time. Sometimes I feel very negative about myself. It's not as bad as it used to be, but one of the worst times for me was when I felt terrible about myself as a woman. I felt that I wasn't complete. This was not because I hadn't given birth to a baby, but because something was wrong with me . . . that I *couldn't* have a baby.

The social pressure placed on me to become a mother is one of the most upsetting and annoying things for me. Social occasions, especially those connected with my husband's work, where I have to meet new people are difficult. Most people, especially after you've been married a few years, expect you to have children. This assumption from others is very difficult to cope with. At one function recently a woman sitting at the same table asked me whether I had any children. This was her first question. I thought to myself: 'Here it comes *again!*' That's always the first question I'm asked. When I said 'No', she then asked if I had some kind of career. When I said 'No' to that too, she asked me what I did all day. If you're not a mother, or have dedicated yourself to some worthwhile career, and plan to have a baby later, then there is a total lack of acceptance of your situation. You are either a career woman or a mother, but you can't just be a person – there's no middle ground. People don't know where to put you. There's nowhere for me to simply *be*. A lot of people ask: 'Well, what are you going to "do" with your life?' Even my family, in the beginning, would ask me this. For a while I had this idea that because I was not going to be a mother I should go out and do some volunteer work, at the hospital, or for some charity. Now, after years of this sort of advice, I think that people direct me to do things in my life because it makes them feel better. They like to think that if you are not a mother, then you are doing something useful anyway.

I usually just answer 'No' to questions like that, or answer very abruptly, because I got to the point where I found myself going through it over and over again. Why do I have to justify, to all these people I don't know, that I don't have any children? I get so tired of people asking me that question. It creates a very vicious circle really, because I suppose I answer them abruptly now, and they might think that I am very sensitive about the subject. Well, I am, according to how I feel, but it's more that I am so tired of that question being the first one asked, the first contact from strangers. That makes me tense.

People find it very difficult to cope with someone who says 'No' to all these questions. Having children is so taken for granted. You don't go into a long conversation with somebody as to why they do have children, but people always want to know why you haven't.

If I do tell somebody that I can't have children, that I have a fertility problem, they usually say something like: 'Oh, I'm so sorry!' People pity me, and that's not what I want. In these situations, people don't know what else to ask you, what else to talk about, so that's the end of the conversation.

When you don't have any children you get isolated from people, especially your friends. You are no longer really accepted into the things that they do. They don't mean to exclude you, of course, but if they're having friends over for a barbeque, for example, they're not going to invite you because they think you'll feel out of it because you will be the only ones without any kids. They think that because there are children around, and you don't have any, that you will be upset, so it's best not to invite you. Our old friends have grown away from us. The friends we have now are divorced, or people whose children are in their teens. We have no real friends with toddlers or young children any more, so I have less and less contact with children, which I regret too.

I get angry when I make comments about children and people say: 'How would you know? You're not a mum.' Although they don't always say it this strongly, that's the message I get. I'm made to feel as though I don't have the right to make comments. I know you don't have to experience something to be able to know something about it, or to look at it from the outside and have a point of view. And I think that point of view is no less valid. Usually I feel strong enough to resist getting upset by that kind of comment, but some days . . . well, on some days, everything gets to me.

I feel that I have lost a lot of closeness with women friends, friends I have had for a long time. As soon as one friend became pregnant, for example, she cooled off completely. There were fewer phone calls, fewer meetings. When I asked her how she was, she would answer with one sentence, and then try to change the subject. I knew that all she wanted to do was talk about the pregnancy, so it became a false situation for both of us.

Friends who become pregnant are very hesitant to tell me. They might tell my husband, so that he can 'break the news' to me, as if I were very fragile. I resent that. Even members of the family who have become pregnant would tell my mother, and then my mother would tell me. They assumed that I would get upset, that I couldn't handle the news. I resented that too because I was trying to get to the stage where I could accept it myself, whether I got upset or not. Why do people always assume that I will get upset? So what if I do get upset? I'm still the same person. Sometimes I would get upset, other times I wouldn't, but I was still the same person. I would rather not be treated with kid gloves all the time.

Friends and family tend to avoid the subject of pregnancy and children. When I was around it was so obvious sometimes that people were really trying hard to not talk about it. I was very conscious of the tension around people. I could feel how uncomfortable they felt. I could feel the tension arise as soon as I arrived, especially if there were children around. I used to wonder whether I was imagining it, but I'm not. People just don't know what to do, how to handle the situation, and that made me tense. It's another vicious circle, this time with people closer to you.

I feel a lot of resentment. In a way I can understand their behaviour. They think they are doing the 'right thing'. They thought they were helping me by not discussing it, but it was hurting me more, because it would make me more aware of it, more conscious of the fact that I was different. In the end, you tend to want to avoid people. As I said, our newer friends are those people whose lives are not focused on children.

I consider myself lucky because I can go with my husband on his business trips. If my husband's situation had been different, if he worked a nine-to-five job, which involved no travelling, and no possibility of advancement, the decisions I would have made would have been different. I enjoy travelling with him.

Since I decided a few years ago to stop 'trying', I think I've accepted my situation much more than ever before. I decided not to try IVF because it got to the stage where my life was completely centred on my body, on having a baby. I had to stop. After all those years of tests and surgery, I realized that I've been poked around and pulled at so many times that I was losing . . . that I had lost . . . that part of my body which was mine alone and private.

I don't know how other women feel, but once I found out what was really happening, that my chances of becoming pregnant were very small, I felt relieved. We didn't have to have sex according to a timetable. Life started to change, and get away from dates and timetables. I could tear up the charts, throw the thermometer in the bottom drawer, and try to have some sort of normal life.

It's taken me a long time to get to the stage where I don't envy women who have children. It's been a long time since I've felt that terrible wrench and ache. Years ago I had no confidence in myself. Years ago I hadn't the courage to go into a coffee shop, sit down, and have a cup of coffee by myself. I felt self-conscious about it. Two years ago I took up an interest that I had off and on, for a long time. Before that I had tried to make friends by joining different classes and clubs, but those things go in phases. Anyway, I actually walked through the door by myself; it took a lot for me to do that. You see, by the time I had reached that point I was more confident. Now that I've found something that I can really express myself with, something that no one can take away from me, it *is* me, I don't want to give it up – not even for a baby.

EVERY MONTH A LITTLE MISCARRIAGE

·

ANDREA BELK-SCHMEHLE
West Germany

As my thirtieth birthday approached, the 'baby question' became unavoidable: soon it seemed like 'now or never'. My decision was quickly made – now. My partner needed a little longer, but finally it became clear, we wanted a baby. According to women friends, steering fat bellies or prams before them, it was quite easy: the woman stops taking the pill or has the coil removed and after one, two or three months she's pregnant. We too were certain that it would be just the same for us and everything would run according to plan. But in neither two, three or four months, nor in the following two years did I become pregnant. I began to read literature on the topic and gathered that one of us must be infertile and that we were a case for the doctor. 'Good, if that's so,' I said to myself, 'then the doctor will sort it out.' My great confidence was fed by the many reports on the steady progress made by medicine. Nothing, it appeared, remained untried, in order to help the more than one million involuntarily childless couples. Enormous sums were being devoted to research, and medical assistance showed no sign of baulking at experiments with test-tube babies and surrogate pregnancies. Why shouldn't it be able to help me too?

What my actual problem and suffering would amount to and how little this all had to do with so-called medical progress was not yet clear to me, when I confidently set off to the gynaecologist. 'Doctor, I want to have a baby.' That's what the nice, fatherly doctor likes to hear, that's as it should be. And when I added: 'But we've been trying for two years now without success,' it didn't phase him for one moment. I got a 'WB' mark for

'Wants Baby' on my medical records and he began playing the keyboard of his medical possibilities.

As I had a nice gynaecologist – it took me some time to find him – the examination began with what is least drastic and painful. First it has to be ascertained whether I do in fact ovulate. From this moment on the thermometer is the sceptre ruling my life. Morning after morning, always at the same time, I have to take my temperature before getting up. The results are entered in a graph book, in which the ideal curve is shown resplendent. After a few months of daily measuring it emerges – apparently I do *not* ovulate. My curves don't look a bit like the example to be aspired to, but like a mixture of Alpine peaks and valleys. 'So that was it.'

I feel in need of repair work and am certain that the doctor will have the necessary tools available. I willingly swallow the prescribed hormone pills that are supposed to force my body to ovulate. My body is finally forced, but in addition to the desired ovulation it also produces all sorts of things that I find strange and unusual. I become fatter, my breasts become larger and heavier, I am convinced that I must be pregnant.

I am already leafing eagerly through books describing the first development phases of the child and stare enthusiastically at photos of embryos in the womb. I start knitting a tiny jacket. My period also fails to make an appearance. On the twenty-eighth day I feverishly long for the thirtieth day, when I can do an early test. On that day I start the test off, faithfully following the instructions and for two hours hypnotize the test-tube to show the longed-for ring which proves pregnancy. The tube remains unchanged and I go off angrily to do the shopping, thinking I will look again later. On my way I realize already: it's over. I defiantly spend yet another hour running around, I don't want to admit it but I know even before I convince myself at home: hope is past.

And so it goes on, month after month, cycle after cycle. Around the fourteenth day, when the temperature curve drops sharply, thanks to the hormones, and the doctor has convinced himself of the right moment after an expert look, he sends me home to conceive a child. Whether or not we are in the mood for it, is a question shoved aside as irrelevant. Mostly we don't feel like it. Who does on command? But as the procreative capacity of my partner has meanwhile been affirmed and my ovulation forced into operation, it must work. So we are obedient. After the monthly enforced act I run around divided, observe my body, listen anxiously to myself. A voice tells me: 'Perhaps, perhaps it has worked this time. Haven't you got a bit fatter? Isn't there a suspicious ache in your breasts?' But a second voice immediately intervenes and warns: 'Don't fool yourself, it won't work this time either. If you start hoping now, the disappointment afterwards will only be greater.'

This voice gets a boost when punctually one week before my period I notice a pulling sensation in my lower abdomen. The first voice is then heard, hesitantly reminding me that many happy mothers also told of stomach pains in the first month of pregnancy. On the twenty-sixth day at the latest the temperature curve drops downward and on the twenty-eighth day the faint doubt of whether I had perhaps measured wrongly is removed: my period flushes my hopes bloodily away. Every month my future child bleeds to death, hope is driven painfully from me, because I don't want to let go. I want to hold on. Every month a little miscarriage, an abortion of my hopes. These days are gloomy and despairing. I withdraw into myself. I don't like going out into the streets, where I am constantly noticing pregnant women carrying their bellies proudly with an inward-looking expression. Countless women are pushing prams, carrying their babies pressed close and tenderly to their bodies, showing that they can do something I can't do, they have something I don't have.

For I am sterile: sterile as a hospital, white, tiled, shining and clean, smelling of disinfectant. Not a speck of dust, nothing living or which could live. Sterile just like me. Or in plain English: unfruitful. Like a drought-ridden field with thick, cracked clods of earth, where nothing grows, nothing flourishes. Sterility – that is also impotence, for potency means possibility. Sterility, that is a 'cemetery belly', as a woman friend once said to me. A cemetery belly, in which countless possible but defunct children, never to be awakened to life, are buried. Hard to accept.

My women friends are not much help. First there are those who get pregnant almost casually. What is there to it? It just happens, that's all. 'Perhaps you don't know how it's done?' one such friend once asked me sympathetically. Thank you, perhaps

I really don't know. By now it seems an absolute miracle to me anyway that such things as pregnancies and babies exist, when so many imponderables have to be taken into account and so many obstacles stand in the way. Books on this subject, which pile up on my desk, constantly point this out. When I still wanted to prevent a pregnancy, it seemed possible at any time that the then unwanted event could occur. Now that I believe that I have prevented it much too effectively and enduringly, getting pregnant is a laborious process. The mothers among my women friends don't look at it like that, of course. They don't know the problem, and don't want to hear anything about it either. 'Look how baby is staring,' says one friend. No, I don't want to look, I haven't got a baby, and if she doesn't want to share this sorrow, then I don't want to know her worries about her baby either. I can't hide it, I am jealous of the mothers with their children. When they cuddle, play with one another and laugh, it hurts me. Although I know that they aren't trying to provoke me, that it's only natural, I still nourish bitter thoughts: why them and not me? I feel shut out from their happiness and avoid associating with friends who have become mothers.

But those women friends who quite deliberately don't want children, are not very helpful either. They don't understand: to let oneself be investigated from top to bottom, sex according to the calendar, just to have a screaming little brat. My family is not exactly much comfort either. Not that I am put under pressure with intrusive questioning: 'Now, when is it going to happen?' But there is the constant talk about the progress of ex-schoolmates or the daughters of friends, to the great joy of grandma and grandpa she has married and has just had her first/second baby/son/daughter/twins. Report after report of mission accomplished rain down on me. And between the lines I hear: 'But from you that's not to be expected.' Of course, this talk is only normal. That's life. To be born and to die, that's the natural course of events. I find it normal too, only I am not normal. And I can't shake off the uneasy feeling: no professional success would ever be as precious to my mother as the announcement: 'I'm pregnant.' Of course, there's no shortage of good advice on how to get pregnant, 'Take a holiday.' We've often gone away, but it hasn't helped. 'Don't think about it, switch off, don't get tensed up, then it'll happen all right.' But who can tell me where the switch is, to simply turn off my desires and hopes?

I seek refuge in the Women's Movement. There I have finally learned that problems are easier to cope with if they are shared with those similarly affected. But my visit to a Women's Health Centre is a failure: 'Sterile?' The woman counsellor squirms, embarrassed, she is sitting between shelves on which there are all sorts of books on pregnancy and having children, while next door pregnant women are preparing for natural childbirth with gymnastic exercises. 'I don't know what you should do. Best thing is to go to the doctor.' Furious, I leave and pin up on the bulletin board between invitations to exchange baby-clothes and join breast-feeding groups and appeal: I want to find other infertile women for a discussion group. The next day my notice has been torn down, as though I have been advertising something obscene.

With resignation, I turn to my doctor again; he now resorts to more extreme measures. In hospital, under anaesthetic, with barium meal pressed into my fallopian tubes, I am X-rayed to ascertain whether or not they are blocked. Only when I am already strapped onto the table and she is injecting the anaesthetic into my vein, does the anaesthetist ask: 'How much do you weigh, by the way?' But I am already too far gone to answer her. She must have assessed me as very strong, because her anaesthetic sends me off drifting infinitely through dream worlds. Only hours later am I finally capable of taking in the result: everything is in perfect order, the fallopian tubes are not blocked.

Again there's the temperature-taking and trying and hoping, until, when my next period arrives I am lying in bed crying and decide – enough. Otherwise, it will go on like this for ever: examination, hope, bloody monthly rejection of a child. Artificial insemination, test-tube baby method, everything that could still be tried seems to me like the laboratory of Frankenstein's creator. A pregnancy forced into being with such means would only be unnatural and anything but carefree. I would certainly only lie in bed for months and ask myself: can I keep it? Will it even be healthy? I don't want that sort of pregnancy.

I withdraw from the medical merry-go-round, even though my doctor protests. Ultimately my intractable body shows him the limits of his possibilities anyway. He would still like to try this and that and holds out straws of hope to me. But I've had enough. The thermometer is thrown into a corner, a calendar for sexuality is no longer followed. It's high time we gave ourselves the chance again to enjoy sexuality as a pleasure instead of just regarding it as a procreative act. Of course, it won't be easy to lose the reluctance that set in owing to medically prescribed sexuality. We have to learn again to accept our bodies which we have so long regarded as a recalcitrant something opposing our desires. And we also have to learn not to let ourselves feel guilty along the lines of: perhaps subconsciously you didn't really want a baby, or, perhaps there's something wrong with your relationship. It's well known that children do occur even in extremely unhappy and disturbed relationships. And of course we too have our ambivalent feelings where children are concerned. Much as we want a baby, we are also aware of the worries and fears involved. But these ambivalent feelings are known to couples who have babies with no problems. Of course, I have to deal with my regrets about the never-enjoyed experience of pregnancy and birth.

In the meantime I have learned how to speak about my problem, how not to shove it shamefacedly into the taboo zone. In this way I have encouraged others too, who suddenly confessed that it was exactly the same for them. I have learned how many couples submit for years and even decades to the medical mills from which they emerge crushed, with a destroyed relationship.

I don't want that. So I have joined together with other women in the same predicament. We talk about our experiences, our wishes, our sorrows and try to cope with our pain together. In this way we have become more assertive and can face the pressures of an often thoughtless world with more self-confidence. This group strengthens my resolve, and, since my desire for children is not dead, we have decided to adopt a child (see chapter by Ute Winkler and Traute Schönenberg 'Options for involuntarily childless women'). Not because we secretly have an eye on the 'adoption effect' and expect that I will suddenly become pregnant when the child is here, but because we have decided that we want a child. Not just with the belly, but with the head too. We know that if we get our child through the Youth Welfare Department, then it will not be merely a second-class substitute but an eagerly awaited child.

PS Since writing this article we have adopted two little daughters. The irony is that although I do not look like any other family member, Maresa – one of my children – looks just like me when I was a little girl!

Adoption has totally fulfilled my desire for children. This became very clear to me when, a year after our first adoption, the cause of my infertility was discovered. After a most painful period which I had checked out, they found that the corpus luteum did not produce enough hormones to sustain a pregnancy. This is a problem which can be fixed by administering a progesterone/oestrogen mixture. So I sat down and asked myself whether there was still the desire for a pregnancy. I didn't feel any such thing and therefore rejected the offered medication. Instead we proceeded to adopt a second child (and thanks to our stubbornness – and perhaps our honest decision *for* an adoption – were successful again within less than a year).

And so now I am a mother: sometimes happy, sometimes unhappy, stressed and full of remorse, because not everything with children runs as smoothly as I had imagined it!! In short, I am just like other mothers.

MOTHERHOOD HAS A HISTORY: AMENORRHOEA AND AUTOBIOGRAPHY

.

MAGGIE HUMM
England

I would never be a mother. Mothers went mad.

My grandmother was deserted by her husband just after giving birth to my mother. Depressed and despairing, she lived the rest of her life in a mental hospital. Or mothers died. My mother died the month before I began to menstruate. Mothers talked only about their children and had to sit separately with them in cold rooms in Newcastle pubs. From the age of fourteen I sat in pub saloons, with my dad and his mate Johnny, drinking snowballs and port and lemonade. We argued about socialism and Johnny taught me to play 'The Red Flag' on his tin whistle. I was the only girl from my secondary school to go to university. The other girls left to become mothers. At university, girls who became mothers failed their finals. The pill was free in 1963. I would never be a mother.

My education demanded that I separate myself from my femininity as well as from my class and regional identity. Much of feminist thinking and writing deals with this marginalization of women in a partriarchal world and tries to describe alternatives that somehow validate that separateness. Like Adrienne Rich, I too grew into consciousness in the late 1950s and 1960s, the place and time now located as the period of sexual liberation. I was beginning to think of myself as a feminist. I was not a mother, and I was enjoying marriage.

I think that part of the desire to reproduce lies in an acceptance of what one understands oneself to be and a need to perpetuate what one is. At thirty, my sense of not belonging, of feeling like an outsider, could be eased intellectually, even emotionally, by feminism. I had begun to know myself. But, without a baby, women who uproot themselves from class or region will always have an additional sense of not belonging because it is motherhood, traditionally, which initiates women into culture.

At thirty, securely employed as a lecturer, the obligatory hitchhiker's guide to Europe behind me, I found myself reconsidering 'motherhood'. I was meeting women, strong interesting feminists who were mothers *and* worked *and* sat in pubs. Of course, I had known about intelligent mothers before, had vaguely believed they could exist outside of Newcastle and Margaret Drabble, but I had realized neither that I needed motherhood, nor, conversely, that to be a mother even for me was to be a woman. Fear of reproduction overcome, I 'came off' the pill to become a mother and climbed down into pain.

> Basically, the hypothalamus (a part of the brain) stimulates the pituitary gland in a cyclical fashion to produce two hormones. These hormones are released into the blood where in different proportions they stimulate the ovary to produce a ripe ovum (or egg) and release this ovum into the genital tract where it can be fertilized. In your case the oestrogen in the Pill has switched off your hypothalamus so no ova are produced! (Letter R.N. Hospital, November 1973)

My post-pill amenorrhoea had been discovered at M. Hospital in a brief afternoon's examination but I was assured then that in several months my periods would re-establish and I would easily become pregnant because I had perfect ovaries and was otherwise healthy. I decided to give up smoking and wait. It was the letter asking me to join a questionnaire survey of post-pill amenorrhoeac women and fill in six monthly charts, which made me suspicious that my case was not the individual and temporary condition described to me by doctors at M. Hospital. A good friend G revealed her own post-pill amenorrhoea. How many are there of us I wondered? Will future social historians describe us, not only as the first generation of working-class women to have experienced class mobility through education but also to have been moved by technology into a different biology. G recommended a private gynaecologist who would prescribe

Clomid: 'Clomid, or Clomiphene, acts at the level of the hypo-thalamus, indirectly stimulating it to stimulate the pituitary to stimulate the ovaries.' (Note from Dr H, September 1972.) The guilt of spending my way out of the National Health Service was ameliorated by Dr H. She was the perfect initiator into a version of motherhood that I could inhabit. I wanted 'motherhood' that could take a feminist, or at least a working woman, and the contradiction of someone who made her own yoghurt and read *Vogue*; recognize these as contradictions and refuse to celebrate the initiation into motherhood as a rite of passage to a 'better' identity. Dr H was kind and herself a mother, but very professional and invitingly collaborative.

The courses of Clomid were to be combined with temperature charts of daily readings taken 'before you put a foot out of bed'. The difficulty of reading a thermometer in the dark early mornings of winter before I could put in my contact lenses was a good apprenticeship for the horrific difficulties ahead. For several months, Dr H and I thought the temperature charts looked promising and that higher dosages of Clomid would easily produce the right peaks and troughs of temperature on the magic ninth and fourteenth days of my cycle. But the chart's zig-zag lines were lie detector readings and the increased dosages gave me only migraine, and dizzy nauseous reactions to bright lights and white walls but *not* a stable cycle.

Dr H told me that Clomid often stimulates the development of two eggs, hence twins. I did not tell her that my husband's father was a twin because I was learning not to tell myself what could not be heard. The beginning of silence. I would never be a mother.

Dr H transferred me to R.N. Hospital and *Mr* H (pretending to be gentlemen, British consultants refuse to be addressed as Doctor). Every instinct of survival told me that this was a danger zone. The regular humours of this densely institutionalized world were the male *bonhomie* of doctors always arriving late, women, as usual, sitting for hours half-naked and cold in ill-fitting towelling robes; and unnecessarily frequent blood tests; and vaginal exam-inations often done by several male doctors one after the other like a gang rape. The weekly examinations were tiring, extremely intrusive and physically demeaning. The Clomid regime began again with the addition of injections of Pregnyl on the ninth and fourteenth days of what might be read as cycles. 'Pregnyl, or human chorionic gonadotrophin, is given to stimulate ovulation by intramuscular injections. You are advised to make love on the day of the Pregnyl injection and the next two days, other days don't matter.' (Note from Mr P, *S.H.O. Medicine*, September 1973.)

There is a male professional mentality which is inherently sexist and élitist. To have the injections I would need, the doctors asserted, to visit R.N. Hospital on the two days of each cycle in addition to the weekly clinics. I was teaching full-time in a Polytechnic precinct in Barking, trying to write a Ph.D with a supervisor based at King's College in the Strand who preferred to tutor me in his home in Brixton, and I did not have a car. I could not talk to colleagues about the treatment in case my teaching/research was adjusted for an anticipated pregnancy. It is not only the sexual politics of the New Right who cannot tolerate a working woman. I persuaded the consultant to allow my doctor to inject me and simply have a weekly hospital visit.

> 7. Side Effects
> These have been very rare and include pains in the
> joints and local reactions at the site of injection.
> (For Hospital Use only S.S. Services, July 1969)

Or, in my case, an inability to walk without shuffling for several hours the morning after. 'Making love' on the day of the Pregnyl injection was as unpleasant. There were still the daily temperature charts to fill in.

Medical treatment is not often described as a lived experience. Infertility presents a particular problem here. For whilst everything that has been written on the subject of mothering can fix on an imagery of archetypes, the vocabulary of 'primary', 'secondary', 'dysfunctional amenorrhoea' is a depoliticized language from a masculine science too small to capture the biological, symbolic, and emotional traumas of infertile women.

Most contemporary feminist responses to medicine are informed by Barbara Ehrenreich and Deirdre English's discussion of what the medical establishment has done to women in *For Her Own Good* (1978). Ehrenreich and English document very clearly the increasing control of women's birth processes by masculine medicine, and the horrific effects on women of early technology like forceps. While a crucial account of medical history, the book becomes the vehicle for a savage rejection of institutionalized medical technology. Medicine is a metaphor for all that is wrong with a masculinized science as conqueror and classifier of women who are portrayed as victims of male doctors throughout history. An account like this denies the ambiguities of infertility except where the condition can be used to stand for a general argument. It denies women, particularly middle-class white women, their need and ability to consciously collaborate with, and perhaps transform for themselves the medical meanings presented to them. We do not discover from this book, nor from others, what women might think and what they might come to know as they are passed along the medical assembly line. Under such circumstances there exists the specificity of each woman's situation, and the understanding of herself as a medical object, which exist in a complicated and contradictory relationship. Writing that does somehow represent infertility, although it is not directly about it, is in fiction about body imagery and female identity like the opening of Maxine Hong Kingston's *Woman Warrior* (1980).

I was encouraged by that reading and by my knowledge that the essence of being 'a good patient' is to simulate the perspective of those who are more powerful than you. And teaching had taught me how to act. The hardest contradiction to accommodate was knowing that the depiction of motherhood being presented to me on each hospital visit was deeply conservative and yet, paradoxically, very appealing. 'Would I mind multiple births if I moved onto Pergonal?' For the first time, and at thirty I had stopped being a marginal woman. I was the centre of doctors' attention, their research needs and their medical world. I wanted to be a mother.

The second year

> We suggest Pergonal therapy. Pergonal is obtained from the urine of menopausal women. The intention of Pergonal therapy is to bypass the hypo-thalamus/pituitary part of the pathway and to stimu-late ovaries direct using the same hormones. When

the ovum is considered ripe an injection of Pregnyl is given. The Pergonal is given in a course of intra-muscular injections on alternate days. Different women require different doses of Pergonal and the starting dose is an inspired guess.

(Letter from Houseman T.)

Again the battle to be injected at home rather than give up teaching and research to make daily visits to the hospital. Yet, even though I think I was able to resist institutionalization so vehemently because I was already uncomfortably aware I could 'pass', the injection routine was fraught with guilt.

My doctor arranged for district nurses to inject me at home, and together, the nurses and I designed a system in my bathroom where, bent over the bath, I could tap the thick glutinous liquid in each ampoule while I was being injected very painfully with another. Awkwardly, I had to initiate each new nurse into the process. The fridge was full of ampoules which we hid from our lodger in case he suspected heroin. The anxiety of waiting each evening to see if the nurse would actually arrive was exacerbated by the class guilt that as a 'non-ill' person I was taking valuable nursing time away from local elderly working-class patients. It was only by midday that I could walk with ease when the stiff leg muscles (I alternated thighs for injections) stopped feeling rigid. And I was nauseous a great deal. Would I be a mother? At least the daily thermometer readings were discontinued. But they were replaced by the only method of assessing doses of Pergonal – urine collection.

The adequacy of the dose is assessed by assay of samples of 24-hour collections of urine in the labora-tory. The estimation takes a day, and with the vagaries of the post, it is usual to be in possession of a result which refers to less than two or three days beforehand.

(Houseman T.)

I have no way of writing calmly about the regime of collecting all my urine for twenty-four hours to send each daily sample. All that counted were the details of heavy containers sloshing with yellow liquid, hidden at work (I must smell like an incontinent

person); arriving straight from work for an evening film trying
to pack the bags around my feet hoping desperately that no one
would stumble over and spill them; of finding special French
bicycling bottles but having to learn how to piss into their two
inch tops; of postal strikes disrupting cycles and injection days.
They were all grotesque shapes in a dense fog of silence that I
was made to keep very indistinct from feminist friends, work
colleagues, even close friends and family because we could not
bear regular 'Is Maggie pregnant yet?' questions.

It was the control that I found most suffocating, although
without it I could not become a mother. There is no way of
being an infertile woman *responsible* for one's own body and its
treatment without creating a self control that in the end becomes
a psychic endurance test capable of absorbing everything by way
of difficulty. I carry with me the tattered remnants of this psychic
structure in my current quasi anorexia (certainly I am food
obsessive). Ingestion has replaced injection as a similarly difficult
event. This analysis is, of course, retrospective. Making sense of
it now has been a long and painful process. Any neatly encapsu-
lated version of infertility cannot take account of the untidy
contradictions in how it was experienced. The daily muscle pain,
sickness and extreme tiredness were layers sandwiched between
the doctors' invasive attacks on my body and the gang rape of
the weekly clinic.

There is, too, a tension between this case study as I present it
and the compulsion of feminist theory to play down a woman's
overwhelming need for her own biologicial, not adopted, child.
My tension, then, is not a mere rhetorical device but a real
problem that I cannot resolve. I simply do not know enough
about the issues described to explain the connections between
them so I am unable to design the perfect pattern for another
infertile woman. I desperately wanted the experience of *my* child
as a product of my own labour. If that posits some psychic need
or existential yearning so be it. I would be a mother.

If the oestrogen levels obtained are too high there is
a risk of hyperstimulation of the ovaries. Hyperstimulation is rare however. Symptoms are, in the mild
form, of abdominal pain with ovarian enlargement; in

> severe forms, accumulation of fluid in the abdominal
> and lung cavities.
>
> (Letter R.N. Hospital)

The 'inspired guess' was wrong. The day after an increased
dosage my waist size increased one inch every hour. Breathing
asthmatically and with my legs swelling perceptibly I was
admitted to the casualty ward. I preferred to trust the 'For
Hospital Use Only' booklet I stole earlier from the hospital.
In it it said: 'Criteria for diagnosing Hyperstimulation. Severe
hyperstimulation – pleural effusion, intravascular thrombosis.
Multiple pregnancies.'

The drip saved my life, reduced my waist and legs but not the
asthma, and the doctors refused to tell me if I might be pregnant.
Would I be a multiple birth mother hiding from *Sun* photogra-
phers? I had to wait five days to discover that my innate good
luck (was it my positive nature or just the gold chain I wore as a
talisman around my neck?) held me clear of multiple pregnancies.

Waiting in the ward, stretching my legs gently in secret exercises, I became a listener. Listening comes easily to the powerless.
To listen, and write down personal observations was a necessary
weapon to fight the unseen observations in the notes at the foot of
my bed. Lying naked for examination, I listened to the consultant
describing my case to his housemen:

> Edinburgh uses the Gamzelle method which worries
> me, because, like his colleague Dr C. in Birmingham,
> G. *unfortunately* induced sextuplets and his assistant
> leaked it to the press. Dr S. had a method of over-
> stimulation – selecting one egg and transplanting it in
> embryo transplant – but wombs often contract too
> quickly and abort. We are all geared up to replace
> Perganol treatment with embryo transplants. Ward
> 10 is already converted and Mr H. is very keen
> because the French people in Paris are geared up.
> We've all agreed to hold back until Dr S. has five
> successful pregnancies.

So my months of pain, in an almost impossible to organize work
routine, were to be discarded for a medical *nouveau* race? Implicit

in the application of infertility treatment is a belief that infertile women are inevitable victims, machines to be tinkered with and adjusted. This appropriates the imagination and experience of others. We all keep hospital diaries.

> Women's Casualty Ward. January 1974.
> Bed 4: 'Bombs, go away, bombs.'
> Nurse: 'These are tablets, they're good.'

I visualize the drug fantasies listening to the calls of patients. An old woman, drugged, talks to her mother, first as a child then as a grown-up. They live together again in the way she repeats 'Mother, help me!' with subtle differences.

How are mothers made? Is motherhood a gift or a slow creeping disease? A Scandinavian woman sounding, as all Scandinavians seem to, like Ingrid Bergman, had suspected cancer. They opened her in the ward with only local anaesthetic to remove a sample for analysis. She was in great pain. Phoning her family that night she said to her husband: 'She was so sorry to hear that, it always was such a good shop, could he keep the wrapping paper and she certainly would take them straight back'; to her son: 'She was so sorry they'd been such beastly hamburgers, hadn't they, and spoilt his evening'; to her little girl: 'a kiss from Mummy for your tummy, rub it hard and the pain will go'. And the phone call was over!

There are no easy devices to give expression to the feelings of infertile women. This private glance into my history stands side by side with the moments of pain and personal knowledge of feminism, I think the knowledge of us all; that feminist theory is still evolving. I see my account as evidence that can be used. I think it is particularly useful as a way of gaining entry to ideas about infertility, what treatment is *for*, why women want to be mothers, that aren't written about in the textbooks of medicine or sociological descriptions of working mothers. Somehow such a piece of writing must incorporate contradiction and non-linear movement into its centre. Coping with the overdose and hospitalization *and* surviving made the subsequent cycles of injections, urine collection, silence and humiliation possible, paradoxically only because they were not the ultimate event, could never be as frightening or painful.

There were four more months of cycles with the ampoules increased to five for each injection. I had another endometrial biopsy, the metal tube cutting into my uterus was an uncomfortable procedure without general anaesthetic and very painful. One day I translated the Italian print on the side of an ampoule container to discover that I depended on a chemical synthesized from the urine of menopausal nuns. Brides of Christ who would not mother. Another contradiction to add to my already doubled consciousness. Yet the experience of infertility is similar in the way it displaces women from their unique control over, and certainty of, genetic continuity and the universal relationship of all women to new life.

I was called early into the clinic one week to see Mr H in person. The prognosis of my treatment was not promising, he said. The hospital could afford to give me only one more cycle of Pergonal. It was too late for the 'inspired guesses' of doctors. I decided to choose dosage levels myself by telephoning the laboratory and pretending to be Mr H's housewoman. I felt certain that the odd day's delay in assay readings allowed a temperature drop which then inhibited the full effects of Pregnyl. If I was wrong the effect would be another, and probably extreme, overstimulation. Certainly my lungs would fill with fluid.

Re: Mrs Maggie Humm 263375
Details of 6th course Pergonal (successful)

Date	Ampoules of Pergonal	Urinary Oestrogen Secretion	HCG
May 24	4	11	
May 26	4	11	
May 28	4	8	
May 28 continued	4	10	
June 10	5	17	5,000 units
June 12		20	
June 15		52	5,000 units

Pregnancy test 16th July – Positive.

I was a mother.

I know autobiography can easily become special pleading. I do have a wonderful thirteen-year-old son. And the treatment was a long time ago. The compulsion of autobiography is to give private experience a public importance not simply a public expression. This can work only by drawing on devices that readers can handle and giving to readers, in part, the messages they want to hear.

For a feminist audience the story of my infertility should, in some manner, connect to their fears of a medicine shaped by masculine ideology into the image and reality of machinery. It should provide an explicit story of how a woman was harmed by medical science with all the misogynist details in explanatory order. I have not been able to hold together the details, have mixed letters, medical reports, metaphors and comment, because I did not want to tell feminists a story they think they already know.

Infertility *is* problematic because of the ways in which it has been technologized by male-dominated medicine. Yet an experience of infertility must be kept problematic, must deliberately not cohere, if the individual who brings it forward is to see the contradictions honestly. But to rely on the apparent passivity of infertile women as a basis for a feminist explanation of the development of medical technology is the narrowest kind of rationalization. To grow is to repudiate the closure of explanation.

My moment of infertility is now detailed and historicized. But making the point of my odd history the complexity of infertility in the medical situation in which it figures is not easy. Elsewhere there are interpretive devices. Infertility demands its own symbolic model, a Judy Chicago Infertility Project, in a biological reality and medical meaning that art co-joins. Then the pain of infertility will become, simultaneously, an understanding of In-Fertility.

SOMETIMES PERGANOL KILLS

.

ALISON SOLOMON
Israel

On 3rd March 1988 an article appeared in the
Israeli weekly magazine *HaOlam HaZeh* entitled
'The Medicine Killed Rivi'. The article was an
interview with the husband of a woman who
died following treatment with Pergonal and also
includes some of the text of a seven-page letter
sent by the husband to the Ministry of Health.
The following is my summary of the article in
translation.

Dr Emanuel Berman may submit a claim against Dr Gavriel
Elsner for negligence in the treatment the latter gave to his wife
Rivi Ben-Ari following which she died a sudden death.

Dr Berman, a psychologist, has sent a seven-page complaint
to the Director of the Ministry of Health detailing the negligence
and the events which led to his wife's death. Rivi Ben-Ari, a
clinical psychologist, died following treatment with Pergonal
which she was taking to help her ovulate. Ben-Ari was being
treated by Dr Bukovsky and she had succeeded in becoming
pregnant once but the pregnancy terminated after three months
when there was no heart beat. Dr Bukovsky went abroad in
March [1988] and suggested to Ben-Ari that she delay treatment
till he return, but she was anxious not to delay treatment and so
she turned to Dr Elsner, a highly recommended doctor who
works at the Tel HaShomer-Sheba hospital. She was treated in
his private clinic.

Both Berman and Ben-Ari were forty-two years old. They were married five years ago and Ben-Ari had a daughter from a previous marriage. Ben-Ari decided to undergo infertility treatment to enable her to have a child from this marriage.

One of Berman's complaints is that neither he nor his wife knew the possible dangers involved with Pergonal. Dr Bukovsky, Ben-Ari's regular doctor, explained in this article the dangers of Pergonal and how important it is that the dosage be given according to the patient's reaction to the drug. He says all doctors know that the drug can be treacherous and that for this reason it is very important that a woman undergoing Pergonal treatment undergo ultrasound approximately every two days. If there is any sign of overstimulation of the ovaries this can be seen immediately and the treatment halted. Overstimulation of the ovaries can create a change in blood-clotting. Overstimulation is always a dramatic condition and sets off a chain of reactions as a direct result of Pergonal. Early hospitalization can overcome these problems says Dr Bukovsky.

In Israel, Pergonal can be given only on prescription. Accompanying the drug is a long list of warnings, contraindications and adverse reactions headed 'For Doctors only' and printed only in English. The drug manufacturers 'Teva' claim that it is not necessary to print the information in Hebrew since Pergonal is administered only by the doctor, and that in the case of doctor-administered drugs the Ministry of Health does not require any accompanying explanations in Hebrew. Berman claims that if he or his wife had seen this list or been aware of such dangers, they would not have relied solely on Dr Elsner's assurances when Ben-Ari became ill. 'What Dr Elsner told us was in complete contradiction to what is written on the list of adverse reactions. We would therefore have at least turned to another doctor for advice.'

Ben-Ari was injected with Pergonal on 10th March. She had two ampoules a day. Her estrogen count on 17th March was 438, three days later it was 1084 and one month later it was 213. The ultrasound showed several follicles in the left ovary and an enlarged womb. Between 19th April and 23rd April she was injected with three ampoules of Pergonal a day. During that week Rivi felt very ill. She had already complained of swollenness, nausea, diarrhoea and stomach-aches. These worsened in the week of 29th April. She was completely swollen, and had put on so much weight her clothes did not fit her. At this point says Dr Bukovsky, Rivi should have been hospitalized as it was already a clear case of ovary overstimulation.

On 1st May Rivi felt so ill she cancelled an important appointment. She called Elsner at home but he was out. His wife asked her not to call him at the hospital but promised to pass a message on to him. He called her and told her to come to his clinic at 4.30 that afternoon. By then Rivi was throwing up all day. She could not drive but went to his clinic by taxi. She told him in detail all her symptoms. He examined her and advised her to lie in bed, drink a lot, and take painkillers as necessary. He did not mention hospitalization, he did no blood test or ultrasound. She continued to feel terrible and to throw up and only because Dr Elsner had assured her that the symptoms would pass did she not go to the hospital.

The following morning Berman found his wife completely confused and incoherent. He called Dr Elsner who told him to bring Rivi to the hospital. 'The doctors crowded around her in anxiety. They had me running with her tests. When they tried to do a blood-clotting test they couldn't because the blood was clotting in the syringe' says Berman.

The medical report states that Rivi was admitted to the hospital in a state of shock with blood pressure that could not be measured. The ultrasound showed extreme overstimulation with many large cysts on both ovaries and with an enormous accumulation of fluids, states Berman.

The last ultrasound Rivi had done was fourteen days earlier, contrary to the fact that most doctors treating with Pergonal do ultrasounds every couple of days. Elsner also did only two blood tests a month, instead of every two to three days.

After two hours in the Emergency Ward Rivi was transferred to the neurological ward and given a brain-scan. The family was told that she was suffering from aphasia and temporary paralysis of the right side. The doctors were anxious about the brain damage suffered so far but did not believe there would be any further damage. Three days later the doctors told Berman they believed that in two weeks she would be recovered and would then go to Bet Levinstein for rehabilitation. At this time no further brain scans were done and Rivi was not connected to a monitor says Berman.

On the night of 4th–5th May her condition worsened. Her father who was sitting with her realized that she was having difficulty breathing. She was given artificial respiration. She completely lost consciousness which never returned.

On the afternoon of 5th May a further brain scan was done which showed an edema in the brain which caused herniation of the brain. She was transferred to intensive care. On 8th May she was declared brain-dead and on 9th May she was declared clinically dead.

Berman's letter of complaint to the Ministry of Health includes the following complaint: that at no time was it explained that Pergonal can be a dangerous drug; that at no time were any possible danger-signs explained to them as symptoms of negative reaction to the drug; there was insufficient follow-up during the Pergonal treatment; the doctor increased the dosage of Pergonal without first doing the necessary tests as recommended by the manufacturers of Pergonal; the doctor ignored the serious symptoms the day before she went into a state of brain-shock.

The Ministry of Health has said it will set up an investigating committee to examine the chain of events following her hospitalization to see whether there was any negligence during this time. Dr Berman insists, however, that in addition to this they should examine Dr Elsner's treatment of Rivi as a private patient before she was hospitalized.

There has been no comment so far from Dr Elsner, who is not allowed to react to these claims while the investigation is taking place.

On 16th September 1988 an article appeared in the weekend magazine of the daily paper *Maariv* entitled 'The Third Grave of Yaakov Volkovitch'. The article was an interview with Rivi's father, who lost his wife to cancer, his son in the Yom Kippur War, and now Rivi. Volkovitch is quoted as saying, 'in all my life I never thought that the alternative to giving birth was death', 'the Egyptians took my son, the doctors my daughter'.

What is notable in this article is the wording of the death certificate, 'Immediate reason: Herniation of the brain, brain death. Illnesses or situations leading to the immediate reason for death – Overstimulation of the ovaries syndrome'.

Part of the article is concerned with Berman's claims and the doctors' counterclaims. Berman is quoted as saying, 'Dr Elsner's reactions to my claims have led me to the conclusion that he is trying to save his skin at any price. If this is so, I may be forced to go to the police and ask them to investigate the incident.'

In the article the doctors claim: (1) that Rivi did not have a particularly bad case of ovary-overstimulation and that (2) there is no direct connection between the Pergonal treatment and the brain-shock and its aftermath:

> It is odd that a doctor who has dealt with thousands of cases – and hospitalized hundreds of women for cases of ovary overstimulation, would not have recognized the phenomenon. (Professor Ser, Head of Ob/Gyn at Tel Hashomer)

> Many women have been hospitalized with cases of ovary overstimulation following treatment with Pergonal much worse than Rivi's . . . (Dr Elsner)

> Our department is the most experienced in the world in Pergonal treatment because use of the drug began here . . . it would be laughable for someone to try to tell us how to use the drug . . . if there have been two or three cases of death [over the past 25 years], that is an existing risk but irrelevant. We have to keep things in proportion and act for the good of the public. This is a treatment which gives life. (Professor Mashiach, Head of Ob/Gyn at Tel Hashomer)

WAITING FOR A CHILD

.

PETER HUMM
England

Waiting rooms at the hospital, waiting at home for the district
nurse to give Maggie the injection of Perganol, waiting for the
laboratory to report Maggie's oestrogen level, waiting for the pain
of her Pregnyl injection to subside a little before going to bed
and trying once more to conceive. Cartoon images of expectant
fathers have traditionally placed us outside, pacing the corridor,
but the long rituals of infertility treatment put me even more
anxiously on the edge. My memory is still of waiting outside,
downstairs, by the phone while Maggie was examined, injected,
tested, monitored and advised that one more course of treatment
might mean that the waiting was over.

Waiting now to read what Maggie has written about this time
in our lives takes me back in two ways. Once again it is left to
her to describe what the men in white coats were doing; again,
I can only construct my account around the fraught gap between
imagining and knowing. I know a good deal now about the
medical treatment of women's infertility but I can never know
how it *feels* to receive that treatment. Once or twice, an enthusiastic junior doctor took the time to explain to us both what he
could pass on from the case notes he had just inherited. More
often, however, I would only hear later about the lecture by the
consultant which had taken our predicament as a text. That
lecture was given around the hospital bed: medical etiquette is
nervous of any lay presence during a medical examination and
so I could never know or help what Maggie was enduring from
the repeated investigations.

Which is why it is hard even now to read of the clinical
procedures to which Maggie and women like her were subjected.
It is more than the immediate instinct to protect someone against
attack: I have to be honest in recognizing my own fear of those

images of rape. I am held by the image of Maggie's vulnerability as she lies under the words and the gaze of the consultant and his housemen but I also know that the scene cannot be simply translated into an icon of feminine subjection. It was Maggie who showed the bravest endurance in all this trial, it was her refusal to be reduced to an object of medical attention that gave us both the courage to continue.

I want to write something for this book so that I can describe what I know about this experience and discover what needs to be imagined. But I am wary of settling too easily into a recognizable narrative, finding a pattern that makes a familiar and soothing sense. It has taken a long time to register the ways in which infertility has affected our lives; it is hard to let go of the story and pass it over to somebody else to read. I am still unsure what those years of waiting did to us. Writing it down now may be a way to find out but it may also tidy things away that still need to be left lying awkwardly around.

I do know that I always expected to have children. I have a younger brother and sister and then a much younger brother born when I was sixteen. I was a very serious eldest son: photographs show me frowning responsibly at the camera while Richard and Janice smile chubbily beside me. The family was close – both grandmothers lived within a mile or two and I moved back and forwards between that grown-up world and the familiar intensity of children. I have always been used to children whereas to Maggie they seemed as exotic as the pub snowballs of Newcastle did to me. If Maggie had to act as my interpreter in the North-East, I was confident that I could pass on what the children we met were saying. At friends' houses I headed away from the work conversation and towards the comforting clutter of Lego trays and wooden bricks. I genuinely admired friends' babies, and thought the babies quite liked me.

So it was a shock when fatherhood did not come naturally. Shock is probably too sudden a word. Just as we had wandered into marriage after three years at university together so we had never consciously settled our attitude towards having children. I guess I was just waiting for Maggie to discover the same attraction I had for being part of a large family. Reading the doctors' letters that explained the damage done by the pill forced realization that what seemed natural was only going to be achieved with deliberate effort and the dismaying involvement or intervention of many others. Becoming parents was not going to bring us together in a world where I felt comfortably at home. Instead, deciding to have a child was going to send Maggie off every week to a world that had always made me feel miserably out of place. The desire to have children, so 'natural' to me that I had not ever thought it out, was immediately surrounded by the technical language and alien procedures of medicine.

We were not immediately threatened with the remote technologies of artificial insemination. The sperm test I had early on still allowed me to take part. I waited anxiously for the result and know how easily a sense of sexual uncertainty can be racked up by scales of measurement. I still do not know the full significance of my motility factor and have to argue against any instinct to invent insecurities. My masculinity was tested in other ways – I was entrusted with the provision of sperm but only at times and in conditions dictated by temperature charts and laboratory readings. I followed the advice of a friend who had waited five years for a child: I was to keep testes coolly efficient, sperm energetic by giving up tight jeans and splashing myself with cold water before bed. It seemed little more than folklore but I wanted to do all I could to help. If the ritual felt a bit foolish then at least it was being carried out at home – I was not the one whose body was being scrutinized in the crowded clinics of a teaching hospital.

So here as in everything else, the experience of infertility sharpens the differences which always have to be negotiated in any heterosexual relationship. The woman was held responsible for the success or failure of conception; the man was reduced even more swiftly than usual to the momentary provider of sperm. This, of course, is true only of cases such as ours where it is the woman's reproductive system that has been damaged. There were times when I wished that we were among the 40 per cent of infertile couples where it is the man who requires treatment. Then at least there would not be the continuing strain of being somehow complicit with the masculine order that had hurt and was still hurting Maggie. Looking back, I can see how this is double-edged; my wish to be more involved adds a further twist to the male jealousy of conception and childbirth. I guessed that Maggie was sometimes able to balance the humiliations of the treatment with a sense that here in the clinic attention was focused upon her essential part in the process. But guessing is the problem. All that I knew was that she was suffering the treatment and that I was removed to a distressing distance.

As the drug treatment became more intensive, Maggie was being hurt at home as well as at the hospital. On the nights when the regimen demanded, I was part of the hurt. We had known that the mechanics of sex by temperature chart would be difficult but now we had to give up all we had learned about the subtleties of shared sexual pleasure. To someone still bruised from that evening's intramuscular injection, the quickest, most pragmatic sex had to be best.

It's difficult to write about this but it's also important for me not to leave all the awkwardness of explanation to Maggie. Infertility is not easily talked about. People who have had difficulty in conceiving know that there is no common pattern and that every experience of infertility must be respected as distinct. Those whose pregnancies have followed a normal course can be taken aback by an insistence that what is normal has to be achieved with so much difficulty and thought by others. And those friends who have chosen not to have children might wonder why anyone would endure such pain and exhaustion in order to have what they have decided to do without.

Those years of thinking intensely about the importance of children in our lives meant that we had to move between all three imagined states. We learned the routines of Pergonal therapy but those routines in themselves are loaded with risk and uncertainty. Either side of that gamble lay the unpredictable prospect of how we would cope with such an exhaustingly contrived pregnancy or with the final admission that we could not have a child.

Swinging back and forwards between these possible futures, we were suddenly and dangerously tilted out of any control by Maggie's rushed admission to hospital. I was phoned at work and told to come at once to the casualty ward at the hospital. Adding to the fear was the fact that none of our friends knew about the treatment. I quickly invented stories to cover what I was frightened to admit: the desire to have a child had now resulted in the dangers of multiple pregnancy or even death. The hospital visits over the next few days removed those fears but still nobody told us what they had learned or how we could decide what to do. It certainly seemed to me too dangerous and painful to continue. I could only imagine the pain and so I was the one to suggest that we give up for a time: Maggie knew what she was having to undergo and how long she could endure it and why it was important to her that she should. The doctors kept their knowledge to themselves and refused to imagine what we might think or feel.

A lot of this, I have now realized, is about separation and exclusion. Medicine still separates mind from body, our fears and hopes around sexuality from the workings of the reproductive system. Because the doctors were interested only in putting right a dysfunction caused by the pill, there remained a complete separation between the physical tests and any attention to what we might be feeling. Textbooks might mention the documented psychology of infertility but all we ever heard were descriptions of the workings of the pituitary gland and how the hypothalamus might be triggered by doses of hormone.

The doctors had their explanatory terms and stories; we needed our own. At the time, Maggie was too close and I was too removed for us to find a common ground on which to explain what was happening to us. Just occasionally in the thirteen years since Dan was born, there has been a sudden rush of confidence in finding someone who knows something of what we have not been talking about. I listen to people's stories about their children; avidly to accounts of clinic encounters between friends and the infertility doctors. It is the detail that brings me close: the consultant who told a friend preparing for a laparoscopy to be sure to wear a favourite perfume for him on the day of the operation immediately became an anti-hero reassuring me that I did not invent my own memories of medical condescension.

It is the unrelenting insensitivity of medical procedure that needs to be challenged by men as well as by women. It is politically urgent to connect the glassy language of test-tubes and deep-frozen fertilization to the daily trial of physical endurance. Consultants can slip away into the lecturing projection of their ideas of a 'brave new' future. The women and men who need to consult that medical knowledge and experience must always remind the doctors that we exist not in some science fiction but in real distress and pain experienced every day.

That is why it is important for men who have experienced

something of the anguish of infertility and its treatment to add their own witness to the testimony provided by women. Men need to come out of the waiting room and argue against the conventions of medicine dictated by a masculinity, which in its narrow notion of scientific objectivity excludes our feelings as well as our partners'. There obviously need to be many more women doctors and gynaecologists but it is also important for men not to evade responsibility for their present actions (or inaction) by leaving all difficulty to be solved by a female future. Men and women need to admit a common vulnerability in this alien, clinical world and to consider common strategies of resistance. There is a long masculine silence to be broken about these insecure areas of feeling. Men need to join women in resisting the medical profession's readiness to reduce those they treat to the stoic silence expected of a 'patient'. I can see now how much more useful it would have been to Maggie and me if I had admitted my impatience, had come in from the waiting room and forced those cheerful young housemen to recognize my anxieties. If I had been there during the tests and consultations, then Maggie might have been recognized as more than a test site for pioneering and risky therapies and I might have been seen more than – on every ninth and fourteenth day – the provider of sperm.

This is to do more than repeat the necessary for a holistic approach to medical practice. Wanting to say something from the father's side – then at the hospital and now here – is part of a politics aimed at questioning the assumptions of patriarchy. I want to resist the easy guilt-tripping retreat into accepting as inevitable the division between male agency and female endurance. Men need to be involved in the arguments over reproductive technology, not as bed-side sympathisers but as allies of those women who are actively challenging the economic and institutional structures of this and every other part of the health service. My discomfort in the presence of those junior doctors came from an inherited working-class distrust of their confident authority: I felt nothing in common with their effortless assumption of masculine certainty. When one registrar missed an appointment because of a ski-ing accident, it confirmed all my back street suspicions of the distance between the doctors' world and mine. When another was unable to examine Maggie because he had broken his wrist practising karate, it made him suddenly human but still uncomfortably masculine. What kind of doctor moves from the infertility clinic to the ritual of chopping wood by bare hand?

Women doctors, I know, can display the same authoritative manner but within the infertility clinic theirs can more often be an authority of experience and that I want to learn from. I do not mean some kind of 'natural' knowledge distinct from intellectual and psychological understanding; that would push us back to the most unhelpful separation between female and male. The politics of infertility for me are to do with resisting any separation of knowledge from imagination in the name of an outmoded masculinity. Infertility disrupts all the carefully considered equations that we have been persuaded to consider natural. It does seem natural for me to have wanted to be closer to what was happening in the clinic, but I can see now how much that came from fear of losing my place as a husband. Writing about it here has made me recognize how much is still invested in the inherited icons of protective husband and protected wife and how difficult I found it to reconsider that role. I was a part of this history and have tried to be part of its telling but it is a part which is hard to learn. Infertility teaches men the difficulty of learning to live on the margin, an 'unnatural' place for us to be.

The women students and teachers with whom I work have taught me a great deal about the issue of women's visibility in this masculine-looking world. Thinking back over those years of waiting for a child has helped me to understand something of the contradictions surrounding women's vulnerability to experimentation. I still do not know how Maggie endured being looked over by those teams of doctors. My own invisibility, outside in the waiting room, offered me an obscure protection. But it left me vulnerable to the fears of imagination. Writing about it now for the first time has shown me how important it is for men to imagine and do, to put in words what they can never know.

When Maggie was three months pregnant we went to the hospital for a scan. The technician's camera was broken that day and so we could not collect the promised Polaroid record of our future child's first appearance. The aquarium flicker which proved the moving presence of a growing human being was a wonderful moment but I still would have liked a permanent image to mark the time I first knew I most probably was going to be a father. The technology of scanning has, I am sure, been particularly welcome to men: we can never feel the developing child inside us but now at least we can see something of the mystery with our own eyes.

Seeing Dan being born was the most vivid happiness of my life. I took a photograph of Maggie holding Dan a second or so after he was born. We sent copies to the two midwives and to the woman gynaecologist who had first advised us about possible treatment. We did not send any to the consultant at the teaching hospital or to the relays of junior doctors whose treatment had ended in success. We had not heard from them throughout the pregnancy. They remained in a separate world from ours.

ACCEPTING INFERTILITY IS A LINGERING PROCESS

■

TITIA ESSER
Holland

In 1979, when I was twenty-nine, I gave birth to a healthy, lovely daughter named Judie. My husband and I were very happy with her. Conceiving her hadn't been that easy – one year after we had decided that a baby would be welcome, I finally became pregnant.

As teenagers, my girlfriends and I often talked about marriage and having babies of our own. We amused ourselves with a trick with a needle and thread that would foretell the number of children we should get. The needle along the palm of my hand predicted three children for me.

When I was a student, one of my worries was how *not* to get pregnant. At that time my periods were sometimes very irregular and I didn't use the contraceptive pill yet, so I often worried about possible pregnancies. When I went to see our family doctor about my periods, he prescribed Primolut. Nowadays I regret the fact that he didn't send me to a gynaecologist for further examination. It could have saved me a lot of trouble later on.

After I graduated I became a teacher at a secondary school. I married and started using the contraceptive pill. While using the pill I was regularly checked by a medical doctor. I kept on working part-time after Judie's birth. The combination of child and work seemed ideal to me. Judie was an easy, happy baby. The only drawback was that she definitely refused to drink from a bottle. She preferred the breast. So I had to take her with me to school. After half a year I stopped the breastfeeding, with Judie's consent of course. My periods came back one month later.

When Judie was one-year-old my periods suddenly became

irregular. Our general practitioner told me such things were not exceptional in a busy life. Half a year later, however, the situation had not changed for the better. My gynaecologist prescribed Primolut. He explained that some women had difficulties with their periods after childbirth. There was nothing unusual in that. The unusual thing for me about this explanation was that my daughter was almost two at that time. Anyway, I hoped he was right. I also hoped that Primolut would set my periods right again.

After some months, however, the effect of Primolut decreased and the trouble started all over again. Again and again we thought I was pregnant. Again and again we were disappointed. Another baby would be more than welcome by now as Judie was almost three. Eventually, our family doctor, whom I frequently visited with complaints concerning my periods, sent me to the gynaecologist again. My period at that time was very heavy and I lost a lot of blood because it lasted much longer than usual. I began to worry, which made me feel depressed and vulnerable. I had lost a certain regularity in my life and felt uneasy without it. I began taking my temperature again in the mornings just as I used to do before Judie had been conceived, so that I could immediately show the chart to the gynaecologist at my first visit.

It was January 1983. The gynaecologist concluded from the temperature chart that I had no ovulation. Considering my first pregnancy he was not pessimistic about the possibilities of another one. In fact he was very optimistic. He told me it was probably fairly easy for me to conceive with the help of a small dose of Clomid. In his opinion, Clomid was an absolutely safe medicine. He had been prescribing it for several years without complaints or problems worth mentioning. The only drawback he could think of was the possibility of a multiple pregnancy. I had never heard of Clomid, so I was quite relieved that my problem seemed so easy to solve. One of my girlfriends, a nurse, warned me. She explained that hormone drugs could be dangerous. At that time I didn't know what to do about what she had told me. I desperately wanted to believe the gynaecologist. He was the authority and I thought he would know best.

In February I had my first Clomid treatment. One tablet a day for a five day period. It didn't work. Two tablets a day didn't work either. Still no ovulation. Actually I did not feel unhappy yet as I was finally having regular periods again. At least some regularity had come back into my life. I was happy about that. What remained was my anxiety about having no ovulation. Physically I didn't feel too bad either. The first signs of possible side-effects of the drug showed but I didn't want to recognize them as such. I wanted a baby. A close girlfriend told me that she thought my face had changed. To her it looked unhealthy, not like it looked before. I didn't agree with her. But when I asked my mother about it after I had stopped using Clomid she confirmed my friend's opinion. I started having a constant vague pain in my belly which I tried not to feel.

In September the gynaecologist suggested three tablets a day. I asked him about possible side-effects of such a long and now heavy Clomid treatment. He assured me nothing much could happen. My husband always accompanied me to the gynaecologist as our experience was that medical doctors would take more time and answer questions more seriously if we went together. Our gynaecologist would get irritated at certain questions as his goal was to get me pregnant as soon as possible.

After having taken three tablets a day for a month, a blood test proved that my hormones had gone back to their normal level. I could also read it from my temperature chart. I was happy with the result. On the other hand, I couldn't deny the side-effects any more. I had dizzy spells, a constant pain in the left side of my belly and a funny feeling inside my head, which I couldn't define. I couldn't see sharply any more. I saw lights and colours and I felt strange, funny inside my head. I remember one time at school when I began to panic because I couldn't see clearly. It made me feel unbalanced and insecure. While working with pupils I suddenly couldn't remember the simplest things. Was that a side-effect of the drug as well? I almost couldn't believe it. I also suffered from a pain in my belly which dragged on and on. Emotionally, I wasn't stable any more.

By the third month, I had to take one tablet on the first day of the treatment, two tablets on the second day, up to five tablets on the fifth day. This way of taking the pills would intensify the possibility of a result, it was said. By the fourth and fifth days I felt awful. I was anxious and had vague pains all over my body. But my gynaecologist had been right, I was pregnant at last.

How happy we were and how quickly I tried to forget those

awful feelings. Everything I was feeling now, I thought, was due to the pregnancy: that constant pain in my belly and stomach and the feelings of dizziness. Meanwhile Judie was four. We decided not to tell her until the dangerous months had passed successfully. After my first feelings of extreme happiness a vague feeling of anxiety overcame me. Was that pain in my belly a normal thing so early in the pregnancy? I decided to cut my negative thoughts out and tell our parents and good friends the hot news. Everybody was overwhelmed with joy. Except for me. Suddenly I didn't feel pregnant any more. In the eighth week I had a miscarriage. They told me I had had a multiple pregnancy. The dreams about our baby ended in hospital. Friends tried to comfort me by saying I should be glad that I now knew I was able to become pregnant with the help of Clomid. It didn't comfort me. The only comfort for me was that I wouldn't have known how to cope with three or more babies.

After a month I had a spontaneous ovulation. It would remain the only one. Clomid treatment started again. A low dose at first. The same old story again. No ovulation. After four months I had my three tablets a day again. It was now one year and three months since I had begun with the Clomid treatment. Still no baby.

With three tablets a day for a month I did ovulate but the side-effects returned as well. I had become so afraid of Clomid at that time that I hardly dared to make love any more, concerned as I had become of the effects the drug would have on the developing child. The drug was making me feel more miserable every month.

In May 1984 my husband and I decided to stop the Clomid treatment. The effects of the drug on my physical and mental health had become too costly. I wrote a letter of explanation to my gynaecologist as I didn't dare to confront him with my doubts. I felt he couldn't (or wouldn't) understand. He never responded to that letter.

From June 1984 until now, November 1987, we have gone through various alternative therapies. I visited homeopathic general practitioners who prescribed pills, tablets and drops. I started on acupuncture treatment. Chinese, Japanese, electric acupuncture and acupuncture of the ear. All to no avail. My condition is improving however, but my ovulation has not yet come back. My periods are still unstable but most of the time I can handle it by taking homeopathic pills combined with regular Chinese acupuncture.

In August 1986 I had another gynaecological check-up. Disappointed as I was that the alternative therapy hadn't worked either, I at least hoped that my condition had improved so that I could get further treatment. I chose a female gynaecologist. I hoped for more understanding. It turned out that I didn't feel more at home with her than I had felt with my former gynaecologist.

The only remedy, according to her, remained Clomid combined with Pregnyl. The blood test had proved that I lacked certain hormones. I suggested that she should work together with my acupuncturist. She said she couldn't as she didn't know anything about alternative treatments. I asked for time to think everything over.

Meanwhile I started to gather information about Clomid (see Part Five for more on Clomid). In medical magazines nothing was to be found about dangers connected with Clomid. Friends of ours who had studied medicine couldn't say much about it. They looked in their medical books: nothing alarming worth mentioning. I talked to a lot of people about it and gradually critical articles and stories reached me.

I heard stories of acquaintances who had been using Clomid some time ago. One friend who was having donor-inseminations in a hospital had to use Clomid although her period was normal. It was 'only' the one-tablet-a-day cure, but she remembers that she was feeling depressed at that time.

Another friend had used the three-tablets-a-day dose and stopped after several months as she had been feeling very miserable. Yet another acquaintance had also stopped after half a year. She too had had the three-tablets-a-day treatment and had been feeling awful.

In the course of this year I decided never to use a high dose of Clomid again. I am feeling rather balanced now and I don't want to lose that balance. I am continuing my acupuncture treatments although they haven't been successful as far as my ovulation is concerned. I still don't want to abandon hope. Hope for another baby. Sometimes I wonder why there are so many women who do use high doses of Clomid without complaining and why I have to be one of those women who does not want to

do so. It makes living much more complex. I feel I have made
the right decision. I don't want to run risks of which I don't
know the range, either towards a future child, or towards myself
and my family.

PART TWO

.

Experiencing IVF

When I came with my list of questions, Dr X patted me on my head and said: 'now don't you worry your little head off . . . we know what's best for you, so if you co-operate and stop worrying you'll have a good chance.' Later, however, he stopped being so 'nice' and once, when I complained about his assistant being too late for egg pick-up – which meant that I had missed my chance that month – he commented sharply that 'doctors' wives always cause trouble' and 'you want a child, don't you? – if you do, then give up your job, stop being a problem and co-operate.' So I felt I had to shut up or risk delay on the programme.

I felt so nervous and tense all the time I really doubted it would work. Somehow I managed to juggle work, house-work, taking the kid [her child from a former marriage] to school and *then* rushing to hospital every morning for a whole month for blood tests, urine samples and ultrasound. And often my veins would not come up . . . I remember worrying so much that because of this it wouldn't work and I had to give up. You see it depends on each procedure; if part of the procedure doesn't work you are a failure again!

It became a battle even doing part-time work. I could never let them know exactly when I was going into hospital and they naturally resented this. I felt that they would have preferred my resignation, but I didn't feel I could give up work even though my doctor had suggested this. But I thought, if I give up work and don't have a baby, then what will I have? What would I do with my time?

I remember the first embryo transfer I had. At the time there were visiting doctors from IVF programmes around the world, and I happened to be one of the guinea pigs going in for the transfer on the day they were at the hospital. It is embarrassing enough lying there with your legs up in stirrups without a roomful of people staring at you and with a huge spotlight (theatre light) shining on your genitals! When my doctor said to me that after that day I would have an 'international fanny' I was really annoyed at this remark, and the innuendo that I should somehow be thrilled at the prospect of being seen by all those international doctors.

THE PRODUCTION OF EGGS AND THE WILL OF GOD

·

ANITA GOLDMAN
Israel

She never really wanted it to succeed. Not really. Didn't want it to happen this way. Too much technique, too many hormones, too little feeling and privacy. An absolutely public conception. Something in all this sickens her. Part of her wished it would fail. Yes.

She is lying, head down, feet up, waiting for the embryos 'to take'. The position is awkward, humiliating, ridiculous. As if she was a test-tube in a stand and one had to be careful not to spill its contents out. She is the first woman in history lying this way, the head of the hospital-bed downward instead of upward and the end of the bed up instead of down. She has an urge to cough, but keeps it in, so that the stomach muscles won't press the embryos out. Why did she have to have a cold exactly this month?

The month of baby-making. Of egg-production. Of fertiliz-ation. But there is going to be no baby. She knows it. She has known it inside all these weeks, since the morning she arrived at the hospital for the first blood-tests and ultrasound-screening. Veins blue and black from the many needles, every morning at 7.45, testing blood-levels and then drinking the ill-tasting water in hospital paper-mugs until the bladder fills, exploding. And waiting. For the other women to finish their screening, for the doctor to come by and look over the results. Waiting with full bladder, talking about other treatments, other successes, other failures. Talking about the pain in the behind from the many hormone-shots, about the tense belly, about the disrupted workday. Talking and keeping the legs pressed together, so that the pee won't trickle out and then you'll have to start it all over again. Drinking, waiting, exploding with the bladder full of fluid.

And the doctors sweep by, smiling graciously to you, the guinea-pigs, swollen with water and hormones. Ready to burst.

And nothing will come out. Nothing. No. Except for a higher tendency to have cancer at the age of fifty-five. Maybe. They all reassure her, but she doesn't trust them. What do they know? How many cases have they been able to follow up? How many women in the world have had their blood pumped with hormones, their ovaries enlarged, producing dozens of eggs, instead of one? Or two.

Two. Her mother was a twin. Her grandmother gave birth to ten kids, plus surely a few abortions and miscarriages. Natural twins, identical. She herself was the second of her mother's five children. A fertile family. Full of women with broad hips and big breasts. Be fruitful and multiply. All of them, aunts and cousins and sisters, drop out little babies whenever the urge comes upon them. And sometimes when it doesn't. Everybody except for her.

Infertile. She doesn't like the word. It is too smooth, too objective, too much connected with fertility. She prefers the biblical language. Barren. Arid, dry, empty, hollow, void, fruitless, wasted. She is an emptiness, a nothingness, a no one. Even though, this week, her ovaries were filled with approximately a dozen eggs of different sizes. Before They sucked them out and put them in test-tubes and made a cocktail of her eggs and his seed.

She worries about the enlargement. How blown-up can ovaries become, without it being dangerous? What are the limits in this case? The other day the ultrasound technician seemed alarmed when looking at the screen.

'Your ovaries are huge', she said.

She didn't answer, couldn't ask, couldn't talk, because her bladder was too full, she had to concentrate on not peeing, while the technician called the doctor, who swept in (they never walk, they always glide through the corridors, their white frocks standing out like sails in the stale hospital wind). Sailed in, yes, and said: 'Nothing to worry about, I have seen much larger than these' and then angrily to the (female) technician: 'Why did you call me from the operating theatre for this!'

And the technician went red and he went away and she went mentally into her body, measuring the ovaries. Can they burst?

Will they ever sink back to normal size? Will this destroy their capacity to produce eggs – will they store the memory of this, producing in time, not babies, but cancer?

The technician liberated her from the pressure and she rushed out in the corridor, her pants half down under the long blouse, quick, quick, into the WC, and ooohh, release, emptying the bladder, the one and only pleasure during these days of pain and humiliation.

She returned more dignified to the corridor, the women asked '*Nuuu?*', meaning 'Well?' in Hebrew slang, and she answered 'Thirteen', feeling an absurd pride when seeing their envious faces. She is the great egg-producer of this group. The others have 'only' four or six and poor Hava only two, which lowers their chances for a successful fertilization. Thirteen eggs. Yes, mixed pride and shame. She is a freak of nature. A hormonized egg-producing monster, hatching like a master-hen in Their laboratory.

'But the ovaries are enlarged', she excused herself, trying to diminish her advantage.

'Oh, that doesn't matter,' Rivka calmed her, 'I was hyper-stimulated last time and had to lie still for two weeks . . . but it goes away afterwards.'

'Hyperstimulated,' she gasped, 'and you still came back for a second try?'

'Of course,' said Rivka, surprised, 'of course I did. One has to try everything, one can't give up, right?'

She turned to the other women for assurance and they all wiggled their heads, like so many hens.

'Never give up, no . . . trying everything . . . be in good spirits . . .'

'I'll never do it again.'

They looked at her, unbelieving, ill at ease. Then they decided that she was only upset and shouldn't be taken seriously.

'Of course you will. Everybody does. You go home, disappointed and tired. You let your body rest. Then you come back. After two months, three months. We all do. You'll see . . .'

'Never,' she said, looking straight into Rivka's eyes. 'I think this might be dangerous. Enlarged ovaries can't be exactly good for you. And all these hormones . . . who knows . . .'

Rivka averted her gaze and moved an inch closer to Hava.

'The doctors wouldn't give it to us, if it was dangerous,' she said. 'They have been doing this for a long time.'

'A long time! Hah! What is ten years in the history of mankind?'

The doctors wouldn't . . . oh they would . . . she knows . . . she knows. . . . Here she is, thirty years old, lying with her head down, waiting for the embryo to take, to stick onto the walls of her uterus, to stay. To stay and develop. Here she is, all agony and anguish, all bitterness and heartache, all pain and grief. Here she is, debased and degraded, embarrassed and humbled, shamed and subdued. Their guinea-pig, their hatching-hen, their hormone cow, their willing victim. And why? Because, fifteen years ago, when all she willed was sex and not babies, the doctor put an IUD in her almost virgin womb and the threads of plastic sticking out, attracting all sorts of germs and they entered her and her fallopian tubes became inflamed and her passages became clogged up and the little eggs couldn't pass any more and she didn't know until ten years later, when sex was still important, but babies even more. And the eggs never stuck. Never stayed. And the walls of her uterus, built up every month by the hormones to hold the egg, crumbled and puked out its content. Spewing, throwing up her blood. Blood and blood. And no babies.

No, the doctor didn't know that such young girls weren't supposed to walk around with a copper IUD in their young fresh uteruses. Didn't know. The recommendations from the Ministry of Health came only a few years later. When they had the statistics. Of which she was a minuscule part.

So what is it the doctors don't know about this time? About the hormones? About the long-term effect of so much ultrasound-screening? About the possible defects of embryos which have been out of the womb? What?

She had decided to ask to look at them, but she forgot as usual. The stress when the doctor arrived, always the same pressed atmosphere, no time, no time, the doctor is busy. She only caught a glimpse of a pinkish jelly concoction. Then she slid awkwardly onto the tilted bed, spreading her legs and thinking how she forgot to shave them this morning. The lab assistant gave the doctor the pinkish thing – was it really hers . . . haven't they mixed them up . . . how *did* they store them – and when he tried to push them in, she felt how futile the whole endeavour was, felt the meaninglessness of these awful weeks of screening and testing. They are not going to stick on, to stay. She felt it all the time. But now she knew it.

So why is she lying here, head down, trying not to listen to Rivka's whispered conversation with Hava? Lying still, like They instructed her, waiting for the embryos to take? Why, when she knows they won't? Because this is what had to be done? Because it would be absurd after two weeks of torture to quit now, at the final stage? Because They had taught her that intuition was not a real category and that logic is everything?

Still, she knows what she knows and slowly the disappointment seeps into her, filling her with its familiar mixture of rage and defeat, pulling her between desire for rebellion and utter subjugation and in the end leaving her only broken. A broken vessel. A barren land. An empty shell. A nothingness, a nullity, a non-being. But non-beings can't feel pain, can't cry, like she is doing now, into the hospital pillow.

'It is all right, don't cry,' says Hava, who has already completed her still hour and is up and moving.

'It is not all right and it is not forbidden to have feelings. Everybody doesn't have to be a cheerful girl-scout like you . . .'

She can feel the stomach-muscles tense up in anger, as Hava turns away, hurt. She tries to relax the muscles with some breathing technique she learnt in some workshop at some time in her life when she still believed it was all in her head and that she had the power over her own body.

Power, it all boils down to power. Power over one's life. Or power over life. That is the difference between her and them. She only wants to be able to influence her own life, but they want to dominate hers, everybody's, life itself. When she signed the form of consent, granting Them the right to 'undertake any procedures necessary', she warned them:

'If I get hyperstimulated I'll sue you, I won't let it rest.'

'Are you threatening us!' exclaimed the youngest doctor in the team, reddening down his throat where a prominent Adam's apple bumped nervously.

'Yes I am,' she wanted to scream, 'of course I am.'

Instead she smiled, mysteriously, mischievously, forcing the other doctors on her side, forcing them to smile with her, against him. And she signed away her power over her body, again, for which time . . .

But it is deeper than that. It is not only between Them and her. It is between her and her. She is defeated by herself, by her body, puking its blood and pain at the end of each month, the temperature chart declining steeply and her plans and projects and designs decreasing with the lowered heat of her body. No, next year they won't rent that little house by the beach and be with the baby. For there will be no baby. No, she can't tell Deborah that she will be giving up her role as fund-raiser for the organization, now when she is pregnant. For she won't be pregnant. No, she won't make all those triumphant phone calls to family and friends, imagined in detail, all their 'hoos' and 'whats' and 'reallys' and 'fantastics' carefully spaced. For there will be nothing to tell.

So how can she walk down the street, under a banner proclaiming her right to decide over her own body? When she is denied that right not only by herself?

She did decide. She decided she wanted to have a baby. And unlike so many of her women friends she even had a wonderful man to have it with. Decisions, resolutions, determination, will. 'Vanity, vanity, all is vanity,' as the humbled king sighed after fulfilling his desire for women to such an extreme that nothing was left but the knowledge that it wasn't women he craved.

Infertility is the final blow to all those brazen, self-assured, demanding, self-realized, liberated women of her generation. Professing to the world that it is theirs to grasp, to turn, to mould.

Self-determination, self-realization, self-domination. Self, self, self.

It's fine with her, she supports it all, she has fought for it since she was fifteen, that year when she thought that sex was more important than caution, that liberation was to jump into bed with every handsome pair of jeans that she encountered, that warnings of cleanliness and moderation were oppressive, that the world was hers. She got a little shaken when that beautiful Grace Kelly nurse sketched her insides on a notebook, in order to explain to her the gravity of her sickness and the importance of keeping still.

'Sterility,' said Grace Kelly and sketched many tiny little lines over the fallopian tube.

That word scared her. So she lay still, although she already wanted to get up and out, away from the hospital, out to the spring, where the handsome men in faded jeans demanded nothing from her, but freedom. For her to be sexually free. That was the cry of the day and she took it seriously, worrying much more about her 'hang-ups' and 'orgasm failures' and 'bourgeois jealousies' than about her inflamed tubes.

But now she is thirty and the demonstrations have died down and next to her sits Hava, who punctuates her speech with 'God willings' as naturally as she herself had once cried 'freedom'.

Had it all been an illusion, she wonders, turning now, for an hour has passed and she doesn't have to lie any longer with her head down and her legs up. Maybe Hava and Rivka were right with their humble acceptance, their trust in fate, their cheerful submission, their 'God willings'? Maybe they are the 'real' women and she herself actually on the other side, with Them? Doesn't she share with Them the Great Western Delusion about man's rights as Master of the Universe? Yes, OK her master is a mistress and she seeks only to govern her own life, not others. But still. She also uses words like control, management, government, command ('Women's command over their language' – she led that workshop).

She 'took control' over her own body, didn't she, she decided that she should be free to fuck without having babies, to sleep with whoever she wanted, without worrying about morals, health, consequences. Then she 'determined' she had had enough of that, now she was going to have those babies, now she was ready, mature, self-realized. And then. Bang. Her world shattered. Her decisions meant nothing, her philosophy went on strike, her body rebelled. Against her.

Now she has tried everything They have to offer. This is the last station, the last treatment, the last project. Now there is nothing left but hope.

She gets out of bed, into the bathroom, some of the pink jelly trickles down her leg.

'Goodbye little babies', she whispers, wiping them up with a paper towel, 'goodbye efforts and pains and mornings on the bus to get in in time for the 7.45 blood test. Goodbye. Now I am free at last. Of all those plans and pills and Pergonal, of all that pain. Now it is only between me and fate. Between me and me. No more doctors. No more treatments. I give up.'

'You shouldn't walk around like that.'

Hava and Rivka look worried.

'You have to rest in bed.'

'I am not sick,' she answers. 'And it didn't succeed anyway.'

'You can't know that!' exclaims Hava. 'God willing it can happen to any of us.'

'Yes, I know,' she says. 'It can. God willing.'

THE INSEMINATION CIRCUS

·

CHARLOTTE BÖHM
West Germany

Anna (thirty-two) and Hans (thirty-four) live in a medium-size town in the Ruhr district in West Germany. Both go out to work, she in a laboratory, he in a government job. In October 1986, at the time of this interview, they had just celebrated their eleventh wedding anniversary. The first ten years of their marriage were fully absorbed by attempts to have a child. Now they have finally had enough. How they reached this point and what they experienced, they both willingly and openly describe. For long sections of their story they give the impression of not being involved themselves, as though what they were telling me was not their personal fate at all.

'Of course we wanted children right from the beginning,' they both say in unison. When each one speaks alone, however, the impression is different. Anna says: 'I like children, and I would have liked to have had a baby. But I won't sink into a depression if I don't get one.' Hans says, 'After a year we wanted children.' That sounds as matter-of-fact as the diagnosis of reproductive specialists, who try to treat the 'unfulfilled desire for children' as an illness. Hans has adopted this way of expressing things. 'Our social environment demanded or desired a child,' he continues. 'In our circle of acquaintance, suddenly they all had children. If we wanted to do something in the evening, our friends always had to think about their children. Furthermore, we have a lovely house and garden here. And if you achieve something, you also want someone to inherit it all.' Hans never indicates in any way that he likes children.

One year after the wedding, there begins for the young couple what the well-known biochemist and critic of reproductive technologies Erwin Chargaff has called the 'insemination circus'. Both submit to examinations. Their general practitioner tries hormone injections, measuring temperatures and temperature graphs. It doesn't work. Anna changes her doctor in the hope that another might achieve more. She undergoes examinations at the University Clinic in Münster and submits to operations, for example a laparoscopy, in order to test whether or not her fallopian tubes are blocked. The result: no organic evidence to the contrary.

She finds the anxious waiting when her period is a few days late worse than these procedures. A period is easily delayed after the hormone doses have been reduced or suspended. 'And even if the waiting lasts only three days,' she says, 'it's still three days under constant mental tension. I don't know now how I stood it for years. I just don't think about it now, and that's nice too.'

In the early years of their marriage, however, the desire for children was so strong, says Hans, that they were fixated solely on this one goal and grasped at every straw. When they heard that there were two doctors in Essen specializing in artificial insemination, they drove there. 'They have a sperm bank too. We knew that their methods were pretty controversial, but they made a very positive impression on us.'

For months Anna and Hans attend the practice in Essen, so that she can have his sperm injected shortly after ovulation. 'They examined us several times and found we were both perfectly healthy.' Finally a cross-test was undertaken which was very expensive and had to be paid for privately: one of Anna's ova was put together with the sperm of a donor, Hans' sperm was used to fertilize an ovum of another woman. Result: both are fertile – with another partner.

'A clear diagnosis on sterility is possible within two to three months,' says Professor Piet Nijs of the Belgian University of Louvain, who has carried out intensive studies on the problems of infertility. But as a rule the couples go through tortures that can drag on for years because the doctors are not sufficiently trained or show too little interest. The story of Anna and Hans confirms this statement. They had been undergoing treatment for six whole years before they learned the result of this test. But they also confirm the experience of the Belgian specialist, that those concerned for the most part simply cannot give up, but, driven by the hope of a miracle, keep looking for new possibilities. At this time, in the middle of 1983, there is in fact a new 'message of salvation': *in vitro* fertilization (IVF). First successful in Britain in 1978, IVF, they were told, had now also been carried out in West Germany.

Anna and Hans did not waste much time enquiring whether IVF was any use at all in their particular case. They threw themselves on it like 'drowning people clinging to the wreckage'. Anna was frightened off a little by the fact that she had to undergo the treatment in Kiel, which was a long way from her home town. In the University Clinic at Münster, which she already knew, IVF was also being practised. But the doctors in Essen advised her against it. 'Go to Kiel. They already have a lot of experience there. In Münster you would just be a guinea pig. In your difficult case you need a clinic that has already shown some successes.'

At the gynaecological clinic of Kiel University the only woman with an international rank and name in the field of reproductive medicine is Liselotte Mettler. This militant IVF pioneer draws on her private mother-image (one child of her own, four adopted children) in public and employs it very effectively in her missionary media campaign for IVF as a 'healing method for sterile couples'. A professor at Kiel University, she depends on successes. She has a difficult battle against criticism and competition, even in her own clinic, where her boss, Professor Kurt Semm, tries to challenge her reputation. Anna and Hans get a taste of this conflict during treatment.

At first, everything seems to go quickly and smoothly. In November they apply to Kiel, and by January 1984 they already have their first appointment. But after seventeen days they have to return home with nothing achieved. No ovulation took place. In April 1984 the second attempt begins. This time it works: seven ova are extracted from Anna. The couple have learned from the depressing experiences of the first stay in an ugly hotel room and have rented a small holiday flat. They have their dog with them, and go for walks, feeling almost as though they are on holiday. 'We were really high,' Anna recalls. 'Everything seemed to be running perfectly.' But then comes the rude awakening. The ova and sperm cells do not fuse. All for nothing.

'For another couple fertilization was carried out in the same nutritive solution,' says Hans, 'and it worked for them. So we were told it couldn't have been the fault of the nutritive medium.

The upshot was that there must be an incompatibility of our ova and sperm cells.'

Yet again the see-saw of hope and disappointment, but it had never been this bad before. For the first time Hans acknowledges doubts as to whether what they are both doing is right. It had already begun when he was sitting all alone waiting for Anna to wake up from the anaesthetic, after they had removed the ova from her. 'The thought suddenly entered my mind: "all that for a baby. Is it really worth it?" My father had said to me long ago that children are not everything in life. "Don't let them go carving your wife up," he said. "You have such a good wife, I would never exchange her for another. Just live your life as it is." And I've tried to talk to my colleagues at work about it. But somehow they don't understand me. One colleague, who has four boys himself, said: "What will you do when you are old and have no one to look after you?" Always, just as we were about to give up, we have heard of other people who have been successful. And at the back of our minds there was the wish to go on.'

During the treatment in the clinic Anna talked a lot to other women. The doctors don't like this, because they think that the women only drive one another 'mad'. But Anna believes that she would not have been able to hold out without these talks. There were a lot of women there who had gone through a whole procession of tests. She mentioned one woman who fell into deep depressions every time it didn't work. 'She bawled the place down. After the tenth time she gave birth to twins. She now only concentrates on the children. Her husband doesn't exist for her any more.'

For Anna and Hans that would be unimaginable. Hans is one of the few men who have stood by their wives every step of the way. 'Sometimes I felt really funny, all on my own with all those women,' says Hans. 'But for me it was completely natural that we did everything together or not at all (except that of course I realize that it was Anna's body that had to undergo the procedure, not mine).' Both believe that this helped them to keep their relationship intact in spite of the crushing burdens. 'We often spent whole nights discussing it. But we never quarrelled to the point that we would have thought of separating.'

And after the experiences in Kiel they did not think of giving up, either. There was still a hope 'in the back of their minds', although they were terribly disappointed that no more examinations were carried out and no new tests planned but instead they were simply and quickly discharged. They felt rebuffed. 'We were sent to Münster for genetic counselling,' says Anna. 'They were to examine whether perhaps a hereditary factor had something to do with the infertility.' After this consultation, for the first time she was 'really fed up'. 'The counsellor asked a bit about our family history, he drew some diagrams and then said there was nothing wrong. We should come back when I was pregnant. At that stage one could do an amniocentesis, to see whether the child was healthy.'

Anna feels cheated. 'You're sent from one doctor to the next. No one tells you anything definite, and they just leave you dangling. "Come back again when you're pregnant." As though we hadn't been trying for all these years!'

For the first time, Anna says, she wants to stop. But it is difficult to get the thought of a child out of her head. She and Hans have become active in the ECB (an association of former Kiel patients and their husbands), which has already recruited about 600 couples country-wide and militantly and aggressively campaigns for IVF as a 'cure' and a method of salvation. At a general assembly they re-met one of the doctors from Kiel and discussed their case with him again. 'It sounded as though something had gone wrong for us,' Hans said, 'and as though there was still a chance.' They wrote to Liselotte Mettler and asked her to check their records again. But there was no answer . . .

Another hope, another disappointment, how many times now? Whoever is not in a position to improve the success rates of IVF doctors is thrown out of the IVF programme – Anna and Hans share this experience with many other couples. For the IVF success rate remains around 10 per cent. At the congress 'From men to gene, from gene to men' in autumn 1986 in Florence, a British reproduction expert says to a molecular biologist: 'Formerly the doctors didn't particularly concern themselves with sterility, but now, with money and a career beckoning, they're all scrambling after it.'

Since this last initiative in autumn 1985, Anna and Hans have begun structuring their life in a completely new way. 'We deliberately looked for new friends who were also living without children. That helped us a great deal. We play a lot of sport, three times a week. We don't want to give that up.' But in their closer circle there are also couples with children. They have a good relationship with Anna's sisters' two little daughters, often going off on weekend trips with them and spending holidays together.

They have already settled the subject of adoption. Anna is in favour, but her family have advised against it: 'Leave it alone.' Hans baulked at the 'snooping' of the authorities which adoption entails. He also has misgivings that such a child 'might not develop as one would wish. I think that I in particular could accept any problems more easily from my own flesh and blood than from an adopted child,' he says. 'Rather than treating a child unfairly, for whatever reason, I would prefer to give up the idea of adopting one.'

Meanwhile they enjoy being released from the pressure of having to have a child. They show no signs of being disappointed or even angry about what they have gone through. 'It wasn't a bad experience,' says Anna. 'At least it cleared things up for us. We can have our say, and we know the score.' Anna is not alone in this cool attitude. Again and again, as an outsider, one is struck by the coolness with which IVF 'patients' accept the fact that they simply must not let anything go untried, in order to be able to fulfil the prescribed role of mother. 'I wanted to avoid the reproach that I had left something out, before I reached the menopause,' said one woman from Hamburg, who had had a daughter at forty-three by IVF. She likes to refer to herself as a 'test-tube grandma'. A fellow patient of Anna's in Kiel gave up after the eighth attempt, at which IVF appeared to have worked. But then her period came after all. Her conclusion: 'At least it has been proven now that my body can produce a pregnancy.'

Anna and Hans have tried to tell other affected couples of their experiences, in order to be able to advise and help them. No one contacted them after a newspaper article in which they gave their name and address. That IVF can be misused is not something they ignore. In Anna's case she thinks that all her removed egg cells were fertilized and implanted. But they know from discussions with other women that egg cells are also frozen or used for other purposes. 'If you immerse yourself in the desire for children as we did for a long time,' Hans justifies himself, 'then you don't allow yourself to be put off by any reservations, no matter how obvious.' Nor does he believe that personal renunciation would have any effect. 'They would just carry on the experiments in secret, and then the whole thing would be even more difficult to check up on than before.'

For them personally, the matter has been concluded. Hans says: 'If a relationship doesn't survive without children, then it's not a good relationship.' Anna says: 'Even if new methods were to be developed now, that could give us fresh hope, I wouldn't go on.' For the first time in the woman who spent ten years of her life under extreme stress in order to become fertile, something of what must be happening deep inside her breaks out: 'If I were to become pregnant now, I wouldn't have an abortion. After all, I did once want a child. But honestly, now, it would be a shock.'

IS IT WORTH IT? I JUST DON'T KNOW

.

ANNE STUART*
Australia

I've been through three IVF cycles: two full ones and one with frozen embryos. In each case I had a successful embryo transfer. No one knows why it didn't work. I still have three frozen embryos in storage and if the next frozen cycle isn't successful I don't know if I will continue with the programme.

In retrospect, I wonder why I didn't realize I had a fertility problem earlier. But I didn't and it came as a shock when I found out that I was infertile. In fact when I didn't become pregnant I assumed my husband was having problems.

I'd had a Copper Seven IUD inserted when I was nineteen. I thought it was a responsible act of contraception. Right from the beginning the IUD was very painful and I had a lot of bleeding. I lost weight rapidly and I was tired and listless. So I asked my doctor to remove it but he told me my problems would settle down. I also told him that I found sexual intercourse very painful. He put my complaints down to emotional problems and referred me to a psychiatrist. The psychiatrist told me that there was nothing wrong with me, but a year later I still hadn't convinced my doctor to remove the IUD. I changed doctors and my new doctor removed it on my first visit. He started treating me for thrush and mentioned that he suspected that my womb may have been ruptured by the IUD.

---

* This piece is based on a discussion between Anne Stuart and Renate Klein. Anne Stuart is a pseudonym. She feels that being critical of the IVF programme in public could jeopardise her chances of continuing on the programme.

I went from one doctor to another trying to find a cure for constant vaginal infections and pains in my sides. Meanwhile my tubes were becoming badly infected, and I was starting to believe that I was neurotic.

I stopped taking the pill when I was twenty-five. Two years later I still hadn't become pregnant. This didn't worry me at first, but after two years my husband and I started having tests. Despite my medical history, I still didn't think that I had a fertility problem – I assumed it was my husband.

I had blood tests to see if I was ovulating and my husband had a sperm count done. Then my tubes were injected with dye to see if they were blocked. They must have been in a very bad way because none of the dye went through.

I finally had a laparoscopy which showed that my tubes were completely blocked from years of infection. Though my gynae-cologist wouldn't openly support my theory that it was caused by the IUD, he didn't discount it either.

I feel that there is stigma attached to the word 'infection'. The doctors gave me the impression that they suspected my constant infections were related to sexual promiscuity. I had to undergo all sorts of tests, including tests for AIDS, chlamydia, and venereal diseases. The results of all of these tests were negative but my infertility is still described in my doctor's medical notes as pelvic inflammatory disease (which to my knowledge is nearly always associated with chlamydia). Also, coming from a small town, where everyone knows everyone else, it was quite embarrassing to front up to pathology for a barrage of tests which are linked to social diseases.

I almost felt vindicated when my first laparoscopy showed that I did have a physical problem. Although I was very disappointed, it proved that I wasn't merely neurotic.

I still wasn't having a very good run with doctors though. When I came out of the anaesthetic, my gynaecologist wandered over to my bed and said in front of the other patients in my ward, 'It doesn't look like there's much chance there. I think I'd better send you to Professor X'. This was totally unexpected yet I couldn't even show any grief over the news because I was surrounded by three other patients recovering from wisdom-teeth operations.

So Professor X performed microsurgery on my fallopian tubes.

The right tube was beyond repair and he removed it altogether. He did his best to repair the left one. He didn't give me any details about the consequences of the operation but I found out through my own research that I would be more likely to have an ectopic pregnancy.

I was glad that I had found this out because two years later I actually had an ectopic pregnancy. As soon as I realized I was pregnant I felt that there was something wrong. I had a dull ache in my left side but again I had to convince my gynaecologist that I wasn't neurotic. I started bleeding but his receptionist wouldn't let me speak to him. In the end I rang my GP and asked him to contact the gynaecologist on my behalf. He convinced my gynaecologist to see me and I had to undergo emergency surgery that same afternoon.

After I came back from surgery, my gynaecologist, true to form, said 'It was really bad luck about that pregnancy; the foetus was only a quarter of a centimetre away from the uterus'. This really upset me. It would have been better if he'd said nothing. I changed gynaecologists after that.

I waited twelve months to get on the IVF programme's waiting list and then it took me another twelve months before I started the treatment. It seemed that every month when I rang up, another obstacle would be placed in my way. My husband would need another sperm count, or I would need an AIDS test, or I'd be waiting on the phone for so long to get through to the infertility centre, that that day's quota of women would be filled. Their regulations seemed to change from month to month but nobody told me what was going on.

Finally all my tests were ready. That's when I discovered I was pregnant. I was pregnant for three months, then I had to have a three-month break before I could start on the IVF programme; and then the nurses went on strike.

Two years after placing my name on the waiting list, I finally had my first treatment. The whole procedure was very stressful, both from a physical and emotional point of view. I'd get up at 5 a.m. to drive to Melbourne for HMG injections and blood tests. I also had to take Clomid tablets twice a day for the first five days. As my ovulation time got closer I had blood tests in the evening also. Just prior to the egg pick-up I was also given an HCG injection.

When I had to have blood tests done in the evening, I'd sometimes do the one hour drive to Melbourne after work and stay overnight. Then I'd drive back to work after my morning blood test. The hospital to which the infertility clinic is attached won't treat outpatients any more, so now I have to have the evening test done at my local hospital and take it with me in the morning.

I had two vaginal ultrasounds to check on the progress of my eggs. I still have visions of a technician telling me to relax while he inserts an instrument that looks like a giant dildo into my vagina. It's not supposed to hurt if it's done properly but I found it very uncomfortable.

The ultrasound was also used to collect the eggs during the pick-up. Eight eggs were collected and six were fertilized – three were transferred and the other three were frozen. My first treatment took place during the nurses' strike and for some reason operations could only take place after 6 p.m. I was the only one left in my ward who actually got to the stage of having a pick-up and transfer. In several instances other women ovulated before their operation could be scheduled.

I was very nervous the first time I had an embryo transfer. My cervix was scraped and a long, thin catheter was inserted into my vagina and the eggs were released into it. It wasn't really painful but it felt like a very strong cramp.

I wasn't supposed to move for at least half an hour after the transfer but after lying in the recovery room for ten minutes I was wheeled down the corridor at top speed and rapidly transferred to a bed. The bed was then pushed back against the wall. I was aware that I had to lie still until my cervix had closed and that this probably would have happened within the first ten minutes after the transfer. But I feel that my rapid trip from the recovery room to the ward couldn't have helped the situation.

I went home and took things quietly but five days before my period was due I started to bleed. I was quite upset that the treatment hadn't been successful and yet I was surprised that I *was* so upset because I hadn't really expected it to work the first time.

My husband was quite supportive but I knew he was disappointed. We really didn't discuss the issue. I know that it's supposed to be better to discuss these things but I didn't want to think about it.

We had to pay a $250 storage fee for the frozen embryos. I couldn't claim any of this on my health insurance. I suspect the fee is not only charged to cover the cost of storage but to encourage couples to undergo frozen cycles as soon as possible.

In fact my three IVF attempts have cost us A$10,000, over and above what we could claim on our health insurance. And the costs are increasing all the time. There is a surcharge on IVF consultancy fees and I can't even claim for Clomid tablets any more.

Four months after my first treatment, I tried a frozen cycle. The three eggs were defrosted but only one was suitable for transfer. I really hadn't expected the frozen cycle to work because I knew that the success rate was very low, so I wasn't very disappointed when I got my period.

On my last full cycle, six eggs were collected – three were frozen and three transferred. I was more optimistic this time because I had lasted right up to the due date of my period without bleeding. I was disappointed when my period arrived because I thought I had passed the critical stage. I still don't know why it didn't work. In hindsight I wonder if they were experimenting on me, because on the form I received specifying the number of eggs that were frozen, I noticed that two had been frozen at the 4-cell stage but one had been frozen at the 5-cell stage. If the embryos that had been transferred were also at the 5-cell stage I don't think a pregnancy would have been possible.

Apart from the fact that I have never achieved a pregnancy on the IVF programme my treatment has always gone like clockwork. After the last treatment was again unsuccessful, I didn't bother to pay a visit to Professor X, although I've since found out that this is compulsory. I resent paying $50 to be told that he doesn't know why the treatment isn't working.

The infertility centre has now introduced a system where patients must have a consultation with an IVF doctor when they come in for their blood tests each morning. This means that I have to pay for a consultation every day while I'm on an IVF cycle, even though the doctor just checks my hormone levels on a chart and tells me to come back the next day. Last time, even when my own doctor, Professor X, was the consulting physician,

I had to remind him that I was due for an egg pick-up. He was very vague. He forgot to tell one of the women who started with me that she needed an ultrasound. By the time she had one, it was too late. She'd already ovulated.

I think that Professor X is more interested in the research side of IVF than its humanitarian aspects. I suppose for a lot of the people on the IVF team, the procedures have become routine. This was really brought home to me when I had my last embryo transfer. The doctor who did the transfer didn't acknowledge my presence. He spoke to the sister standing next to me but gave no indication that I was a participant in the procedure. When he had finished, I was wheeled out and he didn't even look up.

One of the most frustrating aspects of the programme is the lack of information. As soon as my name was put on the IVF waiting list I started to research the programme. Professor X is the co-author of a book on *in vitro* fertilization, which gave me some basic information. But I wanted to know why it was essential that I take hormones to superovulate. I know that I won't produce as many eggs naturally, but they may be of a better quality without chemical interference. I also wonder how my body could be physically able to accept an embryo after my hormone balance has been chemically altered so drastically. After all, this is not the way a woman's body would normally function if she were pregnant. One of my major concerns is the long term effect of the drugs I am using, both on myself and on my child if I were to become pregnant.

I don't have a medical background but I don't think that these are such strange queries. I feel that my questions have been played down. I have been told that there will be no long-term problems but I still haven't received any satisfactory answers. This is one of the reasons I have long breaks between treatments, so my body has time to recover. After each full cycle you must have a three month break, but I don't know if this is long enough. One woman I spoke to had had eight treatments in a row and she was a nervous wreck. I don't know whether she was suffering from the normal stresses associated with the programme, but I'm sure that the large doses of hormones wouldn't have helped.

I'm also worried about the IVF's higher than usual rate of abnormalities. One woman I met had had triplets through the programme. Two of her children were fine but the third had spina bifida. I also know of a woman who has developed cancer of the womb after taking clomiphene citrate. She wasn't on the IVF programme but she was taking it as a fertility stimulant.

Perhaps I'm over-sensitive, but I get the impression that I have no right to question the IVF procedures or to ask the staff to simplify any of the routines for my benefit. For example, many of the tests which my husband and I have had to undergo could have been done in our own town. But this is not acceptable to the infertility centre. So we have to take time off work and spend an hour driving to Melbourne, sometimes for the sake of a ten-minute procedure. I must admit that I haven't been very assertive about my rights because I feel that if I were known to be a troublemaker it could jeopardize my chances to continue on the programme.

My greatest frustration in being involved with the IVF programme is the lack of information available to me. It also entails a great deal of stress – physically, emotionally and financially. It's meant that my whole life – my work, my study and my marriage – is at a standstill until I become pregnant or give it up.

Having children is important to me but I still feel that I can lead a fulfilling life without being a mother. But being childless has really affected my husband. He doesn't discuss it very often but I know that to him a marriage is not complete without children. I've even thought about being altruistic and giving him a divorce so he can find someone who can give him a child before it's too late. But I guess I'm too selfish to really do that. So, for as long as I'm married, I'll probably never accept that we'll be childless.

We haven't seriously considered adoption. Mainly because the adoption lists in Australia aren't even open and even if they were, by the time we reached the top of the list, we'd be too old to qualify. Also, it is very important to my husband that he has his own, genetic child.

If my husband and I were to split up, I wouldn't persevere with the programme. I am going through this because I've put ten years into our relationship but if I had another partner he would just have to accept that I can't have children.

When we were first married we both had certain expectations, one being that eventually we would have children. My infertility has changed many of our expectations. Financially, we're better off than if we had had children. And I've had to really think about my career, whereas with a family I may not have been able to make certain career choices. I may have just stopped working and stayed at home. It has also meant that I've been able to take on a much more independent role than I would have done with family commitments. But socially, we're in limbo – we just don't fit in. Of course we have friends, both single and married, but none of them can really understand our situation.

Perhaps I should have joined the IVF Friends but I really feel that my infertility is a personal problem. Part of the reason for this is that I didn't want it to dominate my life but I also think that, deep down, I'm ashamed of my inability to produce a child, especially when it seems so easy for other women. I've been aware that I am infertile for six years and I still find it difficult to discuss it openly.

Being infertile has forced me to take control of my own life. I can't just drift along and let things take their course. I have to make decisions – about my career, about my marriage and about children. Superficially, the IVF programme offers me a simple choice – the chance to stay on the programme and perhaps have a child, or the chance to stop and accept my infertility. But my decision is not so clear cut – the stress, the constant uncertainty, my fear of the treatment's long-term effects and the lack of control that I have over the treatment, make me wonder if I would have been better off not having to make a decision.

Is it worth it? I just don't know.

HE CALLED ME NUMBER 27

■

UTE WINKLER
West Germany

Inge M. (thirty-two), a full time homemaker with two adopted children, went through IVF in 1982. The procedure was not successful. The interview was conducted and edited by Ute Winkler (twenty-nine), in 1987. Inge's husband Peter (twenty-six) was present during the interview.

Ute: Could you please begin by telling me how you came to IVF?

Inge: We got married in 1979 and wanted children as soon as possible. We waited for two years and then it did not work. A laparoscopic examination showed that my fallopian tubes were completely blocked, and full of adhesions and scar tissue. Microsurgery would have been possible and we were told that the chances for success were about 5 per cent. But my gynaecologist advised against such an operation. So, at that stage there were three options: No children at all (but that, of course, was not offered as an option); IVF (a procedure which is called 'extracorporal'), or adoption.

   Upon hearing this, I went into a deep depression. Then we started two things at once: I made an appointment with Professor T in X and at the same time we put our name down for adoption with the Youth Welfare Department.

Ute: You contacted Professor T yourselves?

Inge: Yes. At first we were told that there was a waiting list of four to five years; that, too, was a reason for my depression. The Youth Welfare Department had also given us a waiting time of four to five years, the same as Professor T. But then we got a phone call from T informing us that I was going to be accepted onto his programme immediately. I think my age was very important, and also the fact that I was physically fit and psychologically balanced, except for those depressions. I was ovulating and my hormones seemed OK. It is very important to be fit and well for IVF. If one is already totally out of order, there is little chance of success. We were then asked to send in my temperature charts.

Ute: Up to that time you had never been in X and you had never spoken to Professor T? All you had done was to send him your case history which you got from your gynaecologist?

Inge: Yes. I sent all my surgery reports, and everything else. Next we were asked to come for an examination to make sure that the reports we had sent were correct. This preliminary examination was done by a biologist. He said that everything was OK and that my treatment was to start in September. He gave me a prescription and I was to swallow hormones – Dynerik tablets they were – for three to four days beginning five days after my period. I had terrible reactions to them! Well, I took these tablets for a while and then we went to X. We took a room in a hotel and I had to go to the clinic every day for a blood test, to check my hormone levels. And every day I had an ultrasound to monitor the development of my ovaries. I am very regular, as I know that I'll get my period every twenty-sixth day in the afternoon. It was quite clear to me why they were so keen to have me on the programme. The hormones they gave me speeded the whole procedure up. But in my case they were able to calculate everything very well in advance.

The ultrasounds were agony. One has to drink a lot of water so as to have a full bladder, because only in this way are the ovaries visible. There we sat, about seven or nine women. At first we could not stand each other. We felt like enemies. We did not speak to each other, just exchanged hostile glances, because each of us wanted to be the first. Each expected to be the one who was successful. None wanted one of the others to start egg collection before her. I knew that I would be one of the first because of my regular twenty-six-day cycle.

Well, after a while we got to know each other and things were less tense. Once the women started to speak about themselves, the things that came out really required strong nerves. I can understand that none of the doctors want to have anything to do with their private lives. If they did, they probably could not do their job. Professor T was rather cold.

Ute: But in public he acts as if he were a great benefactor.

Inge: Until he gets his people! Maybe he has improved since I knew him four years ago. I also think that he wants to advertise his cause. One of the problems is the fact that many of the women who sit in his waiting room have already reached the upper age limit. People who try for a test-tube baby are usually desperate. Mostly they are no longer young women. Between twenty-five and thirty one can say, well, I've still got time, I can try this or that. But if nothing happens at thirty-eight, thirty-nine or forty, then this is their last chance. So these women sit in his waiting room, because at their age they are also too old for adoption. So there are only the Professor Ts and they know that they have got you, because by then all the other medical possibilities have been exhausted. It's the last chance and if it fails a whole mountain of hopes and dreams comes tumbling down.

So there we were – women drinking water and none of us dared to go to the toilet. Now, say the appointment was at 9 a.m. Ten women come in at 9 a.m. with a bladder so full you think it's going to burst any minute. But the doctor only appears at 10.30. Try yourself to wait for an hour and a half with a full bladder: one feels like exploding! I remember how one of the women could not control herself any longer. She went to the toilet and passed a little water. Unfortunately, she was called in immediately after. You should have heard how they shouted at her in front of everybody: 'You are just sitting here with nothing else to do the whole day and you can't even control yourself' etc., etc. And these women are thirty-five to forty years old. They really should not have to put up with this kind of treatment.

Finally, after all those daily ultrasound check-ups we were all called together and each woman was informed how far she had come in her monthly cycle. One woman was told that she had been ovulating the previous day. She should try again in two months' time.

Ute: So you are saying that you had a meeting where each woman's cycle was publicly discussed?

Inge: Yes. Every woman's cycle was public knowledge. So we all sat there and Professor T called me Number 27. I must have looked rather puzzled, so he quickly added my name. I think he mixed us up with his numbers. We all looked around and thought what was it that we didn't understand this time? And we were all so nervous. I don't care how he identifies me in his paperwork but in public he has no right to address me as a number.

Well, I was to be done the next day. I had to go to the hospital at 3 a.m. and the nurse on night duty gave me the hormone injection. Then back to the hotel and on the next day I was admitted to the clinic. This was the time when the eggs had to be collected within twelve hours, that is to say as late as possible, but not too late, because the egg membrane could break and then the egg would be lost. To catch an egg just before ovulation, that is T's great speciality. He is really good at that. I suppose that's why IVF requires a cool scientist, not somebody who messes around with feelings.

Ute: He must be prepared to take risks. I mean he must postpone the moment as long as possible without, however, missing it.

Inge: Yes, that's right. But with many women he *did* miss the moment. These women can then only try again in two to three months. Many of them cried. One woman had noticed her ovulation during the night, but the doctor said that was not possible. They just did not believe her. But at the ultrasound they discovered it too and the woman was sent home in tears.

Ute: So what happened next, once you were admitted to the hospital?

Inge: First I had another blood test to check the hormone levels and another ultrasound. But this time it was different.

The bladder had to be full again, but because of the general anaesthetic that was to follow for egg collection, it could not be filled via the stomach. So they put me on a drip with a sugar solution. Normally they allow two hours for the bladder to be filled up. But they were late putting me on the drip so they hurried it up – it took only half an hour. My arm got terribly cold!

Once on the drip one cannot walk any more and so they took me upstairs to the ultrasound in a wheelchair.

The room adjacent to the ultrasound was again full of women I had met before. They all waited for T or his assistants. It was clear to them now that I was the first to be done and they were all curious to see how I would do. But this time there was neither envy nor animosity, only interest and tension. The ultrasound went well and the doctors kept saying to me 'look here' and 'look there', but I could not see a thing. Then I was taken out of the ultrasound room and the women outside clapped their hands and said 'Quick now, downstairs to the theatre!' That was a great demonstration of solidarity. The rivalry was only in the beginning when everyone wanted to be the first.

So I was taken to the theatre and they gave me an injection. This made me very anxious and frightened. They also put me on the heart machine but that guy, that T just would not appear – it was disgusting. Here I was, semi-conscious and they left me completely alone in the room. Finally I screamed that somebody should come and stay with me. I could not bear to be left alone with all those machines. Because of the monitor, I felt that my heart was somewhere in the room, and it went faster and faster. But nobody came and I got into a total panic. So I said that I was going to leave, that I could not cope, that I wanted to get out. I would have torn off all those tubes, but at that moment T arrived. It is no good if a patient is in a panic because of the anaesthetic.

So the anaesthetist told T that I had gone crazy. And T said: 'What's the matter with her? I am here!' And he signalled to them to put me out. I had had to wait for him for an hour and a half and my feet had gone very cold. It was a very long hour because I was terrified that I could have ovulated. I was lying on the operating table and fantasized that the eggs had jumped out and that T would open me up and find that the eggs had gone. Then he could have told me any old story.

But luckily everything went well, just as he had expected. He found two egg cells and one of them began to divide. They usually find two to three egg cells, never just one. Often there are many more, but they don't like that very much. Because every egg that divides has to be put back. That is because of the law or ethical principles I think. In any case that is what they told us: everything that is taken out and that divides has to be transferred to the woman's womb.

Ute: Would you have preferred it if they had found more egg cells?

Inge: I would not have liked it for instance if they had taken six egg cells which all developed. Nobody wants that much good luck! Just imagine what it would be like to get six children all at once. Twins would have been all right, but six! And usually one or more babies from multiple births have health problems, that's another risk one doesn't want.

Well, they took me back to the ward and I had to rest for forty-eight hours. Then they transferred the one egg cell which had divided. That too was quite an impossible business, though not from a medical point of view. Peter wanted to be present at the transfer. He wanted to come with me in that room where the gynaecological chair stood. In any case, he was the father, or would have been. But they absolutely refused and the way they did it was anything but tactful. They looked at him as if to say 'Who do you think you are?' T was terrible. So cold. In the end the room was crowded with people who were allowed to watch: a professor from Australia, a student, three female assistants and two nurses. People everywhere, but there was no room for Peter. Then they started talking as if I wasn't there. During the whole procedure T never said anything nice or encouraging to me. I had the feeling that he never noticed that I was even there. Not that I had expected much in the way of empathy, but T did not look me in the face once. I heard him saying: 'Oh look how beautiful!' But it was always the others who were asked to look how beautiful I was down there. How would I know what was so beautiful! 'And now we insert the probe' . . . and this and that. But of course I could not see anything as I was lying on my back. I found the whole procedure really inhuman. If only they would do it in a more humane way! I am sure they would be more successful. From a psychological point of view the whole business is so complicated and hard to take that one just has to reject it, both from a rational and from an emotional point of view. It is just so artificial; so alienating . . . I could only go through with it because one of the nurses was just so totally nice.

Another thing was that they had put us in the maternity ward. It didn't matter much to me, but for other women it was just the last straw, it really finished them off. Our nice nurse always saw to it that we were reasonably happy and comfortable and she laughed and joked with us. We used to call T 'God Almighty'. Well he was, wasn't he? So we used to say: 'Here comes God Almighty . . .'

Later, when T took over a clinic closer to where we live, he wrote to us and asked if we wanted to try again; especially since I had such a good cycle, and it would be so handy for us now . . . After the laparoscopy (for egg collection), T had also advised us to have microsurgery: 'it wouldn't be so bad . . .' he said. My own gynaecologist, however, suggested: 'Do whatever you like, but they are all researchers and scientists, they need guinea pigs, the microsurgeons included. They need people on whom they can practise.'

If I had become pregnant, I don't know whether I would have told T about it at all. Under no circumstances would I have wanted him for the birth. The whole procedure, the things I lived through, the other women and their sufferings and the way they were treated. At twenty-seven it is probably easier to cope with these things than at forty!

Ute: I cannot understand why T does not take the women seriously, particularly when he must know that the success of the transfer of the fertilized egg has a lot to do with how the woman feels.

Inge: T believes he can trick the psyche. That's the whole point. Can the psyche be tricked or can't it? I don't believe it is possible. I found the whole thing repulsive. One really has to believe it; and perhaps if one doesn't see any other way, it might work . . .

Ute: Were you very disappointed when it did not work for you?

Inge: I didn't really believe in it ever! Perhaps this is why it did not work. The disappointment was really like the other monthly disappointments when, again, it had not worked. But in the first few months afterwards it was very hard for us to speak about it, because of our hurt feelings about how we had been treated. But the more time passes, the better I can cope. I don't think I would do it again. We would very much like a third child and it is hard to make up one's mind. I would love to be able to decide for myself whether I'll have a third child or not. I think that I have a right to have ten children, but unfortunately there is this problem . . . Sometimes I wonder if we should try again . . . But then we would again be dependent on some professor who would torture us in the same way, or even more, because there would be the whole medical procedure again.

Ute: Is it important for both of you to have your own biological child?

Inge: When the gynaecologist told me that I could not have any children of my own, it was terrible to think that I could never have a child around me of whom I could say 'Look, it is just like me'. Childlessness causes suffering, sometimes it hurts, sometimes it doesn't. I have times when I cry a lot. This will always be so – we will always have our ups and downs. That's quite normal, one is always mourning for something that might have been. Sometimes I don't feel it for a year and I think all is well. And then, suddenly, it is there again. It can be caused by anything, a birthday, a certain smell, anything that reminds me of a child.

Ute: Just to return to T once again. Were you told about risks and success rates? Or how the whole IVF procedure is done, in detail?

Inge: Not much. I understood things most of the time and I asked questions. I can look after myself reasonably well. But there was a woman from another country who didn't understand a thing of what was happening to her. Her husband was the same. A young doctor, whose job it was to explain everything to that couple noticed that they had a language problem, but he was not prepared to spend more time with them. With the woman they could do as they pleased, as we were in the clinic. But the husband had to understand when he had to bring in his sperm, or else the whole procedure would have been useless. We were not really informed about what would happen. They told us very briefly about the whole physiological procedure. The ethics of the whole thing was not discussed.

Ute: Did they tell you about the success rates?

Inge: At the time we were told that the figure was about 25 per cent. Later we understood how this figure was calculated. If one takes into account all the things that can go wrong the final figure that emerges is about 5 per cent.

Peter: What is meant here is that cell division and implantation is successful in about 25 per cent of cases. After all, if all goes well up to that point, this can be counted as success, too.

Inge: But if you take it up to the real thing (a live baby at the end), the rate is only 5 per cent. When I first heard 25 per cent I thought 'that's not bad, I'll try it, perhaps we'll be lucky'.

Peter: At that particular time there was a general euphoria in Germany. The first test-tube baby had been born in the Federal Republic only a few months before. And Inge was immediately accepted because she was young and healthy.

Inge: We thought that it did not entail much surgery. I did not want to have a full-scale operation. The laparoscopy was a bad enough shock for my system. I am no hero when it comes to surgery and a full anaesthetic takes a lot out of me. When we heard that no major operation was involved we thought that we could risk it.

Later we also had moral scruples. For instance when T told me that there were two egg cells and only one was to be put back as the other had not divided, I began to agonize over the thought that T might not have told me the truth: had he really collected more than one egg cell? And had he perhaps put them all back? How come only one had divided? What about the other(s)? I had this horror vision that somewhere a test-tube was bubbling over with a baby of mine! I know this is a mad idea, but I just cannot help imagining it; it has become an obsession: a baby appears, is suddenly there all alone in the test-tube . . . terrible, I could not sleep while I was thinking about it. And then it dies. Of course, what else can it do in a test-tube? Nothing happens with it, so it dies.

Peter: I must say, we were quite worried about how little support the women received. For instance, when they had to wait with a full bladder for their ultrasound test.

Inge: Fortunately, I was never alone, my sister was with me. But those others! When they talked about their lives, the hopes they invested and the way they were treated! They tried to do everything right, to please T and his assistants. They were totally at their mercy. Disgusting! I thought, no, I am not going to be like that. I won't let them do that to me. I never had the slightest confidence in T. I did not know him, and he never behaved in a way that could have won my confidence. So why should I have believed him?

We tried IVF in September, and in the following spring we read about the controversy in England about how long embyros can be kept alive for research. The very thought made me sick! That is the reason why it is so important to trust the doctor, and see a gynaecologist whom one knows. I must be convinced that he does the job as an alternative for me and not for research.

Ute: After what you've experienced, would you advise other women against IVF?

Inge: I could not say to a woman that she should not try it. I can understand why she would want to go for it. So I would say to her: 'OK, it will be nasty and you will suffer.' But I would not say that she should not be allowed to try.

Ute: Do you sometimes think that you would like to have another try for yourself?

Inge: Not for myself. For myself I would never do it again, only if Peter insisted, would I do it. But I don't think he would. I think of all the things that can go wrong, and the direction into which they are moving. And with every woman who volunteers the doctors have won something. It helps them to improve their routine. No, I would not like to be part of their machinery ever again.

WE ARE NOT JUST EGGS BUT HUMAN BEINGS

■

LENE KOCH
Denmark

In the autumn of 1986 I began researching the experience of infertile women on IVF programmes at a large Danish hospital.[1] After a couple of months, I had a call from a thirty-five-year-old woman, Elizabeth, who wanted to talk to me about her experiences. The story she told revealed such important issues concerning the emotional and psychological consequences of IVF that it made me revise some of my original beliefs about its benefits.

The next months of my research were thus influenced by the story this woman had told me and increased my sensitivity to similar issues with the other women I was interviewing. She had been in the IVF programme for longer than most women. To begin with she participated in a special experiment that was carried out in the first half of the 1980s. Later, she joined the regular IVF programme of the hospital. When IVF was accepted as ordinary medical 'treatment'[2] in 1986 by the Danish Health Authorities, she continued to be on the programme.

Initially, my interest in IVF was primarily concerned with the possibilities this technique provided for genetic manipulation of human gametes, on a long term basis. This perspective, which I share with many others, is serious enough, but – I have come to realize – it ignores issues and critiques that relate particularly to women and which are only gradually becoming visible to the public.

IVF as a form of infertility 'treatment' has been intensely publicized in recent years. This is certainly not because of its practical results in 'treating' infertility. At best, its real success rates – a baby at the end of the pregnancy – are only slightly higher than those of tubal microsurgery, a procedure often criticized for its low success rate by the very experts who want IVF to take its place. IVF has hit the headlines, however, because of the enormous prestige and complex high technology involved in its research and, of course, because it contains the potential for controlling the creation of life, a potential which has traditionally rested with women.

While the 'benefits' of IVF have had no difficulty in reaching the press, the costs to women undergoing the procedure, e.g. the risks associated with the hormonal stimulation, ultrasound scanning and psychological trauma, are rarely mentioned. Because of the researchers' desire to use fertilized eggs in experiments, infertile women become a vital resource for those scientists bent on revealing the secrets of life and death. The women considering IVF have an optimal motivation for yielding the reproductive material that the scientists need because they expect to benefit from this arrangement and the 'material' can be delivered by no one else. Also, they believe that the desire for a *biological* child of their own can only be fulfilled by the IVF clinic. But their psychological problems associated with infertility and with the IVF procedure are neglected and – with the exception of feminists – receive no attention whatsoever by medical doctors, scientists or politicians.

The women's determination combined with the poor results of IVF, the lack of proper information among IVF 'patients'[3] about these results and the lack of attention to the psychological realities of people with an infertility problem makes the concept of informed consent and ethical procedures in IVF research highly problematic. Elizabeth's story is an illustration of this.

The background

When she was twenty, Elizabeth had an inflammation of her tubes, and as a consequence became infertile. She didn't realize this until many years later, however, and spent a fortune on contraception between the ages of twenty and thirty, including the pill. When she wanted to stop taking the pill, influenced by the growing awareness of its dangers, she had a gynaecological examination which revealed that her tubes were damaged as a result of the earlier inflammation.

During the next ten years Elizabeth unsuccessfully tried every type of 'treatment', and finally ended up on the IVF waiting list of a large Copenhagen hospital. By this time her wish for a child had increased as she had met her present and much-loved husband. But she was also exhausted by the incessant and futile infertility 'career' in the medical system. She felt haunted by family and friends who made her feel guilty that she wasn't doing enough to have a baby. 'It was almost a relief to be on the waiting list' she says, 'because then I could tell all of them that we were doing everything possible to have a child.'

It turned out that Elizabeth was certainly willing to do everything possible to have a child. Having been on the waiting list for a couple of years, she and her husband had a letter from the hospital asking if they would be prepared to undergo an IVF experiment performed in co-operation with the fertility clinic at the hospital. They were informed that they were one of twenty couples who had been selected from the waiting list, primarily because of their alleged psychological strength and emotional stability ('How they ever reached this view of us is beyond me' Elizabeth says). Would they come for a consultation at the hospital about this?

'The whole thing seemed very secretive', Elizabeth told me. 'We had this conversation with the leading scientist in the experimental group, and it took place in a private room secluded from the humdrum of the clinic. The atmosphere was very clandestine, we felt we were among the chosen few who expected to become involved in something very special.' Elizabeth didn't realize what the exact purpose of the experiment was but it was explained to her that the research might give her and other women a better chance of becoming pregnant. Whether participating in the experiment was an alternative to the regular IVF programme or a means of obtaining special treatment before others on the waiting list was not made clear. She remained on the waiting list and later moved on to the regular IVF list.

Elizabeth was positive from the beginning. She welcomed anything that would help her achieve her goal, and felt confident that once she entered the experiment, she would be an 'insider'. She would gain advantages that other women on the waiting list did not have: 'We all had our motives and they all had to do with individual advantages. I was assured that through the experiment they would become familiar with my body and its functions and once they knew my reactions and responses, I would stand a greater chance of becoming pregnant. I felt certain that somehow it would be an advantage if I participated.'

Elizabeth told me that at this first meeting with the scientist in charge of the experiment, Dr J, it was repeatedly stressed that it required a great deal of strength and perseverance to be part of the experiment. No woman was allowed to give her consent until the next day, even though all the women who had been asked knew already that they wanted to do it: 'We wanted to do it, all of us. We were quite giddy, and told Dr J that we would go out to the phone booth in the hall and phone in our consent from there.'

Dr J was doing the correct thing by asking the women to go home and think it over. But at the same time he also offered them what they felt was a 'special treatment'. More importantly, he offered them an increased expectation for a child. 'Once he had given us the impression that this was a better chance of having a child, it was impossible to say no', says Elizabeth. 'This is what is so dangerous, and almost paradoxical. He gave us hope but at the same time told us to go home and think it over. But there was nothing to think about. *He* was the one who should have thought it over. *He* should have gone through the psychological – and lastly physiological – implications of such an offer, because we were completely unable to.'

The daily routine

'They followed us all through four menstrual cycles. We showed up every morning at eight to have blood tests, hormone injections and ultrasound scanning. We collected our urine and turned it in daily. We were a bunch of women who met every day. In a way we had fun – the atmosphere was very congenial, though perhaps a bit grotesque. One morning, when my husband turned up at the hospital to pick me up he was met with this remark from Dr J: "Well, what are you doing here. We can manage this thing without your assistance, you know." It was a joke, and we were part of it.'

Most of the women, however, had psychological problems as well as unanticipated physiological effects resulting from the treatment. 'I put on six kilos from the hormone treatment. No one at the clinic told us of these potential side effects. I am usually a very strong and controlled person, but one day I realized that I had cried three times at work and so I asked at the hospital, "Are you sure there are no side effects to these hormones?" They then began to look into it because there were several of us who had complained about these particular side effects. It turned out that the hormones they had been giving us were not the usual ones. We were finally told that the pharmaceutical firm dispensing the hormones had somehow delivered a different product without telling the hospital. We never knew more.

'Well, after three cycles of "treatment", or what I thought was treatment, I was to have a number of fertilized eggs transferred. I knew from the beginning that one of the problems with IVF was to make the fertilized egg adhere to the lining of the womb. The day before the transfer I spoke to one of the technicians at the lab about my worries and she told me that no one had ever become pregnant from the treatment given to the women in the experimental group. This extraordinary piece of news was a shock to me because I had never thought along those lines. I thought pregnancies occurred among the experimental women at least as often as they did among women on the "list", i.e. the women receiving the regular treatment. But this lab technician told me that I was mistaken. Dr J simply didn't give us the proper information. They all talked about the success rate and the twins that had been born recently, but all this turned out to have happened to the women on the "list". All the glamorous pictures in newspapers and magazines were of women from the "list". Perhaps we were the only ones who didn't know. Afterwards I realized that this may have been the reason why we (the women in the experiment) never met the women on the "list". We always had appointments at the hospital at different times. I believe that they didn't want us to meet them and exchange information. This was the incident that first made me suspicious of the whole thing. You see Dr J had never told us that the pregnancy rate was zero. I had picked up a piece of vital information from a lab technician by mere chance.

'Well, I had my fertilized eggs transferred and I lay at home for five days, holding on to these eggs, but finally had my period. I was completely devastated. I had been one of the women in the experiment who had helped keep up the good spirits and encouraged the others. But once I began bleeding, I was the one who needed help. I phoned the hospital, wanting to speak to Dr J. I got him on the phone and cried and he said to me, "Don't worry, we shall find a solution." He said he wanted to look at my blood tests in the afternoon, and he promised to phone me back. But he never did. He never phoned me back. This was the last I ever heard of him. I still can't believe it. It was an incredible disappointment and a terrible betrayal by a person I had trusted so completely.'

This was the end of Elizabeth's participation in the experiment. She didn't turn up again for renewed experimentation and the hospital didn't contact her for a formal termination with the experiment or to learn of her physical condition after treatment. Instead she went back on the 'list'.

The lack of information about how likely her chances of pregnancy were, and of the nature of the experiments, as well as the lack of empathy from the scientist responsible, became the crucial experience for Elizabeth. It gradually undermined her confidence and respect for the doctors and for the good intentions of the experimental scientists. Her initial feeling of disappointment and betrayal have turned into a mixture of anger, a desire for revenge, and a final realization that she had been emotionally and psychologically exploited. 'I'll get over it, but had I known from the beginning that I would not have a baby after this, I think I would have gone berserk.'

A vital failure of the experiment was lack of information. To this day Elizabeth does not know the purpose of the experiment; its total duration, or its outcome. She has never received any written information apart from the initial letter inviting her to become part of the experiment, nor did she ever sign any papers to prove that she had given her informed consent.

'My lack of information became absurd when I was in hospital after an egg transfer and asked my neighbour, who was also lying-in after IVF, a question about the procedure. She answered: "It's all in the brochure." "Which brochure?" I replied. The women in the experiment were never given the information that the women on the "list" had received.

'It all has to do with respect. They ought to respect not only one's body but also one's feelings. *We're not just eggs, but human*

beings. I remember the time that Dr J told us to think it over
carefully before we went into the experiment. But somehow he
didn't have the ability to explain to us what the risks were. And
I don't think he knows what they are. You don't know yourself
until afterwards. But he doesn't know and he never will know
because he never cares to ask.

'I once met him in the corridor, about a year later when I was
on the "list". He said, "Hello, how are you?" and I replied,
"Fine, thanks, but what about you?" I think he ought to have
had some problems. I think I would have had him fired if I had
the power. Why didn't he send us a letter to say that the experiment was over, what the results were? I should have liked to
know if he wrote a book about this. All the women became so
closely attached to him and worked up a feeling of confidence
that was never returned.

'It's the desire for a child that carries you through this. We
have all been through several operations and we all have scars.
We all know IVF is our last chance of having a child of our own,
and that has made us extremely sensitive.'

Work and life during IVF

After she left the experiment, Elizabeth entered the regular IVF
list and has undergone two of the three cycles that are normally
offered IVF 'patients'. Almost two years have passed and this
long period of involvement in IVF has put a severe strain on
Elizabeth's working life. One of the major problems of being on
an IVF programme is fitting it into one's work life. Elizabeth is
a department head in a large advertising agency, a job with heavy
requirements. 'Fortunately I had my embryos transferred during
the Easter holidays, and when I was in the experiment we had
to be at the clinic at eight o'clock in the morning. It certainly is
difficult to go to the hospital in the middle of the day as we have
to do on the regular "list". Some women take sick-leave and get
a reputation for being unreliable workers. Others try to manage
both the IVF procedure and work. This is what I have tried to
do myself. But it is a very stressful situation, especially when one
considers that each cycle of treatment lasts two weeks and one
may have to commence four to five "treatments" in a year.[4]

'At one time I had to travel to London for a week-long business trip. I was scheduled at the clinic at the same time. I asked the doctor what he thought I should do. I should never have asked him. He was astonished that I could even consider leaving the country when it was about to be my turn! But I knew I could skip a month and come back into the system later – which is what I did. Such a situation makes one feel divided. If I skipped this cycle for business reasons they would consider me odd and irresponsible. Both the hospital and our friends had such great expectations. All the same, I have a life to live which I cannot neglect cycle after cycle.'

Worries

Elizabeth is a woman who basically accepts the idea of IVF technology. But she has trouble when she considers what IVF research and experimentation implies. 'I am worried about the experiments. I refuse to think that they experiment on my eggs. I know they fertilized some of my eggs and never transferred them. I don't want to think that I might have reason to doubt them, and I believe them because of the power and authority they have.'

Elizabeth's feelings oscillate between faith and doubt. 'Once you are in the experiment, you have to have faith in them. We believed in them because we thought we were in their power. The "girls" accepted a lot. Somehow you become dependent on them.' These women were treated and forced to behave like children: 'When I came in to have my hormone levels tested I would ask: "Have I behaved properly since yesterday?" When I was sent home the evening before I was to have my eggs out, the doctor told me: "Now be careful not to ovulate before you come back tomorrow." Why does he tell me that? I cannot control my own ovulation, but it makes me feel guilty and responsible for something beyond my control. One of the other women told me after she had had an egg transfer: "I couldn't help coughing last night, I'm so afraid I have lost the embryos." They ought to tell us explicitly what we can and cannot influence. Everything else results in a bad conscience. Now I don't blame them for not getting me pregnant – I'm sure they have done their best – but I *do* blame them for not taking more care of me when I needed it.'

When I asked her if she had ever considered dropping out of the programme – she still has one cycle of treatment to undergo – she said: 'It's not a question of choice. You cannot say no to IVF. It's a question of responsibility to one's own conscience. I think that I would blame myself for the rest of my life if I said no to this last cycle because it *might* result in a child.'

This epitomizes the dilemma of women who consider IVF. Regardless of the low success rate very few women are able to say 'no' to IVF. Lack of information about the tremendous stress and prolonged period of the treatment plays its part, of course, but once IVF is available as a socially accepted 'treatment' for infertility, the element of individual choice begins to disappear. The wish for a child is almost automatically transformed into a wish for a *biological* child and the alternative of adoption is disregarded or put off. Thus costly time is spent and often wasted in an IVF programme while the woman nears the magic upper age-limit where she is forced to leave the IVF programme and by that time usually has become too old to adopt.[5] Elizabeth and her husband are now considering adoption, as they are on the verge of abandoning IVF.

'Somehow I don't care which child we get. As long as we get one. The thought of abandoning the wish for a child is completely out of the question. It all has to do with the *how*. Everything else is an academic discussion to me . . . I am determined to have a child, either through IVF or through adoption.'

Elizabeth and the other women thought that participating in the IVF experiment would put them in an advantageous position where their chances of pregnancy would be enhanced. They did not receive any information which indicated that this was not the case. Instead, they had to experience, through their bodies and their emotions, the disadvantages, anger, frustration and side effects of the experiments, all to no avail. The women thought they were being given an increased chance of becoming pregnant. For this expectation they allowed the scientists to experiment on their bodies.

If this were a give and take arrangement, the women gave infinitely more than they received. Elizabeth even gave the hospital the invaluable use of her own good spirits since she was a major factor in maintaining a jolly atmosphere among the women participating in the experiment.

The final outcome for a woman like Elizabeth is a hard-earned experience. For the hospital the result may be costly too, as the confidence of a number of women clients has been undermined. Unfortunately, very few of these women have articulated their experience. Elizabeth's story is an attempt to give voice to one.

NOTES

1   For preliminary results of my investigation see Lene Koch and Janine Morgall 1987. Towards a Feminist Assessment of Reproductive Technology in *Acta Sociologica* 30 (2):173–191.

2   Strictly speaking, IVF is no 'treatment' for infertility. Even if the IVF procedure results in the birth of a child, the woman – or her partner – remains infertile. To use the term 'treatment' is part and parcel of the medical (and media) distortion of IVF as a 'cure' for infertility. However, because 'treatment' is the word which is constantly used to describe the IVF procedure, I have chosen to leave it in Elizabeth's story, occasionally putting it into quotation marks to indicate its problematic use.

3   Similar to the word 'treatment' (see Note 2), the term 'patient' is a misnomer: it labels infertility as a disease and treats infertile people as 'sick'. However, I have decided to leave the word 'patient' because I think that in the humiliating IVF procedure the women become patients in all senses of the word and are stripped of 'clients' rights – an alternative term for patients suggested by critics of IVF.

4   Only a completed cycle of treatment 'counts' as a full 'treatment'. Thus a woman may commence several more 'treatments' than three during the period she is in treatment.

5   In order to adopt a child in Denmark one has to have accepted one's infertility, and this requirement is *not* fulfilled if a couple is on an IVF programme.

BABY MAKING IN AUSTRIA

·

BRIGITTE OBERAUER
Austria

The seminar was held in a private clinic in an upper-class suburb of an Austrian city. Dr M welcomed us in the library, over coffee and cream cakes. This is somewhat unusual in medical circles, but clearly the intention was to make a good impression on all the participants (male and female) – future colleagues – as we were all training to be doctors. In addition, making the personal connections would be good propaganda for Dr M's private *in vitro* fertilization (IVF) clinic and result in referrals of women to him. I had gone to the seminar expecting that the topic would be discussed in the usual cool and distant scientific manner. I also expected to hear the mandatory slogans about reproductive medicine's 'help' for suffering humankind; in particular about the 'help' for infertile women and their terrible predicament. What I experienced, however, was not only technocracy, but a demonstration of the most brutal disdain for women, a lack of consideration which manifested itself in the treatment of women and in the most cynical sexist propaganda.[1]

Everything in the clinic was arranged to emphasize that it was technology which could produce life – not the women who had sought Dr M's help and who were introduced to us as 'non-achievers' and 'failures'. What we were told about were parts of the female anatomy and functions of the female body. They were isolated, measured against the technical machinery, seen as 'defective' and cut up into sections. The message was that thus 'vivisected', women can only be 'fixed up' with the help of technology.

The language Dr M used to describe the women reinforced this view. Women who did not respond to the ovulation stimulant clomiphene citrate were called 'clomiphene-failures'. 'Fertilization-failure' was another disqualifying definition. The eggs of women over forty were labelled 'unsellable stock', and Dr M said, 'We are of the opinion that the womb is the best incubator', and 'sometimes incubator conditions are not quite as ideal as those within the body in general'. As an aside he reminded us that 'It could be the father's problem', or 'often the reason for the lack of fertilization can be found in the sperm', or 'as you know, in more than a third of the sterility cases the causes lie with the man, not with the woman'.

This dissection of 'having a child' into body parts – specifically women's body parts – was emphasized by the fact that the button on the container in which embryos are frozen (clearly visible to every woman) was in the shape of a nipple. Women's egg cells, which Dr M repeatedly referred to as '*Eilis*' [Austrian dialect for 'little eggs'], were sorted into different qualities. 'The bad ones will be at your disposal to mess about with [*zum Verwurschteln*] as they will have to be thrown out anyway', or 'when we freeze unfertilized eggs we can practise with the old messed-up ones, the ones which just didn't fertilize, the failures'. Or even worse: 'This one isn't ideal, we'll take her last. That's a real ugly [*ein Schiacha*] embryo, and she got pregnant with it! Ha ha ha!'

Speaking about the one who wasn't 'ideal', Dr M referred to a woman whose case history we had just discussed. It is clear that women are subjected to a range of experiments whose principal aim is to control the female body as if it were a machine. To quote Dr M again as he explains egg stimulation:

> In this way I am able to stimulate the ovaries in isolation, that is to say without the influence of the pituitary. This is – so to speak – the *dernier cri* in ovary stimulation and we are not quite sure yet how it works. In any case, if we give a woman hormones in order to trick her into producing several mature egg-cells the success rates can be improved . . . and if we take her off the pill we can again harvest more and better quality egg-cells. It seems that the ovary does a better job.

Surplus eggs are used for a plethora of scientific experiments such as different freezing techniques and culture mediums. In discussing this, Dr M commented that 'many of these eggs have a damaged set of chromosomes – to put it plainly, the chromosomes are getting mixed up.' He continued:

> Half of them fertilized pathologically, which made us wonder. After fertilization they divided reasonably well, and we transferred some, but none of the women got pregnant. One has to be very cautious if there are so many pathologically fertilized egg cells. Furthermore we got a report from England, where they had tried out this method on rats. After analysing the chromosomes they found that the eggs not only fertilized in a polyploid fashion, but also that aneuploid chromosome sets are found.

I am sure that Dr M had not told the women into whose wombs he transferred the fertilized eggs about the dangers inherent in experimental technology, nor that they themselves were part and parcel of testing these methods because they were the first ones on whom new experimental drugs and procedures were tried out.

After this theoretical introduction, the IVF seminar moved to a practical demonstration of a follicle puncture and the subsequent 'harvesting' of egg cells. The humiliations imposed on women and the disregard for their dignity and self-determination became shockingly obvious.

As the first woman was brought in, Dr M looked at the test results and explained to me with the unnecessary joviality usual among colleagues that the ultrasound test had shown only one follicle and that therefore – in this case – it was to be expected that the treatment would be unsuccessful. The woman was in her mid–40s and had already had five children. But because her second husband wanted her to bear *him* one or more children she came to IVF. Her age and weight problem were factors which worked against any further pregnancy, but she was not told this. Supine on the gynaecological chair with legs raised and apart she was trembling with shame and fear – a mere object: available to all those around her.

As Dr M had already said, there was only one follicle visible in the ultrasound which he then punctured with the vaginal scanner. The vaginal scanner is a rod with a probe attached to it, to which is attached left and right the anchorage for the needle.

The probe shows the exact distance from the anchorage of the needle to the follicle via the ultrasound machine. The follicle puncture can be executed in two ways: either by pistol or by hand. Doing it 'free handed' requires great force on the surgeon's part. It is also much more likely to result in serious injuries. Usually women are given anaesthetics if they wish, but 'the latest thing is' – as Dr M puts it – 'to have them participate and feel the whole procedure'.

This particular woman had opted for 'feeling', but now she was nervous, full of anxiety, and could hardly lie still. The first attempt at puncturing the follicle did not work. Dr M had to try a second time, after which one follicle was extracted. The painful procedure was terminated in a relatively short time.

It took much longer with the second woman. She was a teacher, about thirty-five, slim and beautiful. The ultrasound had shown about seven follicles. If the doctor's conversation with the first woman had been cool and distanced, it was now friendly, even flirtatious. This woman, too, had decided against tranquillizers, and she too lay trembling and visibly distressed on the gynaecological chair. Each time Dr M prepared to prick the follicle with the scanner, he warned her: '*Achtung, jetzt steche ich!*' ['OK: now the thrust!'] The woman winced, but after each attempt his suggestive question was: 'It didn't hurt, surely, did it?'

Standing there watching, I too experienced the woman's humiliation. She lay with her legs apart on the chair. Dr M sat between her legs and introduced the vaginal scanner. At each follicle puncture he retracted the needle and then drove it in hard – a movement very similar to the act of penetration. All the other students had their eyes fixed on the woman's genitals. After the fifth follicle had been sucked out, the woman asked him to stop, because she was in great pain. But Dr M would have none of that: 'There are still such beautiful follicles' and so the sixth and seventh follicles were punctured against her will. And again she winced, again each puncture unmistakably resembled a penetration. Finally, when all seven follicles were punctured, an eighth black dot appeared. Although she implored him to stop, Dr M insisted on continuing. After the puncture it was found that the black bubble was a cyst which was then immediately aspirated. Such a procedure, especially for a woman of thirty-five, can be fraught with danger. In IVF, cysts often result because of overstimulation of the ovaries by the egg growth-stimulating drugs.

This is not the only danger of IVF. Indeed, in this very attempt described above, Dr M had perforated a follicle and damaged the woman's illiac vein. Such life-endangering injuries are laughed off, trivialized and ignored. It was adding insult to injury when Dr M suggested immediately afterwards that she have breakfast or go shopping with her husband.

Such episodes prove that women are not only refused self-determination, but also that the pain they experience is not taken seriously. A woman's body is a useful object for experimentation in order to win academic fame and establish a successful business. As IVF is by and large a failed technology IVF specialists world-wide are eager to continue developing new techniques. Egg collection by laparoscopy, for instance – the most frequently used technique for egg collection – is time consuming and requires a full anaesthetic, which can be fatal.[2] Hence the search goes on for other techniques, e.g. for egg retrieval via the bladder. Although – as Dr M said – 'brilliant people' had warned about the danger of puncturing the full bladder, in performing this operation, he had been reckless enough to risk it: 'Gynaecologists are neurotically scared to damage the bladder! But we said "So the bladder is perforated with a needle, so what? That little hole will close up again." '

The technique, however, did not seem satisfactory after all. So more experiments were undertaken. As Dr M explained:

> We had to try everything, like it or not; to look from above with the ultrasound, and from beneath put a protective finger through the vagina and then to puncture by hand. Well, we had to puncture through the vagina and it went relatively well. With two patients we injured the intestines with the trocar [a stiletto-like needle with a handle and a triangular point]. That usually happens with women who suffer from inflammations, or who have had surgery and are full of adhesions. Sometimes the intestines have attached themselves to the umbilicus – so you just can't help it.

Whatever happens, it is always the woman's own fault if she gets injured. But here, too, women are classified and a dose of racism is thrown in:

> If they are brave they will need no tranquillizing injections . . . Of course much depends on the woman's attitude. Some women don't feel the pain so much. There seems to be a sloping-off effect from North to South. Women from the Northern countries are usually brave, but in the South, Arab women for instance, they tend to dramatize . . . 'O God, will my follicles grow? And now this is too high and this is swelling up, for goodness' sake, *poo, poo, poo*' [imitating the voice of hysterical women and gesticulating wildly].

'Failure' and 'success', then, are clearly defined. If IVF doesn't work it is the woman's fault in one way or another – if it *does* work, it is the doctor who is the fertilizer: 'We are now approaching our hundredth baby! Out of principle we never prevent anybody who wants to try our methods, even if the problem is with the male partner; or if the infertility is idiopathic.'

In our society women have no value as autonomous human beings. Patriarchal ideology is interested only in our child-bearing potential. But this mentality is usually camouflaged: we are told that women have 'urges', or are 'sick', which allegedly originates from the inability to bear our own children. Thus Dr M lectured us:

> The wish for a child comes from the depth of her character, it is her basic function . . . She gets married and loves her husband, and then she wants a baby of course, and suddenly her period stops and hurray 'I am pregnant'. But then she is brought in haemorrhaging and with an ectopic pregnancy. No sooner is she right again, just a few months later ('That was just bad luck, let's try again. I will be right this time!') again the same story, that's how it usually starts; no period again, hurray, this time lucky, even

if she is a little nervous, but everything is all right. She goes to the doctor, he says everything is OK, but in reality it is not, and things get worse, and so on and so on. And in the end she finds out it will never be OK, because by now the fallopian tubes have been taken out, and that really worries her; and then she resigns herself to being childless. But she always thinks about it, and then there are the social pressures: her girlfriend runs around with *her* child, and another one already has her third, and she starts to cry when she sees a pram with a baby in it . . . and she remembers her bad experience. And in the end she hears about it – aha, there is this new method where one does not need fallopian tubes, and she gets this idea, 'Well I am going to try this' and she'll come here and become a patient.

Increasingly, more methods are developed to deal with *male* infertility. This means that a healthy fertile woman has to subject herself to the dangerous and emotionally draining IVF treatment in order to fertilize her egg with often pathological, low or no mobility sperm. Dr M described one such new technique:

There is a new method, called '*zona* drilling'. Drilling means just what it says: an injection needle is inserted in the *zona* (that is the *zona pellucida*, the egg membrane), and the egg is injected with a medium containing mainly hydrochloric acid. A drop of this acid drills a hole in the membrane, then sperm are added. But pathological sperm will also penetrate through this hole. . . . We might ask, will there not be too many sperm to penetrate?[3]

Dr M continued his elaborations:

Well, a fantastic experiment has been conducted: completely immobile sperm were injected through this hole and the egg was fertilized. You will ask how this could happen? Well, the egg just projects its zytoplasma [the basic plasma of the cell which is usually surrounded by the egg membrane] and 'inhales' this sperm. And once it is within the egg, the egg will do its duty and catch it in a truly feminine fashion.

In order to uphold the myth of the 'helping touch' at all costs, all connections with the less positive aspects of genetic engineering are strictly negated. Dr M insisted that:

> IVF as a treatment for sterility[4] has nothing whatsoever to do with terms like 'sperm bank', 'surrogate motherhood' or 'ectogenesis' [the artificial womb]; it has nothing to do with '*homunculi*' or with organ production or selective breeding, etc., etc. So please don't mix up apples and pears!

These statements are patently untrue. Dr M has himself demonstrated his willingness to have frozen, unfertilized eggs checked for chromosome anomalies by zytogenetic testing. This allows him to select genetically 'unworthy' material. Dr M contradicts himself in his own statements:

> We had a pregnancy *in utero* [in the womb] which was abnormal and we availed ourselves of this opportunity to practise the method of chorion biopsy, the latest thing. We are harvesting genetic material: instead of testing the amniotic fluid in the sixteenth week, we can now insert a catheter into the vagina and carefully try to catch some chorion villi which can be pinched off close to the cervix and tested for genetic normality. This test has the advantage that it can be done in the eighth week. If the results are pathological then it is psychologically easier [for the woman] to terminate the pregnancy.

Asked whether this method was likely to cause a higher abortion rate he answered: 'Not that I know of. But we have only tested chorionic villi biopsy with pathological pregnancies and we have not enough patient material for further tests.'

However, IVF specialists have thought of a way to get

'material' to conduct further trials. They are asking women to become egg donors. This will bring them a step closer towards their ultimate goal which is to completely functionalize women and make them into reproduction machines. Answering the question if there were many women who donate eggs, Dr M said:

> To say 'many' would be an exaggeration. They usually do it for money: we pay about 14,000 Austrian Shillings per donation.[5] But in any case this is the best of all possible motives; these women are not under any psychological pressure. A female donor who does it for money is emotionally neutral and her motiviation is unequivocal.

This new type of prostitution and female sexual slavery is yet another form of humiliating women. It is encouraged by the bad socio-economic conditions in which many women have to live. Dr M does not even mention the possibility of the health of the women donating the eggs being damaged because they have to be superovulated.[6]

Finally, there are always plenty of excuses if the IVF procedure does not lead to the desired pregnancies in spite of repeated follicle punctures – one woman had to submit to over ten! In the end, it is the doctor who is the hero. Dr M's final statement was:

> Even if a woman is in bad psychological shape during IVF and no pregnancy could be achieved, IVF was not without sense. It may have given the patient a new life experience and thus contributed to her maturation. We, the physicians, should cease to measure our satisfaction and success merely in achieved pregnancies.[7] I know of several cases where women had their artificially assisted *multiple* pregnancies terminated, as they could not cope with them. So we should accept that grieving over unsuccessful treatments does not necessarily mean medical failure. We should see all our endeavours as meaningful measures designed to help our patients.

NOTES

1 In the following text, passages in quotation marks are taken verbatim from my notes of Dr M's seminar – hence their sometimes fragmentary nature.

2 Several women in France, Israel, Australia and Brazil have died during a laparoscopy in connection with IVF. The cause of death has been glossed over in all cases. The common explanation is 'respiratory failure' due to the anaesthetic. (See p. 231 for details)

3 The penetration of the egg cell with more than one sperm (polyspermic fertilization) causes chromosomal anomalies in the developing embryo/foetus.

4 Calling IVF a 'treatment' is a misnomer. The woman – or her partner – remains infertile even in those rare cases when IVF is successful.

5 14,000 Austrian Shillings equal US$1000/$A800/£stg600 approximately.

6 See pp. 234–40 for further information on superovulation.

7 Measuring 'success' in terms of achieved pregnancies rather than live births unites IVF specialists throughout the world. In so doing they artificially boost IVF success rates – 'failure rates' is a more accurate term!

GIVING UP: THE CHOICE THAT ISN'T

.

KIRSTEN KOZOLANKA
Canada

This is the forty-seventh time I have felt hope slipping out of me in a relentless stream of menstrual discharge. I know it is the forty-seventh time because my computer tells me so. The crisp, cool headings displayed on the monitor were designed to make me feel more in control: 'Number of days in cycle', 'Days of intercourse during fertile period', 'Test performed'. Instead, I feel my life spinning away from me while I obligingly record the symptoms.

For the first time in four long years, I ask myself if it is time to give it up. Despite the continuing physical and emotional pain of my infertility, I have never before taken seriously the idea of giving up. You see, giving up, for the infertile, is not really an option at all. We make our reproductive decisions as members of a society that believes a woman's primary function is motherhood. Our choice to have children takes place within a framework that has always included reproduction and motherhood as our biological destiny. We see this reinforced constantly in television commercials, in designer baby clothes stores, in our Christmas traditions, in our parents' pointed questions, in families strolling through the park. The socialized desire to mother is so strong and so deep-rooted that we rarely consider the option of rejecting it.

For infertile women, motherhood has even more significance. It becomes a central force in our lives, all the more necessary for not achieving it. We have no choice, really, other than to have the pursuit of motherhood take over our lives because so much – self-identity, self-esteem, self-image – depends on it.

This pressure on women to become mothers – pronatalism – is limiting in terms of the options it offers to all women. It is callous in regard to infertile women because we do not even make the highly socialized 'choice' to fill the approved-of role. Society decrees we must be mothers and we are labelled neurotic and deviant when we cannot comply.

If pronatalism makes it difficult for us to choose to give up, then advances in technology make it downright impossible. We are more likely these days to seek help for our infertility. Over the years of our treatment, we invest so much time and energy in our goal that it is not easy to know when to stop trying when almost daily technological breakthroughs offer new hope. The doctors cannot tell us where the end of the road is; they do not know themselves because the limits of what they can do are constantly changing and, besides, they have a vested interest in seeing the success that comes from our conceptions.

Advancing technology means there are always new 'choices' to make. Strangely enough, technology may give us new choices, but it doesn't necessarily expand our options. Barbara Katz Rothman (1986) writes of this in *The Tentative Pregnancy*. In referring to reproductive choices, she writes: 'The new reproductive technology is offered to us in terms of expanding choices. But it is always true that while new technology opens up some choices, it closes down others. The new choice is often greeted with such fanfare that the silent closing of the door on the old choice goes unheeded.'

When we 'choose' to make use of the technology, we are also acknowledging and legitimizing society's view of us as mothers above all. And when we make this choice, the door shuts behind the option of giving up, of getting on with our lives.

It's not a real choice at all. Giving up is not looked at with favour by those who choose to pursue treatment. One woman I know had successful tubal surgery followed by an infection that put her back to square one. Her options were IVF or more tubal surgery. She decided to pursue adoption instead. She gets a lot of flack now when she tells her story to the couples in her pre-adoption counselling group: 'I have been called a "quitter", which is an interesting term that infertiles use,' she says. 'They say, "you could have tried IVF, why didn't you?", but just because it's there doesn't mean it's right for you.'

In a sense, those of us who are infertile choose infertility, because we choose to be treated. We do so, however, in an atmosphere that makes it almost impossible to choose to do otherwise.

It is what Professor Margarete Sandelowski (1986: 439–53) of Louisiana State University Medical Center has called 'Sophie's Choice', a catch–22 situation of choosing between two unsatisfactory options. We can either accept infertility without treatment 'in a social context in which being infertile violates a norm of behavior' or we can submit to treatment, which can lead to 'hardship, the postponement of other life goals, and no cure'.

Damned if we do. Damned if we don't.

My own infertility problem was treated with Clomid. It seemed an insignificant regimen – just a small, innocuous tablet once a day for five days during each cycle. We pop so many pills – antihistamines, aspirin, oral contraceptives, vitamins – that it didn't seem to be a technological fix at all. Women's reproductive histories, with contraception focused on our bodies, makes it seem easier for these small interventions to occur almost without notice.

I knew other women who had started with this small dose of Clomid, but swiftly progressed onto a steeper drug regimen. They took Pergonal to ripen more than one egg, a shot of HCG hormone to release the egg on schedule, Premarin to control the quality of their cervical mucus, Progesterone suppositories to keep the level of that hormone high. They were monitored constantly through blood tests and endless ultrasounds. Sometimes they were also artificially inseminated by a frozen sample of their partner's sperm just to coax things along. 'It happened the very first time I went in for a [cervical] mucus test and I brought in my husband's sperm sample,' one infertile woman told me. 'I remember the doctor saying, "We'll give this a try" and I had no idea he was going to do artificial insemination. He said, "Waste not, want not".'

They, too, had started with five small tablets. I wondered how large a leap of faith it needed to go from Clomid, swallowed with water in front of the bathroom sink at home, to ten visits to the doctor every month.

At the time I started taking Clomid, I joined a support group for infertile women. Smug in my belief that I would be pregnant any day, I listened with growing apprehension to the stories of the other women. Everyone had taken Clomid, and much else besides. No one was pregnant. After the first meeting, I sat numbly in my kitchen for two whole days, successive cups of tea growing cold in front of me.

It wasn't a game any more, a case of take your pill and get your baby. As Dr Pat Gervaize, a clinical psychologist at the infertility clinic at Ottawa Civic Hospital, tells her patients, they are involved in infertility regimens like keeping temperature charts in order to provide data for the doctors, not because they are going to get the reward of a baby for doing it. That is the bitterest pill of all to swallow – the idea that being good and obedient and, well, feminine isn't going to give you that ultimate approval.

But no one in the group thought of giving up. Instead, we watched a video on reproductive technologies and marvelled at the options already available in the United States. I was disturbed by the images of men in business suits deciding women's reproductive futures. They were discussing prices and markets. A woman in the group was astonished at my criticism of the élitism and sexism I saw in the video. 'But couples are getting *babies*,' she protested. Nothing was more important than that.

Many of these women are waiting for the day when an *in vitro* fertilization clinic will open in our city. Already there are 400 names on the waiting list. The screening criteria will shorten the list (right now, for instance, only women with tubal defects are being considered) and the day will come when some of us with ovulatory problems – the Clomid-takers – will get our chance.

So the failure of a complicated drug regimen is not the end of the road it once was. Gamete intrafallopian tube transfer (GIFT), in fact, is touted as a procedure that optimizes chances of pregnancy for women with ovulatory or other problems who still have patent tubes.

Last week, I attended a public meeting on *in vitro* fertilization and artificial insemination. Two doctors from a local clinic gave slide shows and answered questions. The audience was attentive and responsive. They were so hopeful. Do they know how low the success rates are for *in vitro*? Do they care?

Dr John A. Collins (1983; 1201–6), a leading infertility specialist in Canada, has conducted studies on success rates of infertility treatment that are profoundly disturbing. His studies indicate that doctors are getting no more pregnancies by treating infertility than they are without treatment. In other words, there is no significant difference between the rate of pregnancy for those who go through all the treatment, called 'treatment-induced' pregnancies, and for those who do not go through it, the so-called 'treatment-independent' pregnancies. This is not for advanced technologies, like IVF, but for standard treatments (like hormone therapy or drugs for certain conditions) of all kinds of factors involved in infertility.

This is not to say that infertility specialists cannot help women get pregnant. The same number of women will get pregnant with treatment as without treatment, but they will not be the same women.

Dr Collins' studies are not without their detractors in the medical profession. But an important source, the *British Medical Journal* (1987: 155–6) acknowledged in a recent issue that '[m]any doctors and lay people think that the great technical advances in the past twenty years in treating infertility have led to high success rates in treatment, but this is a myth.'

Let's say you do 'choose infertility' by choosing to be treated. It seems the decision, agonizing as it is, leaves you no further ahead. Basically, treatment gives you something to do while you are waiting to conceive. The trouble is that every infertile woman believes she will be the lucky one to succeed with treatment. For this reason, very few infertile women are willing to be part of a control group – those who aren't treated – for the purposes of comparative studies on success rates.

The reality of the low success rates does not deter one of the doctors at this public forum. He says, and I have heard this argument before, he can give a couple a 15 per cent chance of conceiving in an IVF cycle. He points out that a fertile couple has the same chance in any one normal cycle. But it's not the same at all and it is stunningly callous of him to even compare the two.

In order to give an infertile woman her 15 per cent chance in an IVF programme, she must undergo emotionally strenuous and physically painful medical interventions that last throughout her entire cycle. It's not just the extensive drug regimen designed to induce a superovulation, it is the laparoscopy, the extra monitoring through ultrasounds and blood tests, the incredible stress.

It is so draining that often clinics will not allow a couple to attempt IVF conception two months in a row.

This same doctor speaks disparagingly of the feminist opposition to his work. Between slides, he says he doesn't have time to think about the ethical considerations of what he is doing. He'll do that later, he says with a wave of his hand.

But later is too late. Reproduction is being redefined while he shows us slides and airily dismisses ethics. It is a classic 'ends and means' situation. Do you want a baby? Then close your eyes and put up with the pain and maybe, just maybe, they will give you your heart's desire. Whatever you do, don't question your right to have a child any way you can.

That's how American lawyer Noel Keane sees the work he does in his surrogacy firm. 'I don't have any ethical problems with what I'm doing', he says. 'I think everybody's got a right to have a biological child – at least, we do in the United States. I think it [surrogacy] is absolutely right.'[1]

I say nothing at the public forum. I challenge nothing, although I am deeply worried. If I say something the doctors from my clinic might not give me my baby.

And, after all, I am one of the lucky ones. I already have a healthy daughter. Other infertile women don't consider me infertile, but fertile people don't understand either. The worst thing about this secondary infertility is that it pits me against my infertile sisters. I am less needy than they, they think. It also gives me less of a right to speak out. Who am I, already a mother, to tell them what to do?

One woman describes to me a watershed moment in her infertility. For years she had been gathering maternity clothes from her sisters and friends. When she found out that her best friend was pregnant, she gathered up all the clothes, all her dreams, and gave them to her friend. In that moment, she had to admit to herself the hopelessness of her quest for a biological child. I sympathize with her and offer a similar story. My own maternity clothes had been placed lovingly away after my daughter's birth, awaiting my next pregnancy. Years later, I perform the same cleansing act of sending the maternity clothes to a friend. The woman listens to my story then says quickly: 'But you had already used your clothes.' She did not mean to be cruel, but she indicated to me clearly that her pain was greater than mine.

It is not over for me after four years. I sometimes suspect it is just beginning. The Clomid worked, but I miscarried. Blood tests after the miscarriage indicate that my hormone levels are now normal. I am, supposedly, fertile again. But after five months of trying to conceive, I see no evidence of this and I am growing weary. Next month, if I am still not pregnant, I am expected to go back to the clinic.

More than anything else, it frightens me. Now that I am fertile again, if I do not conceive, do I enter the painful limbo of unexplained infertility, where no cause can be found and therefore no treatment prescribed? Will my doctor tell me that GIFT or IVF is my only hope? Choosing technological interventions becomes less and less of an academic question and more of a decision that will haunt me throughout my life. Am I a 'quitter', too?

The world of infertility is a narrowing one. It forces individual solutions to a problem that is so profoundly social. It turns man against woman and woman against woman in the mad scramble to achieve the social goal of parenthood. 'Give me a baby at any cost' is the refrain, and many are willing to leap into the breach to provide that commodity. But a baby is more than just another consumer good to be purchased on an emotion-induced shopping spree. My socially-created desire to have a baby must not blind me to the price I must pay.

I cannot in all conscience divorce the end from the means. I think of the fine Argentinian film, *The Official Story*, about the infertile woman who unknowingly adopts the infant daughter of one of the *desaparecidas* lost in her country's reign of terror in the 1970s. When she begins to suspect her child's origins and the part her husband has played in the terror, she embarks on a personal quest to unravel the past that may lose her her daughter. But the price of ignorance and indifference, of pretending the problem does not exist, she finds, is too high.

I feel like this woman, terrified, pulled every which way by forces beyond my control. If I delve too deeply into the questions, I might not like the answers. And I may lose that chance to have a baby.

I had a dream while I was writing this article. In it, I am at a microphone in a convention hall. (Those of us who work in the media often see our disembodied selves performing miracles in front of cameras and microphones.) My sister feminists are all around me and I am expounding on choice and technology. My words are admired by the crowd. (The mark of a good PR person: Give them what they want to hear.) Suddenly, another infertile woman, my *alter ego*, is at a rival microphone and she is asking me the hard, incisive, journalistic questions I have refused to ask myself. 'You say your ethics force you to refuse technological involvement,' she taunts. 'So easy for you to say here, now. But if it means not having the baby you want so badly, what then?' I try to dodge the issue. 'Well . . . ,' I begin, stalling because I do not want to answer this question. She does not give up, this other infertile woman, this *bitch* destroying my smug little dream. 'Even if it means not having a baby?' There is silence in the hall as they wait for me to answer. I wait with the rest of them to hear what I will say. (The camera zooms in for the kill.) 'Even if it means not having a baby', I say heavily. There is a great cheer. I have said the right thing. I am awake now and I am weeping. Why can't I stop weeping?

As dreams go, it is not very subtle. I receive succour from my infertile sisters. They teach me the meaning of dignity and strength. I do not want to turn my back on their pain, but I must take some responsibility for the future I am helping to create. It saddens me that I must choose one or the other of these two worlds, but as much as I need and want them to, they rarely intersect.

Today, as I write this, I do not want to prolong this agony of false choice. I want – for whatever selfish or altruistic reason – to give it up. I know I will wake up tomorrow and I will go through it all again. Maybe my decision will be different then.

But for today, in this forty-seventh cycle of my discontent, this is what I choose.

P.S. After more than four years of infertility, I am pregnant. Although I expect that I will relax more as the pregnancy – now at fifteen weeks – progresses, the last three months have been a black hole of terror. The overwhelming fatigue and constant nausea were bad enough, but the fear of miscarriage nearly drove me crazy. Every twinge, every gurgle, every discharge was cause for alarm – and if I didn't feel anything, well then, I must be about to miscarry, I agonized. It became clear to me as it never had before that *this was it*, that if I did miscarry, then I could not bear to go through any of this again. So the pregnancy became even more precious. I have done nothing for three months but brood, sleep and feel sick. I am at last beginning to relax, although I live from one obstetrical appointment to the next.

I did go back to the clinic but only to keep the appointment that had been made months earlier. The doctor went over our file in detail from beginning to end and explained that he could not prescribe Clomid (as previously done when my hormone levels were too high) because the most recent blood tests had, as we knew, come back normal. Basically, he reiterated, it was a matter of time before conception occurred. Just to be sure that there was no impediment, he suggested we book another post-coital test. I went away perversely annoyed that he did not want to give me Clomid, even though I knew I did not want to take it. I decided not to book the PCT that cycle. The next cycle, I booked it and then cancelled it several days later. I simply was not prepared for any kind of intervention and doubted if I ever would be. But who is to know, because that was the cycle I got pregnant. It rather leaves it dangling, doesn't it? I only know, as I said above, that I became convinced that I could never, ever go through this (early pregnancy) again, let alone what might be necessary to achieve the conception. In the end, the straw that broke the camel's back was pregnancy itself and the terror it invoked. It was just too damn much.

It's not much of an explanation, is it? But it is an ending of sorts, although I find there are all sorts of new reproductive choices/options to taunt me; my obstetrician suggested (but did not push) genetic counselling, which we declined. That decision, of course, will haunt us until the birth.

NOTE

1   Front Page Challenge, CBC Television, 6 November 1987.

REFERENCES

Collins, John A.; Wrixon, William; Janes, Lynn B.; and Wilson, Elaine. 1983. Treatment-Independent Pregnancy among Infertile Couples. *The New England Journal of Medicine*, 309: 1201–1206; Interview with Dr Collins, 15 July 1987.

Lilford, Richard J. and Dalton, Maureen E. 1987. Effectiveness of Treatment for Infertility, *British Medical Journal*, 295: 155–156.

Rothman, Barbara Katz. *The Tentative Pregnancy: Prenatal Diagnosis and the Future of Motherhood*. New York: Viking, 1986; London: Pandora Press, 1988.

Sandelowski, Margarete. 1986. Sophie's Choice: A Metaphor for Infertility, *Health Care for Women International*, 7: 439–453.

PART THREE

.

Exploiting Fertile Women
in the Name of Infertility

SURROGACY: MAKING THE LINKS

·

GENA COREA
USA

Women's bodies are not only the *recipients* of so-called treatments for infertility like *in vitro* fertilization. In the institution of surrogate motherhood, our bodies actually *become* infertility treatments. Women are hired to be artificially inseminated, to gestate a child, and then to turn that child over to the sperm donor, thereby 'treating' the infertility of the sperm donor's wife.

According to a 1986 ethics report by the American Fertility Society, a professional association of some 10,000 US physicians and scientists who work in reproductive biology: 'The primary medical indication for use of a surrogate mother is the inability of a woman to provide either the genetic [i.e. the egg] or the gestational component [i.e. the uterus] for childbearing. . . .'

A man's desire to conceive his own genetic child is transformed in the report into a 'medical indication' for buying a woman's body.

The report, written by an ethics committee headed by Dr Howard Jones, co-lab parent of the US's first test-tube baby, states: 'For the husband of an infertile woman, the use of a surrogate may be the only way in which he can conceive and rear a child with a biologic tie to himself, short of divorcing his wife and remarrying only for that reason or of having an adulterous union. Certainly the use of a surrogate mother under the auspices of a medical practitioner seems far less destructive of the institution of the family than the latter two options.'

The report medicalizes the sale of women's bodies. It uses the language of 'therapy' to sanitize and legitimate this new traffic in women and to make the suffering of women and the violations of their human dignity invisible.

Consider these medicalizing phrases from the report:

'a situation in which surrogate motherhood provides
the sole medical solution'
'the medical aspects of surrogate motherhood'
'there could be a role for surrogate gestation in reproductive medicine'

The American Fertility Society Ethics Committee recommends
that if surrogate gestational motherhood is pursued, it should be
pursued as 'a clinical experiment'. (If 19th century physicians
in the United States had medicalized slavery, they could have
conducted a 'clinical experiment' to see if slavery were truly
therapeutic for the slave holders.)

Unlike Pergonal and egg suction devices, women are a 'therapeutic modality' with minds and wills of their own that may
interfere with the plans of the 'patient', the man with a desire
for a genetically-related child. The Ethics Committee consoles:
'Although there exists a potential for surrogates to risk harm to
the child by failing to disclose a genetic defect that would
disqualify them for surrogacy or by engaging in harmful behavior
during pregnancy, such risk could be minimized by proper
medical and psychological screening of surrogates.' No fear –
physicians will exercise quality control over the 'treatments' they
use.

Entrepreneurs in the surrogate industry often tout surrogacy
as a practice designed to fill the empty arms of an infertile woman
with a child. But who is surrogacy really for?

Often the 'infertile wife' already has children by a previous
marriage. After bearing her children, she either becomes infertile
or undergoes a voluntary sterilization. When she remarries, her
second husband wants children of his own.

For example, consider three of the cases detailed in the
following pages: Nattie Haro, whose husband used Alejandra
Munoz to gestate a child, has a daughter by a previous marriage.
The wife of the man who hired Patricia Foster has three children
by previous marriages. The wife of the man who hired Laurie
Yates also has grown children by a previous marriage.

Speaking of the 'infertile wife', Elizabeth Kane, the first legal
and paid surrogate mother in the United States, said in testimony
before a Michigan legislative hearing on 12 April, 1988: 'It is her
husband who has become obsessed with his desire to obtain an

heir. In order to preserve the marriage, she must go along with his plan to hire a surrogate wife.'

Is surrogacy truly aimed at relieving the suffering of infertile women? Or does surrogacy create that suffering?

At hearings before a Wisconsin legislative committee on 12 February 1988, one infertile woman, after giving glowing testimony on the merits of surrogacy, was asked how she had experienced the arrangement. To the shock of onlookers, she began sobbing. In the suddenly hushed hearing room, she said, 'It's so humiliating to have my husband ask a strange woman to bear his child.' (Kane, 1988)

We know of at least one woman who left her husband because, she explained, she could not stand the pressure being put on her to go along with the surrogacy arrangement. (Keane and Breo, 1981: 138)

In surrogacy, reproductive technologies, many of which were developed for use on infertile women, are applied to fertile women to make them more efficient breeders. The women, who are generally low-income, become 'living laboratories' for experiments with technologies.[1] These technologies include amniocentesis, sex predetermination, embryo flushing, *in vitro* fertilization, and superovulation.

The women who tell their stories below provide examples:

Patricia Foster: Surrogacy combined with sex predetermination
Foster's sperm donor ordered that his sperm be split, separating out male-engendering and female-engendering sperm, and that Foster be inseminated only with the male sperm. He wanted – not just any child – but a son.

Mary Beth Whitehead: Surrogacy combined with amniocentesis
Although Whitehead was under thirty and not in need of any prenatal diagnosis, she was required to submit to amniocentesis, essentially for quality control over the product she was producing. She bitterly resented this and tried to resist it, unsuccessfully. (The contract called for her to abort if the test found the product not acceptable, the only part of the contract New Jersey Judge Harvey Sorkow did not uphold in the famous Baby M court case.) Elizabeth Stern, a physician and the wife of the sperm donor, drew blood from Whitehead's arm several times during

the pregnancy. Whitehead was not told why this was being done to her.

Alejandra Munoz: Surrogacy combined with embryo flushing
Munoz, a twenty-one-year-old Mexican woman with a second-grade education and no knowledge of the English language, was brought across the border illegally to produce a child for a man in National City near San Diego. She was told that she would be artificially inseminated and that, after three weeks, the embryo would be flushed out of her and transferred into the womb of the man's wife. She was familiar with the concept, knowing that this procedure was used on cows on farms near her home in Mexico. The embryo was never flushed out. Munoz, who had planned to be in the country for only a few weeks for what she thought would be a minor procedure, ended up undergoing major surgery – a caesarian section. She was offered $1,500, well below the already exploitative $10,000 fee generally offered white Anglo women.

Nancy Barrass: Surrogacy combined with superovulation
After an insemination, Barrass contracted a bacteria infection from the baby buyer's sperm. This could have delayed her impregnation. But rather than waiting for the infection to clear up, the surrogate company's doctor prescribed a triple dose of Clomid, the fertility drug. He continued to inseminate her. She suffered serious drug side effects, including a pain in her left ovary so intense she was unable to walk.

Laurie Yates: Surrogacy combined with superovulation
Yates apparently didn't get pregnant fast enough, whether for the doctor or the customer is not clear. She was not an efficient enough manufacturing plant. (When I asked Yates if she had had any say concerning whether or not she would be superovulated, she replied: 'He [the doctor] *told* me, "We're going to give you . . ." He didn't *ask* me.')

Jane Doe: Surrogacy combined with superovulation
Between the ages of fourteen and twenty-five, Jane Doe had nine pregnancies, five of which ended in miscarriage, as reported by Rochelle Sharpe of Gannett News Service. According to Doe,

when the physician who screened her for the surrogate company heard she had had nine pregnancies, he was not alarmed. Instead, he said, 'Good, you're really fertile.' Since she was breastfeeding an infant at the time she agreed to be inseminated, she was not ovulating. Instead of waiting for her to begin ovulating again naturally, the physician superovulated her with fertility drugs. (Sharpe, 1986)

Shannon Boff: Surrogacy with in vitro fertilization

An egg was extracted from an infertile woman, fertilized in the laboratory with the sperm of the woman's husband and then transferred into the womb of Shannon Boff. She gestated the child, delivered it and then turned it over to the couple. (The reason the infertile woman had no uterus was that after becoming pregnant in an *in vitro* fertilization program in England, she had lost the baby during pregnancy and had to have a hysterectomy.)

Pat Anthony: Surrogacy with in vitro fertilization

Anthony, a forty-eight-year-old South African woman, was implanted with four eggs removed from her daughter and fertilized *in vitro* with the sperm of her son-in-law. She gave birth to triplets by caesarean section on 1 October, 1987. Anthony's daughter, who already has one child, had reportedly had her uterus removed as a consequence of an obstetrical emergency. (The son-in-law, a refrigeration engineer, said: 'I couldn't be more delighted than my mother-in-law will give birth to my children.' After the pregnancy had been confirmed an IVF clinic director commented: 'From an IVF point of view, I guess it's all over. It's really an obstetric problem now, and from that point of view I imagine a 48-year-old with triplets would be no picnic.' [*The Australian*, 1987; McIntosh, 1987])

Harvey Berman, the lawyer who took on the defence of Alejandra Munoz, decided at some point during his involvement in the case that it would be a good idea for him to start his *own* surrogacy business. I interviewed him about this on 24 April, 1987. His plans call for using surrogacy with IVF, sex predetermination technology, embryo freezing, embryo flushing, and eventually, cloning. The physicians associated with his firm will use whatever technology they are developing, he said. Of his future clients, he said: 'People that want to be certain what they're getting and are willing to go against the – quote "laws of nature" unquote – and get a product in advance that they have chosen – I don't see anything *per se* wrong with that.'

So the new reproductive technologies are being used, and will increasingly be used, in conjunction with each other.

In the next chapter Mary Beth Whitehead, Patricia Foster, Alejandra Munoz, Nancy Barrass and Elizabeth Kane relate their 'surrogacy' experiences.

NOTE

1   The term 'living laboratory' is one coined by Robyn Rowland of Deakin University, Victoria, Australia, a leading critic of the new reproductive technologies and used for the first time in *Test-Tube Women* (1984).

REFERENCES

American Fertility Society Ethics Committee. September 1986. 'Ethical considerations of the new reproductive technologies.' *Fertility and Sterility*, Supplement 1. 46 (3).

Kane, Elizabeth. 12 April, 1988. Testimony before a hearing of the Michigan Senate.

Keane, Noel P. and Dennis L. Breo. 1981. *The Surrogate Mother*. Everest House, New York.

McIntosh, Philip. 4 July, 1987. 'Experts warn of complications for surrogate grandmother.' *The Age* (Melbourne).

Rowland, Robyn. 1984. 'Reproductive technologies: the final solution to the woman question?' In *Test-Tube Women: What Future for Motherhood?* Eds. Rita Arditti, Renate Duelli Klein and Shelley Minden. Pandora Press, London and Boston.

Sharpe, Rochelle. 1986. 'Surrogate sues lawyer over death of newborn.' *Gannett News Service*.

The Australian. 4 June, 1987. 'Woman to give birth to her grandchildren.'

WOMEN WHO EXPERIENCED SURROGACY SPEAK OUT

∎

MARY BETH WHITEHEAD
USA

Mary Beth Whitehead grew up in New Jersey, one of eight children. In 1973, at the age of sixteen, she married Richard Whitehead. They have two children, Ryan and Tuesday.

On 5 February, 1985, Whitehead signed an agreement to be artificially inseminated with the sperm of William Stern, carry the child, and relinquish the child to Stern for $10,000.

She broke the following provision of the agreement: 'Mary Beth Whitehead, Surrogate, understands and agrees that in the best interest of the child, she will not form or attempt to form a parent–child relationship with any child or children she may conceive, carry to term and give birth to, pursuant to the provisions of the Agreement, and shall freely surrender custody to William Stern, Natural Father, immediately upon birth of the child . . .'.

Whitehead gave birth to a daughter on 27 March, 1986. Shortly after turning the child over to Stern, she asked for the baby back and did not return her. She refused the $10,000 payment.

On 5 May, Stern, a forty-one-year-old biochemist, went to court and asked Judge Harvey Sorkow for an order granting him immediate custody of the child. Whitehead was given no notice of this court appearance and no opportunity to respond. Stern based his petition on the assertion that Whitehead was considering moving to Florida and might flee New Jersey if notified of the court proceedings. Sorkow ordered immediate surrender of the child to Stern's custody.

Later that day, five policemen came to Whitehead's house to get the baby while Stern and his wife, Elizabeth, waited outside in a car. Whitehead managed to hand her baby out a back window to her husband who fled with the child. Whitehead, clad in a nightgown, was handcuffed and thrown into a patrol car while her neighbours looked on. Her daughter Tuesday, then ten, stood screaming and begging Stern and his wife to stop what was being done to her mother.

Whitehead was later released. With her family, she fled to Florida and lived there for the next eighty-seven days. At the end of July, Florida police raided the home of Whitehead's parents, knocked down her mother, seized the child, and turned the child over to Stern.

The famous 'Baby M' trial ensued, with Whitehead trying to regain custody of her child. On 31 March, 1987, Judge Sorkow stripped Whitehead of her parental rights and upheld the surrogacy contract. In his decision, Sorkow referred to Whitehead and other so-called surrogates as 'alternative reproduction vehicles'.

Whitehead's daughter lives with her father and her father's wife. Her name has been changed by court ruling from Sara Whitehead to Melissa Stern.

I have joined with other mothers who have lost their children to urge the United States Congress to ban surrogacy.

I'll tell you how this started for me. I responded to a newspaper advertisement in the *Asbury Park Press* asking for women willing to help infertile couples bear children.

I had always believed we were in this world to help other people. I thought that this was something that I could do while still being at home with my children. I genuinely believed that this was a way for me to help better the world. Looking back, I now believe that this was a form of brainwashing. Over and over they told me that it was the 'couple's baby'. They never explained that everything a woman does to produce her own child I would be doing.

No one ever said to me: 'It's your baby and there's a possibility that when she grows up and finds out you sold her, she might hate your guts.' No. They didn't tell me that and they didn't tell me it was Ryan's and Tuesday's baby sister and they didn't tell me how my husband would feel after taking care of me during pregnancy for nine months. None of this was mentioned. It was just shoved under the rug. They just kept telling me it was the 'couple's child'. It wasn't until the day I delivered her that I finally understood that I wasn't giving Betsy Stern her baby. I was giving her *my* baby.

Noel Keane's Infertility Center didn't make me aware of my rights. I thought because the Sterns had hired me, they could tell me what to do. So even though my doctor said I didn't need amniocentesis or a Tay Sachs test, I had them because the Sterns insisted on it. When Betsy Stern wanted to take blood from my arm several times, and I didn't know why, I allowed it. When we were sitting in a car and she was drawing blood from me, I felt used and exploited.

Perhaps some people think the baby would be better off with people like the Sterns. Many of the newspaper stories made the point that I didn't finish high school. The idea people got from that was that I couldn't be a good mother. I couldn't be a good mother if I didn't finish high school and was married to a garbage man. What they all ignored, however, was that I was a mother and a good one.

Bill and Betsy Stern have money and are educated, and they got to the courthouse first.

I don't think I ever had a chance. I don't think any of us 'surrogates' ever had a chance.

The economics of surrogacy in the US are simple. The sperm donors are well-off and the women they hire to bear their children generally are not. I don't think I have to explain what that means. The wealthy couples are better able to hire lawyers and psychologists to plead their cases.

Before all the publicity, no lawyer would touch my case. When I was hiding in Florida, I called lawyer after lawyer. But I didn't have the money to hire them.

It's true I ran away with my baby. I ran and hid and I called and called, trying to get help. People tell me that there are smarter ways to fight for your child, like the way the Sterns fought against me. But I didn't have any other way. So I ran and I hid. In the end the Sterns with their high-powered legal advice were able to secure temporary custody by court order before I even got an attorney.

In Florida, where we hid, I kept Sara next to me every minute. I figured if she was in my arms, they'd have to shoot me to get her.

I was in the intensive care unit in a hospital in Florida, sick with a kidney infection, when they came to take the baby from my parents' house. The police came and knocked my mother down and ripped the baby from the crib. My family had to come to the hospital and tell me that my baby was gone.

My ten-year-old, Tuesday, saw the police storming our home twice, coming for the baby. She saw this once in New Jersey when they handcuffed me and once in Florida.

I was completely devastated about having the baby taken from me. I felt like I was used for one purpose and was no longer needed or wanted. I was distraught for my child, for my own flesh and blood. I remember the inseminating doctor telling me that I was giving away an egg. I didn't give away an egg. They took a baby away from me, not an egg. That was my daughter. That was Sara they took from me.

Against the power of Noel Keane's surrogate company and the man who hired me, I didn't have a chance. Neither did Patty Foster, who watched what I was going through on television and read about it in the newspaper while she was pregnant with a son she could not bear to give away. She saw what happened to me and she felt she did not have a chance. Now her son is gone and she is fighting for him as hard as I am fighting for my daughter. Alejandra Munoz and Nancy Barrass and Elizabeth Kane – none of us had a chance. It's not just Mary Beth White-head. It is all of us. We have started a mothers' support group to help each other. More and more of us are coming forward and saying that we are human beings. We are not baby-making machines.

There have been moments when the public humiliation and personal pain have been so great that I have thought of giving up. But the joy of Sara's smile when we become cellmates for two hours once a week and her tears as she is lifted from my arms by guards who tell me that 'your time is up', always renew my determination. Even the most restrictive prison-like setting cannot destroy our bond or change the fact that she is still my daughter. There can never be a court-ordered termination of our love. For her sake, I will always find the strength to carry on.

Now, through the National Coalition Against Surrogacy, I feel that I can do something to prevent other women from going through the suffering I have been through, and am still going through. I can work with other women for laws banning this cruel business that sells human flesh and blood and pretends that nobody is hurt in the process.

When all this started for me, I thought surrogacy was a nice way of helping someone out. Now I know that surrogacy is wrong for our society. Now I know it is wrong to sell babies. And I know something else: it is also wrong to *buy* babies. I know it is wrong to use women as if we had no feelings. I know it is wrong to cause pain to the sisters and brothers of the babies who are sold through surrogacy contracts. It is wrong to hurt my daughter Tuesday. It is wrong to hurt my son Ryan. It is wrong that we mothers are not heard because we often lack wealth and education.

I have learned all of these things the hard way, and while I deeply hope that other women will learn from my mistakes, I am not a public crusader. I am simply a mother and a housewife from New Jersey who has decided it is time to speak out.

ALEJANDRA MUNOZ
Mexico

Alejandra Arellano Munoz, twenty-one, has a grade school education. She comes from El Habal, a tiny village near Mazatlan in the north-western state of Sinaloa in Mexico. Until she was brought into the United States illegally to gestate a baby for a relative she had never met, she worked as a cleaning woman in a bank earning $50 per week.

Munoz entered the United States with her young daughter, Nalleli. She gave birth to her second daughter, Lydia Michelle, on 25 June, 1986. She shares joint custody of Lydia Michelle with the child's father.

This is Munoz's story, as told to Gena Corea in many interviews with both Munoz and Munoz's cousin, Angela Garcia.

My story began in June 1985, when my grandmother, Natividad Munoz from Mazatlan, Mexico, came to visit her sister, my great-aunt Alejandra Mendoza. Nattie and Mario Haro, my second cousins, went to see them and explained how desperately they wanted a child. Nattie had a child by an earlier marriage, but Mario wanted a child of his own. Nattie cried and asked if they knew of anyone in the family that might be willing to carry an embryo and then have it transferred to her.

My grandmother said she would ask me. The Haros made it clear to my grandmother and great-aunt that I would only carry the embryo for two to three weeks and not full-term.

Since the Haros were family and what they wanted seemed to be an easy and safe procedure, I agreed to meet with them in Tijuana. They explained to me what they had explained to my grandmother and great-aunt. After that meeting, the Haros made plans for me to cross the border illegally into California.

I lived with the Haros. In September 1985, I impregnated myself with a syringe of sperm given to me by Mrs Haro.

They treated me fine up until the day I found out that I had to carry the baby. When I was about a month pregnant, Tia [Aunt] Alejandra from Tijuana came. She came to the house with my second cousin Angela Garcia, who is Nattie Haro's sister, and Maria Buono, my grandmother's sister and the mother of Angela and Nattie. I call her Tia Lupe. The Haros were extremely angry that they were there. They said it wasn't any of their business and they should not have any contact with me. Tia Alejandra said she felt responsible for me since she had arranged for me to come to California. She wanted to know if we had been to the doctor so the baby could be put into Nattie.

Nattie was upset that Tia Alejandra was asking too many questions. She told her not to be so nosy. Tia Alejandra said: 'She's my responsibility too. I want to know when you are going to the doctor so they can put the baby in you.'

Nattie said: 'That's not going to happen. It can't. I can't carry the child. Alejandra will have to carry the child.'

That's when the big fight broke out. I said I was going to have an abortion. Nattie said: 'Then you must be a whore. That's not Mario's child.' She called me a lot of bad names.

I began crying and crying. Tia Alejandra told Nattie: 'How can you call her that? You yourself gave her the sperm and she impregnated herself. How can you call her that?'

I was in tears because I knew I either had to abort or carry the child for the full term. Tia Lupe and Angela said that abortion was a sin. After I thought about it, I decided not to have an abortion.

Tia Alejandra asked the Haros why they had deceived us all. She said: 'You don't do this to family.' The Haros said they were willing to give me $1,500. Mario Haro said he thought that was enough money for what he called an 'uneducated, uncivilized, ignorant woman'. Angela told him that in the United States, surrogate mothers are paid up to $10,000. He said: 'For that price, I could have gotten someone intelligent.'

I was very depressed and angry that they had deceived me. I had never agreed to accept money to bear a baby and then to turn my baby over to them.

Nattie Haro wrote something on a small piece of paper. She read it to me while everyone was shouting and upset. Mario Haro didn't want Angela or Tia Lupe or Tia Alejandra to read it. I can only read printed Spanish, not handwritten Spanish. Later, Nattie said the piece of paper was a contract.

Mario said, 'Sign it' and I signed it. It was very confusing to me. I had just found out that I had to carry the child and that was a big shock. Then Nattie called me a whore. I was crying and everyone was yelling at each other and then he came out with this paper I couldn't read and said, 'Sign it.'

I remained with the Haros during the pregnancy. I felt they had a responsibility to see me through and make sure I got good care since they had deceived me and put me in that situation. And I was afraid that if I returned to Mexico, no one would believe how I became pregnant. The Haros treated me badly. I never told my cousin Angela this because I didn't know how she would react. I didn't know if she would side with her sister, Nattie. I had never met her before coming to the United States; maybe she would tell the Haros and then they would treat me worse.

The Haros never took me anywhere – to a park or anywhere – and they didn't want me to leave the house. They told me that immigration would pick me up. I think they didn't want me to leave the house because most of Mario's family thought that it was Nattie who was pregnant, not me. Nattie would wear a little pillow under her maternity gown when she visited Mario's mother.

I think Nattie treated me so badly because she resented me carrying her husband's child. She already had another child by an earlier marriage. But Mario wanted his own child. Nattie had had operations to try to give him his own child. He did not want to adopt a child. Nattie said she had to have an operation to repair the damage to her ovaries after three test-tube baby operations that didn't work.

It was hard for me, not leaving the house. I became very depressed. Finally, Angela said to Nattie that I was going to get sick if I didn't leave the house. That was when I was about five and a half months pregnant. She said, 'If she's carrying that child, don't you care that she's mentally well too? She has to get out.' She told Nattie that her sister-in-law needed someone to babysit. Nattie agreed to take me there every morning and in the afternoon the sister-in-law would take me back.

When I was seven months pregnant, I knew Angela better. I was feeling my baby growing and moving in my womb. I told her that I couldn't go through with it. I could not give up the baby. I told her, 'This baby is mine.'

I told the Haros at about the same time. They didn't say very much. They hardly reacted at all. Angela spoke to them about it too but they ignored her. Later I found out why. They were arranging things so that everything would go their way and it didn't matter what I said or that I wanted to keep my baby.

Angela later said to me that the Haros ignored her because they thought: 'Who is Alejandra? She's an illegal poor girl. What is she going to do? Who's going to pay for it?' Mario asked Angela several times: 'Are you going to pay for her lawyer?' That's why they were so confident, Angela said. Because I had no value to them. They saw me as nothing. They have told the press that I am an illegal, uneducated Mexican.

When I first began to go to a doctor during my pregnancy, the Haros told me that I would have to use Nattie Haro's name for insurance regulations and because I was an illegal alien. Because I do not speak English and am not familiar with insurance, I never questioned this. The Haros told Dr Miller and the other people in the hospital that I was Nattie Haro, Mario's wife. In this way, their insurance paid for the medical bill and Nattie was able to falsify the birth certificate. The birth certificate states that Nattie Haro is my baby's mother and it is signed by Nattie's hand.

I knew that Nattie signed all the hospital papers. What I did not know then was that one of those papers was the birth certificate.

On 25 June, 1986, I gave birth to a healthy baby girl by caesarean section. I was not able to fight for my baby then because I was too weak. I couldn't fight because I could barely walk. And the Haros told me that immigration would take me away and I would never see my child again.

I was certain that when Mario and I went to register the child and get the birth certificate, the way we do in Mexico, that I would have my baby. I was the mother and he was the father. At the registration, I thought I would get the baby, beause mothers always get the babies.

The Haros brought me to Angela's house from the hospital and then they drove off with my baby. Angela and her family were on vacation. When they returned, Angela said: 'Where's the baby?' I said, 'When we register her, that's when we're going to get her.'

Then Angela explained to me that's not how it is done in this country. That in the United States, you don't go to register the baby after leaving hospital, that it is all done at the hospital. She asked me, 'Do you have papers from the hospital?' I said no. She said, 'Who signed all the papers?' I said, 'Nattie.' She said, 'Alejandra, you cannot do anything for your daughter because you don't have that birth certificate.'

I grieved for my child. I begged for help. I told Mario that I wanted my baby. He said I would never see the baby. He said: 'If you try to get the baby from me, you're going to sink.'

When I found out about the insurance fraud, he told me that I was guilty too, he did that to put fear into me. But I told him: 'I don't care. We'll both go down.'

Angela tried to help me but because the birth certificate was falsified, things were complicated. She began to search for a lawyer to help me, looking through the Yellow Pages of the telephone book. She called every single lawyer in the Yellow Pages. Everyone wanted $1,000 to $2,000 right away. We didn't have it. It took about three months to find a lawyer. The lawyer said he would help us for $700. Angela got the $700 from friends and from people in the church.

By the time we had a lawyer, the Haros had already been with my baby for three months. It was three and a half months before I could see my child.

In February 1987, a judge ordered joint custody. But my child, Lydia Michelle, lived with the Haros. I was allowed to see her on Mondays from 10.30 a.m. to 1.30 p.m. in the Haros home. The Haros would leave while I was there. At first, they locked the bathroom door and the door to the baby's room and said I had no right to go into either room and I couldn't go into the kitchen. I needed to go into the kitchen to warm the baby's bottle. After we protested to the court, they unlocked the doors.

Later, more than a year after my daughter's birth, I was able to have her stay overnight with me one night a week, in addition to the Monday visits.

In October 1987, the judge decided that I could have more time with my daughter. Now, Mario Haro drops the child off at my apartment every weekday morning at 6 a.m. and picks her up again at 3 p.m., except on Thursday when she stays overnight with me. I'm very happy to have more time with Lydia Michelle.

Before I had permission from the Immigration and Naturalization Service (INS) to remain in this country legally, Mario Haro would tell me that I would soon be deported and lose my child forever. Now I have permission to stay in this country until 22 April, 1988, and maybe after that, I will be able to have that extended. I am very grateful to the INS which has been understanding to me.

Nattie Haro has stopped talking to Angela, her sister, and to her mother, Tia Lupe. She and Mario are upset that they supported me. Sometimes Tia Lupe cries and misses her daughter. Then Angela tells her, 'Mom, you did the right thing. I don't think you could have lived with yourself if you knew you had turned your back on Alejandra.' Tia Lupe says that is true. But sometimes she cries.

I don't know what I would have done if Angela and Tia Lupe had not helped me. I could not have explained to North Americans what had been done to me. I could not have gotten help because I don't speak English. If they had not helped me, no one would ever have known how I was used, how my daughter was taken from me.

PATRICIA FOSTER
USA

Patricia Foster, thirty-two, grew up in Michigan where she lives today. She married at sixteen. She and her husband have two children, aged twelve and fourteen. In 1973, Foster, after having left her school St Mary's Academy, to care for her first child, took a high school equivalency examination and graduated.

She has served as a volunteer at her daughters' school and, for three years, as troop leader of the Blue Birds, an organization for girls. Foster studied computer programing at Monroe Community College for two years. She has worked in a women's clothing store and in a travel agency.

In October 1985, she responded to a newspaper advertisement for a 'surrogate' mother. On 25 March, 1987, she gave birth to a son, Andrew. Andrew lives with his father and his father's wife.

I am thirty-two, married, and at the time I saw the ad in *The Detroit News* offering $10,000 for surrogate mothers, I had two daughters aged fifteen and twelve. Now I also have a son born 25 March, 1987, in Detroit, Michigan.

It was October 1985 when I saw the ad. I placed a call to the number to see what it was all about. The company asked me to come up and learn about the program, with no commitment to actually become a surrogate mother. They asked me to bring a picture of myself and of my children.

I told my husband that we were going to see what this was all about. My husband argued with me all the way there and was totally against the whole thing.

At the meeting, hearing about all these desperate people who want a baby and have unsuccessfully tried everything to have children, you're made to think that you are a saint and that this is the gift of life, the most unselfish thing a human being could give another human being, if you will just agree to do it.

You are told this is the couple's child, not yours. Some women like me think we can do this wonderful thing and save these people from this heartache.

After the meeting, the baby broker even had my husband

convinced that we were doing this wonderful thing for humankind.

So I became a 'surrogate' mother.

I thought (wrongly) that the baby wasn't conceived out of love, that since I was to be artificially inseminated, I would feel differently about this baby. But by three months he was moving and by four and a half months I saw the baby on an ultrasound screen in the hospital and watched his little fist swinging and saw his little legs kicking. I couldn't take my eyes off the screen. He was mine and I loved him no matter how hard I tried to convince myself otherwise.

As it turned out, the couple that hired me was not childless. The wife has three children of her own, by one or more prior marriages.

Two and a half months into my pregnancy I started watching the Stern vs. Whitehead surrogacy case on television every day, watching while 'surrogate' Mary Beth Whitehead struggled to keep her daughter. I began to see what the baby broker forgot to tell us. I began to see what I really got myself into. I had to watch them drag Mary Beth Whitehead through the mud because she fell in love with her baby.

By five months into my pregnancy, I was terrified about the possibility of giving up my child. My own lawyer told me I had no rights to my child. (This lawyer had been recommended to me by the baby broker. He said I could find my own lawyer if I wanted to but there weren't many who understood the surrogate contract and this lawyer did. So I went with him. Later I found out that 'my' lawyer works *with* the baby broker!)

In Mary Beth Whitehead's case, I saw Judge Harvey Sorkow say that the surrogate mother contract was legal. The sperm donor, who is a lawyer, told me over and over that the contract was legal and binding. He'd call me up and say: 'You see what Sorkow did? Face it, Patty. The contract is legal.' I was being torn apart and crying myself to sleep at night because I didn't want to give up my baby, because I was scared of putting my family through another Stern vs. Whitehead trial, and because I was feeling guilty about the contracting couple.

Then Judge Sorkow took Mary Beth Whitehead's parental rights away and 'my' lawyer told me I had to sign the adoption papers turning over my child to the couple who ordered it.

It was the hardest thing I've ever done.

The surrogate company keeps telling you that this is the couple's child. But your body takes over. Your mind and heart don't agree anymore. This little person takes over. He moves. He kicks. He reminds you twenty-four hours a day that he is there. You start to see this little person grow and grow. But you are told you are a surrogate mother. Surrogate means 'substitute'. But how can this be? Where did that ovum come from? And how does this baby get forty-six chromosomes when we know twenty-three – and only twenty-three – come from the man?

The guilt you start to feel because your heart is taking over! Putting your hands on this tummy that grows and this little person who responds to your touch. Praying every night that he's a healthy baby. Crying yourself to sleep at night because you are scared of your feelings, and realizing in the back of your mind, baby or mom or both might not make it. Praying not to go into labor so you and the baby can't be separated.

Then he arrives. After his father cuts his cord, he is layed across you. Looking at his little face as he starts to quiver, you rub his back and reassure him he's safe and you are there. You know by this time he is your son and you will never be able to let him go. But then you feel such guilt because you love your baby.

You leave the hospital with empty arms and feel cheated. Now the suffering, the pain, the feeling of emptiness, the great sense of loss at being separated from your child. How can this be, how can this ever be allowed to happen?

I've been fighting since my son was a month old to stop the adoption. I never wanted that adoption to happen. I've been trying to get this into a court, trying to do everything the legal way. Every day that my son is in his father's household, it's a strike against me. But I am unable to do any more.

The baby broker makes it very difficult for mothers to stop these adoptions. You don't have any idea what is going on because he does the adoption in another state far away. Everyone involved in my case is a Michigan resident and the birth occurred in Michigan but I have to fight the adoption in Florida. Why the state of Florida? To make it easier for the father and his wife and nearly impossible for the mother?

I learned that justice is for the rich.

Now a whole family has been ruined. Only a person in the same situation as us would understand the stress, the pain of being separated from the baby, the sleepless nights, the nightmares of a child.

After her brother Andrew was born last March, my twelve-year-old daughter kept having nightmares. Finally, she wrote the nightmare down as a composition for school, calling it 'Mrs Bates and the Group'. Mrs Bates is the wife of Andrew's father. (I've substituted a pseudonym for her real name.) This is the nightmare:

> One day Holly, my brother Andrew and me, we were all at the park. Then there was four cars that went by slow. The first car looked like Mrs Bates's car so we got up and went to a different side. They went to the side we were at. Then we went to another side. They went there too. So Holly, my brother and I went down South Grove and we were at the end of the street. There were people coming down both ways. They had masks on so we couldn't see who it was so we had to go on Willow Beach . . . They tried to get Andrew. They wanted to get Andrew and keep him. They got him from me. They got off the beach and so did we. We never got to see him again. It was Mrs Bates and the group.

After confronting the father of my son with this story, his reaction was: 'Why? She knew the arrangement.' But this is an innocent child whose nightmares express the loss felt by an entire family.

I stand with many others who call for the banning of surrogacy. Surrogacy may help take the heartache away from one family but it surely destroys another. Infertile women sometimes say they feel pain every time they see a baby, a child. I'm the one who now looks at every child that goes by, at every crying baby that I hear, to check if it is my child. I wonder every day what he looks like or what he is doing – is he healthy or could he be sick? Is he being taken care of? I look at his empty crib and live one day at a time until I see my child again.

NANCY BARRASS
USA

Nancy Barrass, thirty-one, grew up in Marin County, California. After having earned associate (two-year college) degrees in social science and medical assistance, she is studying for her third degree, this one in early childhood education. Barrass has worked in infant/toddler centers, nursery schools, and after-school centers. She has served as leader of a Blueberry troop, an organization for young girls. She lives with her daughter. Her son lives with his father and his father's wife.

I gave up my son through a 'surrogate' arrangement. I am writing in the hope that the practice whereby a woman signs a contract and consents, before she gets pregnant, to give birth to a child for other people, will be outlawed.

The process of being pregnant and giving birth has a profound effect on the woman that are unforseen and unknown by her at the time a contract is made. Legislation should prohibit 'surrogate' businesses from advertising and operating.

The majority of women who have become pregnant as 'surrogate' mothers would not have done so if there had been no economic incentive and if they had known the actual emotional impact this experience would have on them.

Because I became a 'surrogate' mother, my life has been seriously damaged. So have the lives of my nine-year-old daughter, the son I gave birth to as the result of my involvement in this practice, and the rest of my family. Based on my experience, I strongly urge women not to get pregnant as 'surrogate' mothers.

I learned about the Center for Reproductive Alternatives in 1984 through an article in the *San Francisco Chronicle*. I was then employed part-time in an obstetric/gynaecologist office and in a day care center. While employed in the doctor's office I came into contact with many infertile women. I felt a great deal of sympathy for those women. As the mother of a young daughter, I know the difficulties of being a single parent, but also the great joy in being a mother. I love children and I am now a nursery school teacher.

My desire to become a surrogate mother evolved out of my

compassion for infertile women and my love of children. I wanted to bring the joy of a child to an infertile couple.

In August 1984, I was interviewed by an assistant director of the Center for Reproductive Alternatives about becoming a 'surrogate' mother. I met the director, Bruce Rappaport, in October. At that time the center was affiliated with the Independent Adoption Center. Mr Rappaport was the director of both centers. I mention this because I believe Mr Rappaport, who had a birth mother counselor on his staff at the Adoption Center to counsel the birth mothers, was aware of the life-long grief and anguish of a mother who gives up her child for adoption, and of the deep relationship that develops between a mother and her child during pregnancy.

Their 'counseling' did not address these issues. In fact, it was very misleading and totally inadequate. I was ill-informed. I was told I would feel 'nothing but joy for doing something so wonderful'.

During my pregnancy, I asked the director and the center's counselor many times when I would be able to meet with surrogate mothers who had already delivered. They never gave me that opportunity. I needed to meet with those women to have some understanding of the feelings they had about their experience as surrogates.

The center's counseling consisted of group support sessions held twice a month for potential surrogates. The sessions were led by a male marriage and family counselor. We were told by the counselor from the beginning not to consider the baby 'our' baby, but 'the couple's baby'. I was never told about the grieving process that a birth mother goes through or of the long-term negative emotions I could expect to feel after I gave up the baby. I was not counseled about the depth of the relationship that develops with the baby during pregnancy, or that I should expect to feel a great sense of loss and grief when the baby was taken from me. The center did not provide me with the opportunity to be counseled by, talk to, or meet with either surrogate or birth mothers. I now understand that the emotions are very similar, if not the same, for surrogates as for birth mothers.

At my 'match meeting' with the customer couple, I said clearly that I wanted to keep in contact with them and be part of the extended family. The stepmother-to-be continually assured me that my daughter and I would always be part of their family and would be allowed to see our child. The center never told me I would have no legal right to see the child or even to receive information about or pictures of him. The center told me I would receive pictures. The stepmother told me she would send pictures and letters. I have not received pictures from the couple since February 1987 when my son was five months old. Now I am not allowed to see or hold my son – much less be any part of an extended family.

I do not feel I was respected as a human being by the center staff, including the doctor. At one point I was inseminated with a bacteria infection which the biological father had. I was not informed by either the couple or the doctor that he had the infection although the couple knew.

The center's doctor prescribed Clomid, a fertility drug. After taking the drug, I developed a corpus luteum cyst in my ovary which lasted throughout my pregnancy. The doctor then prescribed antibiotics for the bacteria infection. With that particular infection, it is very difficult to become pregnant. However, rather than wait until the infection was cured, he prescribed a triple dose of Clomid and continued to inseminate me.

The triple dose of the drug had serious side effects for me. I experienced dizziness, blurred vision, a severe facial rash and intense pain in my left ovary. I was unable to walk because of the pain. When I told the doctor about the side effects, he told me to continue taking the drug, and asked why I was taking such a high dosage. When I told him that that was the dosage his nurse had instructed the pharmacist to give me, he said it was done without his knowledge.

I was not told I had an infection, but was just instructed to take the antibiotics and an increased dosage of fertility drugs. I was not given the results of the medical tests or told why the fertility drug dose was increased.

But the biological father-to-be frequently telephoned my obstetrician at home and discussed my pregnancy with him, as well as confidential matters I had spoken of with the doctor. For me, there was no patient/doctor confidentiality.

At one support group I expressed frustration over the way I was being treated by the center's doctor. The following day the counselor called and told me it was inappropriate to discuss that matter in the group counseling sessions. He told me I should not discuss problems regarding the center in the counseling sessions if I wanted to continue in the group. I was told I had to attend the sessions but I was not allowed to freely express my feelings and concerns at them.

I was not paid the expense money promised me by the center on time, and had to use my rent money to pay bills for maternity clothes, pre-natal exercise and swim classes.

Two months before my pregnancy due date I told the sperm donor and his wife of my need for them not to be present in the delivery room. I felt no special closeness with these people because of prior conflict with them, and had no desire to share with them something so vulnerable and intimate as giving birth. They responded to my request by saying that their presence at the birth was part of what they paid for.

This incident is typical of how I was treated and made to feel; my feelings were ignored and not taken seriously. I was intimidated and made to feel as though I owed them.

In the center's budget for services due, my medical and therapy expenses were to be covered until the end of November 1986. I received a letter dated 24 October, 1986, from the biological father stating that he would no longer pay those expenses. I later learned that on the day before, 23 October, he had been awarded paternity and full custody of my son.

During a luncheon meeting between myself and the stepmother on 5 November, 1986, I asked her when I could start seeing our baby. I was surprised she had not brought the baby with her. When she invited me to lunch, I accepted because I thought I would see him.

She told me I could start seeing him as soon as the adoption proceedings began and I had signed the necessary papers. She told me I was too maternal and too attached.

A week later, I met with the stepmother again and, as the mother of M, I signed a form for consent to step-parent adoption. I signed the form in front of the stepmother, who was holding my baby. I was so desperate to see and hold him that I was willing to sign over my rights as the legal mother because I believed that my visiting rights to M would then begin. But for five weeks after I signed that form, the stepmother cancelled every scheduled visit, for one reason or another.

The couple took the baby to Europe. They told me I could spend a day with him upon their return. I never heard from them again.

In January 1987 I began calling state officials to stop the adoption. I realized the oral agreement for visiting rights was not going to be honored by the couple. I wanted to obtain the right to remain M's mother and have continuing contact with him so he would be assured a continuing life-long relationship with me, his mother, and with his sister.

In June 1987 the State Probation Department deferred the adoption. To this day, my trial has been continually delayed. The baby remains with the couple.

The 'surrogacy' arrangement has disrupted my family forever. I did not realize the effect it would have on my daughter. When I came home from the hospital, my daughter, aged eight at the time, asked: 'Mommy, if I am a bad girl, are you going to give me away too?'

For months she could not sleep at night and frequently asked if I was going to give her away or if I had ever thought of giving her away. The psychologist who counseled my daughter after her brother was born said this will affect her for the rest of her life.

The professionals at the Center for Reproductive Alternatives assured me that my becoming pregnant and giving up my baby would not affect my daughter.

What I have written here is simply a brief outline of the events and trauma surrounding my 'surrogacy'. This is a process that continues to go on, and that I now know will be with me for my entire life.

TRANSFERRING ONE WOMAN'S PAIN TO ANOTHER IS NOT THE SOLUTION

∎

ELIZABETH KANE*
USA

I am Elizabeth Kane. I became America's first legal surrogate mother in November 1980. It's hard for me to believe that eight years ago I was advocating surrogate motherhood and today I am working with the National Coalition Against Surrogacy. We are working with State legislators to ban surrogate parenting arrangements on a commercial basis.

Let me begin by giving you a little background information about myself to help you understand my motives for having a baby for strangers.

I was the second child, and first daughter in a family of four children. I was raised in a strict middle-class Lutheran home in the 1940s and 1950s in the Midwest. My father and brother were masters of the house simply because they were male. Throughout my childhood, my mother taught my sister and myself the same values her mother had instilled in her as a child. 'Never question the authority of your father.' This order included my older brother, and without saying so, I knew it was because my mother felt they were wiser and stronger and superior to us. During my childhood and adolescence, I remember envying the ability of males to be able to do anything they wanted to without an explanation. They were never asked to defend their behaviour. My mother would shrug and say 'That's a man for you,' or smile with obvious pride when my brother's behaviour was outrageous,

* This is a version of a paper delivered at the National Women's Studies Association Conference, Minneapolis, USA, on 24 June, 1988.

'Teddy is all boy.' Even to this day, my mother frowns her disapproval if I criticize my husband in front of her, while my sister is still a woman of the fifties in her relationship with her husband. Neither one of them can understand my 'rebellious' attitude toward my husband, labeling me 'ungrateful'. They are still trying to figure out 'what has gotten into me' in the last few years.

As children, we were all taught to give and to share with others at the risk of personal sacrifice. The earliest incidence of this I can remember was when I was about four or five. The older boy who lived next door would come into my backyard to play and I would immediately hop off my swing seat. I had learned earlier I was expected to share which meant I stood on the hill and watched him play.

It's strange. Now that I look back, I cannot remember ever feeling angry, or a sense of unfairness, but rather, acceptance.

After high school, I went on to become a physician's assistant and soon began to internalize the feeling that doctors were superior to everybody. The older women in the office would never let me forget I was to tiptoe into his office with a telephone message and apologize for the intrusion. I knew it was my job to serve him and to better his medical practice. I willingly worked overtime without being paid and after the first year I regarded the doctors I worked with as sitting on the right hand of God. So it should not surprise you when I say that my baby broker, who was both male and a physician, could have asked me to walk over hot coals and I would have willingly obliged. Unfortunately, he knew this fifteen minutes after I walked into this office for the initial interview.

My main motive at the time seemed to be altruistic. I had been surrounded by infertility all my life. First in childhood with a favourite aunt who never talked about being barren but the emptiness was etched upon her beautiful face, and later a close friend in high school who discovered she would never bear a child. She was convinced no one would want to marry her.

By the time I was a newly-wed, four or five of my friends were undergoing infertility tests and our conversations revolved around their efforts to give their husbands a child and their feelings of inadequacy at not being able to be a 'good wife'. We all knew it was our husband's job to supply material possessions and our job to take pride in our homes and to fill them with children. Those friends of mine who were Roman Catholic were expected to produce at least four or five children. Not only had they disappointed their husbands, but also their parents and the Pope. My infertile friends soon referred to themselves as 'failures', and I prayed fervently for a fruitful womb.

By 1969, I had given birth to our second child, and had discovered my sister could not have children. Several years later my brother and his wife were visiting her gynaecologist while their baby crib remained empty.

By this time, I felt strongly that infertile women needed a solution to their problems. As far back as 1970, I had talked to my husband about having a baby for a friend. I thought of it as an act of sisterhood. If infertile men had sperm donors to help them, then why was it that infertile women did not have alternatives to their sterility? Did they expect to?

In December 1979, I read a news article about an infertility specialist Dr Richard Levin, who was looking for a surrogate mother. I thought the name was quite appropriate since I would be substituting for another woman for nine months. I felt like a perfect candidate despite my thirty-seven years. I mailed a résumé and photographs of my children and myself to prove to the doctor I could 'make pretty babies'. I did not feel it necessary then to share this information with my husband. I knew full well he would never understand my reasoning for wanting to have a baby for a woman I had never met.

Six weeks later, I was in Louisville with my husband undergoing physical and psychological examinations. During the two psychological examinations, there was no discussion about my bonding with the baby. No one talked about what my three children should be told or how they would feel about having to part with their brother at the end. Because I had had a daughter out of wedlock in 1964 and put her up for adoption 'with no apparent problems' (according to the psychiatric report), I wonder if they thought I could easily do it again? Their primary concern seemed to be about my ability to terminate my parental rights. I know now they thought of me merely as a reproductive tool, including the twenty-three-year-old female attorney hired by the baby broker. She consistently threatened me with 'breach of contract' every time I asked a question or insisted on meeting the contracting couple. I was only a healthy uterus without a brain or a heart. Even today, eight years later, I am amazed at the stories I hear from other 'surrogate mothers' regarding little or no counseling about their feelings during the pregnancy and after the birth. Concerns about the feelings of their children are non-existent.

At the request of Dr Levin, a male photographer from *People* magazine was present during the entire insemination. He promised me it would never be published but was for Dr Levin's personal photo album only. A full page picture of myself with my legs spread, shaking hands with the inseminating nurse, graces the pages of *People*, 14 April, 1980. Weeks after the conception, Dr Levin sent *People* to my home, insisting I wear a maternity top to cover my three-week pregnancy. Two weeks later I appeared with him on my first contact with the television media; the Phil Donahue program. I glowed with warm feelings for the expectant couple and the entire concept of surrogate parenting. I was totally incapable of protesting or even recognizing Dr Levin's increased control over me. The media circus began, with Dr Levin telling me to continue to use the pseudonym Elizabeth Kane 'to protect my privacy'. He screened publicity requests and then called me, *telling* me where to appear. Little did I know at that time, that the photographic diary he kept of the pregnancy and the video camera he had propped in the birthing room would be sold by his agent to the media worldwide. I had no inkling that the next time I appeared on the Phil Donahue program, only weeks after the birth, a video would be shown and I would be forced to sit on stage and watch myself give birth. A few minutes later, the 'new' parents called to gloat over their prize. My son. My face still aches from the smile I forced upon it that morning for the sake of the camera and the audience.

Yet, during the pregnancy, I told skeptical audiences I had the *right* to do as I wished with my body. It took me only a few months to understand that the contracting couple and Dr Levin owned me from the neck down. I was told I could not drink a glass of wine with dinner, I could not smoke or even take an aspirin for a headache without the written consent of Dr Levin, who lived 350 miles away. I underwent numerous blood tests, ultrasounds and an amniocentesis to assure the couple of a perfect child. Before the conception, I had asked about having an amniocentesis because of my age but I was unable to back out once the baby broker decided he liked the idea. The final insult came at the time of the birth when the baby broker, Dr Levin, invited a number of people into my birthing room to watch the 'historic event', including his wife, secretary and cousin.

The couple joined me in the delivery room shortly after the birth – not because they weren't invited but because they were late arriving. Then I willingly let a strange woman hold my newborn baby and call him 'her son'. I had convinced myself a scrawled signature on a contract would guarantee I would never love my child. I told myself daily during the entire pregnancy that this child was not mine, words frequently echoed by my baby broker. The fact that this couple already had an adopted son and were not childless did not bother me until I discovered it was the sperm donor who was obsessed with having a biological child. His wife was satisfied with the son they had adopted together.

I ached for her when she told me how empty she felt, knowing her husband had to hire a surrogate wife to prove his fertility. He had gained a child that had lived only in his imagination and I had lost a son who had been part of my life for eight and a half months. Yet, even after the delivery I could not acknowledge my sorrow at having to give my son to a complete stranger.

After the birth, my baby broker continued to parade me around the country to speak about the rewards of being a surrogate mother. Seven months later, it was impossible for me to face another television camera or newspaper reporter. I told him I would no longer be available to promote his business. At the same time, I began receiving photographs of a beautiful brown-eyed infant with chubby cheeks. He no longer looked exactly like his father as he did at the time of birth. Instead the top half of his face was identical to mine. Only then did I recognize the fact that he was *my* son, too. He would carry my genes with him from one generation to the next. And I have exchanged the right to ever see him again for US$11,500.

I sank into a deep depression and had no interest in being a useful human being. I began to contemplate suicide as the only way to release my family from the shame they had suffered during my pregnancy. The emotional scar tissue on all of us was evident and still is to this day. But I felt without me, they could move to another small town and begin again. No one would ever have to know they were related to Elizabeth Kane.

I struggled for a long time to regain stability and rational thought. By the time my son was two years old, I decided to thank God for the three children I had at home instead of grieving for the son I would never see. I forced myself to actively participate in community affairs, take aerobic lessons to regain my figure and take karate and sky-diving lessons to regain a sense of worth. I returned to night classes at the university to prove to myself through the A's I obtained that I wasn't stupid after all.

In January 1985, I flew to England to speak out against surrogacy only weeks after the first British surrogate baby had been born. I told them we cannot ask women to have babies and give them away to men who are unhappy. That transferring of one woman's pain to another woman is not the solution in any society. Oddly enough, the American press was not interested in any anti-surrogacy speeches until the tragic story of Mary Beth Whitehead began to unfold.

In 1980, my intention was to find an alternative to adoption for young infertile couples. Today I have discovered that the baby business has become an industry and the children contracted for and being born with AIDS or mentally handicapped have become industrial waste.

Many couples are in their second and third marriage, are middle-aged and wealthy. Paying a baby broker US$12,000 to $15,000 to find them a healthy uterus is not a financial strain. Often the wife is surgically infertile by choice and already has children from a previous marriage. Her husband is not childless but is a stepfather to her children. Only because of his obsession with exercising his right to procreate, must his wife submit to his desire to hire a surrogate wife if she wants to preserve their marriage. She too is being intimidated and coerced into signing a contract to have her husband's procreative demands met by another woman.

A woman in Wisconsin recently testified before state legislators. She burst into tears at the end of an otherwise glowing testimony when a Senator asked her about *her* feelings. She sobbed hysterically, 'The experience of looking through a catalog with my husband to find him a surrogate was so humiliating.'

Because commercial surrogacy has been rejected internationally, men from countries all over the world are flocking to America to buy their babies. There are twenty-three baby brokers in the United States and they are only interested in surrogate mothers as reproductive toys. The evidence is the number of women who are superovulated 'to save the couple time and money' and the women who are accepted into their programs with multiple sclerosis, debilitating back problems and congenital heart defects. One surrogate mother from Texas with a heart condition was found dead in her bed on 30 October, 1987. The body of her eight-month-old son was inside her uterus. Today her mother is outraged that surrogacy and its business tactics killed not only her youngest daughter but her first grandchild. Her daughter and grandson are buried on their farm, under the same tree her daughter used to swing in as a young girl. Her loss is permanent. Hopefully mine will be only temporary. There is little I can say to console her.

My son did not ask to be deserted by me at birth. He did not decide he wanted to live in another state with a man I had never met. Today his father has chosen not to tell him he has a birth mother, two sisters and a brother living in Wisconsin. My son's father had the right to separate us during the pregnancy by demanding an abortion and today he has the right to separate us until my child is twenty-one years old. Some day my son might be forced to carry the burden of knowing he was purchased for the price of a new car.

By participating in an act of reproductive prostitution without protesting, I have now taught my daughters a lesson I had never intended. They have seen my pain and have watched me gain a new strength over the years. They will never let any man intimidate them the way my baby broker and sperm donor psychologically coerced me during the pregnancy and in the years that followed. My daughters will never serve as a whipping post for any male because they know they are valuable, worthwhile human beings and they demand the respect that is due to them. My daughter Julie recently spent forty-five minutes after class arguing with her professor about her answer to a test question that she knew was correct. While this man stared at her breasts during her questioning, she never wavered until he conceded. I have never been so proud of her as I was the day she related the event to me. My daughters will never play the martyr role my mother, my grandmother and I were taught by our church and our society.

The only way I can fight back is to see that surrogate parenting is banned in every state of this nation. I do not want any more women with low self esteem to view themselves as reproductive meat whose only role in life is to produce children, preferably those with a penis.

Abraham Lincoln once said, 'The sin of silence rather than the voice of protest makes a coward of man.' For too many years I was silent. Today I am protesting the breeding of American women as though they were bovine.

PART FOUR

.

Rethinking In-Fertility:
Establishing Positive Frameworks

I felt like a baby machine; no one was interested in me as a person. I was just a chook with growing eggs inside – and if they didn't grow properly then it was my own fault.

No one ever talked to us about our experiences in the programme. I mean the psychological side of it. Doctors don't place a great deal of importance on you. For them you are just X, just another number and if you have 'failed', another statistic.

When I was told after the third attempt that my eggs weren't good enough and that I should give up, I was shocked and utterly devastated. I remained deeply depressed for more than a year and I was suicidal a lot of the time. I felt such an abysmal failure, a barren woman unable to give my husband a child and my parents their grandchildren. I had even failed technology.

I cried and cried when I heard that the embryo transfer hadn't worked. Ever since they had allowed John and me to have a look at our embryos in the glass dish through the microscope I had really believed it. Yes, we *could* have our own children, there they were . . . mind you I don't actually think of them as babies but these cells have the potential to become a baby . . . our own baby . . . for the first time that abstract hope 'child' becomes real . . . and then all you get is this phone call: 'Sorry Mrs H, see you next time . . .' and you ache and ache but then sign on again because it seems you were *so* close, close as never before in your life . . . so you *had* to give it another try. . . .

INFERTILITY AS CRISIS: COPING, SURVIVING – AND THRIVING

∎

ALISON SOLOMON*
Israel

Five years ago I discovered I was infertile and infertility became a crisis in my life. It had never occurred to me that I might be infertile and because it does not generally occur to women that they may not be able to have a child exactly as planned, I had to cope with it alone. There was nobody within the medical establishment who helped me and the Women's Movement was also unaware of how to deal with this crisis.

Five years ago I was desperate for a child. I used to look in the mirror and think, 'I'm not a normal woman. I may look like one, but inside I'm not.' Normal women could get pregnant – but I couldn't. This may sound melodramatic – but it is true. I had never thought about infertility and had certainly never read about it. When I decided I wanted to have a baby, I went straight out and bought the *Mothercare* catalogue, a book on pregnancy, and a book on childcare. I started reading the book on pregnancy the same evening, though I promised myself I wouldn't read the book on childcare until I was actually pregnant. It remains unread to this day.

The first period I had after I decided to get pregnant came as a shock. I was furious. For the first time in my life I wasn't using contraceptives – so why wasn't I pregnant? Six months later, instead of reading the book on pregnancy I had reverted to my

* A version of this paper has been published in *Reproductive and Genetic Engineering: A Journal of International Feminist Analysis*; 1 (1): 41–49 (1988). I would like to thank Renate Klein for all her help and encouragement, which started when I first met her and has continued ever since.

women's health manual and was reading a chapter to which I'd never paid much attention – infertility. I understood that infertility could be caused by painful periods, or urinary tract infections both of which I'd suffered from seriously. Armed with this 'knowledge' I visited the gynaecologist, who, without asking any background details, told me to take my temperature every morning for three months and come back with my charts.

Three months later a brief glance at my charts told my doctor I wasn't ovulating. She gave me a popular brand fertility drug (Clomid) and said that this would do the trick. I carried on with my charts and although my temperature didn't rise I was convinced that I must have ovulated – that was what the pills were for, after all. When I still hadn't ovulated after two months she doubled the dose of the drug. Soon I was suffering from hot flushes and gaining weight, but when I mentioned this to the doctor she looked at me askance and said scathingly, 'You do want a child don't you?' (I would soon learn that as an infertile woman I had no right to complain – if I really wanted that baby, I would be happy to suffer any inconvenience, however great or small.)

The last month that I was on Clomid with this doctor my temperature did rise – far too high. Instead of rising from 36.4° to 37° it rose to 38.3° and remained there for a week. When I took this finding to her and pointed out that it was 38.3° and not 37.3° she replied quite simply that it was not possible. When I assured her it was, she said 'Well, you must have made a mistake'. I had been taking my temperature for almost a year by then yet she could still insist that I was wrong. She took me off Clomid, gave me a referral to the local hospital and told me there was nothing more she could do. The hospital said there was a long waiting list and I should call back in a few months. I suppose to them a few months doesn't seem long (in fact, once you're in treatment, and see women who've been in treatment for years, you realize it isn't long at all) but at the time I felt cheated. I couldn't understand why I would have to wait so long since I envisioned a kind of conveyor belt where you went in and within a few months were out the other side happily pregnant.

My whole life was revolving around my intense desire to get pregnant. I wanted to join an aerobics class but thought I'd soon be pregnant so it wasn't worth paying the year's membership. I also wanted to buy a bicycle to ride to work, but once again it hadn't seemed worth it if I was going to get pregnant. I wanted to join the tennis team at work – so many things I wanted to do (to say nothing of larger issues like wanting to change my job), but didn't because I assumed I'd soon be pregnant. So life became one big wait.

After I was accepted at the clinic, one of the first things the hospital doctor wanted was a sperm test from my husband. My husband explained that he'd already done one for the local doctor but this doctor said he would want regular sperm tests every few months. My husband was incensed – all that trouble he had to go to, as well as the lack of dignity and degradation. The first time he had to have a complete genital examination he came home in a state of shock. It occurred to me then that if men had to go through everything we women go through with our gynaecological tests and examinations, they wouldn't sit back and take it so easily. My husband was also extemely concerned about what would be done with all the sperm from the tests. At the time I couldn't understand why it mattered even though it was in that very hospital that one of the doctors was prosecuted for unethical conduct; finding himself short of sperm, he called out to a passing orderly and 'requested' a sperm donation. The recipient had of course been reassured that 'all attempts will be made to match the donor and the recipient's husband'.

Our family and friends were clearly worried by the fact that we hadn't yet started a family. It is not acceptable in Israel to be childless and it is not usual to wait before starting a family. Even couples who can't really afford children are told 'with the child, comes the luck', and economics are no reason to put off having children. (Similar thinking led to the repeal of a section of the abortion law so that lack of means to bring up a child is now no longer sufficient reason for a legal abortion.) Pressure is applied to childless women and I certainly didn't escape it. I felt it in many small ways: at the circumcision ceremonies of friends' children, always 'please God by you'; on 'Mothers day' being the only one in the office not entitled to the afternoon off; being made to feel that riding a bike was irresponsible and that I obviously didn't really want children; when there was a family gathering being given one of the babies to hold (to bring me luck if I did want a child, and to shame me if I didn't).

People sometimes think that perhaps it was because I was married to a 'Sephardi'[1] I felt so much pressure. Although this is true, even women from western, educated families are under tremendous pressure to have children. I recently met a woman who left the kibbutz she was living on because of her infertility. She is thirty-six and had tried to accept her childlessness, but had found herself made to feel a total outcast. The kibbutz has become one of the most family-orientated institutions in Israel. The first fact a kibbutz always boasts about is how many children it has. In town it is no different; my friend Orna, a young Ashkenazi, and modern 'career-woman', feels that even if *she* could accept her childlessness, her family and friends, to say nothing of society, would not.

The morning at the clinic would begin with the ultrasound. We came to the clinic having drunk thermoses of tea and pints of water – and then would begin the agonized wait for the ultrasound technician to arrive. We were scolded like naughty children if we hadn't drunk enough. Each woman would waddle into the room, have the ultrasound, and then rush out making straight for the toilet. Conversations usually revolved around the different treatments we were all going through and the different operations we had had or would be having. After all, what else was there to talk about? I don't think any of us had really good or exciting jobs. How could we when we would be going to the clinic three times a week arriving at work three hours late? Infertility treatment is hardly the best way to build a career.

The actual appointments were always a let-down. I remember once the doctor was examining me internally and asked if I did a lot of sport. By then I was cycling, playing tennis and going to aerobics so I replied that yes, I did. I asked if that was wrong. He answered vaguely, that no, he just wondered. But why then, I thought, was the question asked in the first place? I never really knew what was going on – what treatment I was having or why. When I tried to ask questions based on the reading I was doing, the answers were hurried and incomplete and the questions were clearly not welcome. So I tended not to ask questions – apart from anything else I would think of that long line of women who were waiting to come in after me and who also had to get to work. It didn't seem fair on them to take up more of the doctor's time. (At a recent visit to my local doctor's clinic, I saw that a new system has been introduced whereby the first half-hour of the day is for 'questions and answers'. On my doctor's schedule, someone has erased the word 'answers'.)

During that period I was tense a lot of the time. Every morning I'd take my temperature, waiting for the fourteenth day of the month to see if there would be that sudden drop and rise. Because there was always a slight rise, I would wait anxiously for the end of the month hoping that *it* wouldn't happen – that my period wouldn't appear. I read everything on the subject of infertility – by then the books on childbirth were relegated to the back of the bookcase and their place was taken by the only available book I could find about infertility.

Then one day after I'd done some test or other, the doctor suggested that since the results would take about two months I should just take a rest from everything: stop taking my temperature, planning intercourse, and so on. I was furious. It was like telling me to stop thinking, to stop breathing. Didn't he know that my whole life was guided by one ambition and one alone – to get pregnant? Today, my infertile friend Orna says that she finds these breaks disconcerting – 'sometimes it's such a pleasure I don't want to start again. But of course,' she adds quickly, 'what choice do I have?' Orna says she'll give it one more year and then give up. But she admits that being in infertility treatment is like being on drugs – you always think, just one more time. Today I also feel this way about fertility clinics. I think those fertility drugs are just like any other drug – something you get hooked on. And just like any real junkie, you're part of a whole scene. An addict can't take drugs and carry on leading a normal life, and that's what I was – an addict.

I took the two-month break, and suddenly I discovered that it was actually a pleasure not to have to 'think-thermometer' first thing in the morning, to make love how and when we chose, to stop thinking about babies, and to start thinking about me. For the first time, I began to think what would happen if I did not get pregnant, at least not for the time being. I could start getting involved in many activities that I had postponed for so long. I could seriously think about changing my job. If I stopped being tied to the clinic, I could start doing interesting, exciting things – if I could make that choice.

I talked to my husband about this, but since I was the one

who really bore the brunt of our infertility, he did not realize just how much the treatment was affecting my life. I use the term 'our' infertility because according to the sperm count, he was also sub-fertile. However, we were told that this was only going to be dealt with once *my* problems were solved! I started to think about why I really wanted children and realized that it was partly because of our life-style. In an environment where we were the only ones in our apartment block without children, the only ones in the family without children, the only ones amongst our friends without children there was no viable way to come to terms with childlessness. My husband was part of this environment and would not leave it. In fact, one of the things that most attracted me to him when we first met was that he would make a wonderful father.

When the two months were up, I delayed going back to the clinic. I felt disillusioned. At the beginning I'd been so sure that the treatment would be quick and easy. I had believed that when I took a drug to make me ovulate it would work. By now I knew that fertility drugs didn't always work, and especially not on me. I knew that the drugs themselves made me feel unhealthy.

About a year after I'd started infertility treatment I became involved with the Women's Movement. Even there I discovered that whenever I brought up the subject of my infertility, there would be a total lack of understanding. I would be told (by women who had children, or had made a conscious decision not to have children) that it shouldn't be so central to my life. I felt that my feelings and my reality were being denied. Yet I felt that a feminist approach could be helpful to myself and other women and I began to think about the idea of a self-help group for infertile women. When I mentioned the idea to one of the women at the infertility clinic she said she had enough of her life revolving around her infertility without going to a group devoted to it. I did not then know what kind of approach we could use which would be different from our own spontaneous discussions at the clinic. I felt that perhaps we could examine what would happen if we did not get pregnant, but I remembered my husband's reaction to any suggestion of 'giving up' and I realized that most of the women in our clinic were too far into treatment to give up. Yet I was feeling more and more repulsed by the clinic and all it stood for. After the two month break I had not gone back to the clinic. In the end I decided to stop going altogether.

I still do not know why I could not get pregnant. When I went back to the clinic several months after my husband and I split up, the doctor was no longer willing to treat me. Not, he hastened to assure me, for any moral reason, but only, he told me confidentially, because 'it's really all trial and error anyway'. It was as if now that I had dropped out of the scene he could admit that he didn't really know what he was doing anyway. He told me that I was just as likely to get pregnant without any treatment at all. It made sense – by then I knew only two infertile women who had become pregnant – one in a two-month break before starting on Pergonal, and the other after one unsuccessful IVF attempt and before she started the next. The whole thing struck me as supremely ironic and I felt gladder than ever that I was well out of it.

Once I realized that I wasn't going to have children, my whole attitude towards motherhood and children changed. This did not happen suddenly; it was a gradual process. At first I still could not accept that I was not going to get pregnant. Other women take getting pregnant for granted yet when I hear of a friend who is pregnant I see it as a real achievement. Even when I began to give courses at the women's centre, I still saw motherhood as an essential part of womanhood. I had been a feminist long before I was married, yet it was still not easy to let go of a dream.

Every woman has her own answer on how to cope with her infertility. Many of us change our lifestyles so that motherhood is not so central to the way we live, and others of us find some other way to be in close contact with children. Sometimes we think we've 'really got over it now' and some tiny thing will jolt us into the realization that the forms of longing or desire for a child may change but they never disappear. But we know we're on the way when we can stand up and say 'I am infertile – and I can cope with that' – and mean it.

I strongly believe that not only can we cope with infertility, but we can actually thrive from the aftermath of infertility crisis. I would not have believed this to be true when I was in treatment or even one year later. But today I KNOW it to be true, both from my own experience and also from my work in helping women through another kind of crisis – rape. I believe that too many women are going through painful and dangerous medical intervention unnecessarily. It is these two beliefs – one personal, one political – which form the basis of what I see as a feminist approach to infertility.

I am basing my ideas, obviously, on my own experience but also on my work in a rape crisis centre. Before describing a feminist approach to infertility, I would like first to briefly look at present attitudes to infertility in the medical establishment, in Israeli society, and in feminist theory. By examining where present attitudes fall short, we can then establish a way of looking at infertility which will be most helpful to infertile women.

The medical attitude

Sophie Laws has said that in our society all too often, 'the only way to deal with female experience is to put it into a category which is easy to recognise – sickness' (Laws, 1983:20). This is what has happened to infertility.

For medical practitioners, infertility is a purely medical problem, a malfunction of a system in need of repair. Not only is the system in need of repair, it is the doctor's *duty* to repair it, since this is his[2] job. For proof of this mechanistic attitude we need only look at the terms used to describe infertility caused by tubal blockages or other physiological problems, at least in Hebrew, which are called mechanical causes of infertility.

Infertility is a malfunction of a system, and this is clearly seen in the way hospitals calculate their success rates on IVF programs. In my own survey of IVF clinics in Israel in 1986, all clinics clearly stated that success rates are based on the number of *pregnancies* compared to the number of *laparoscopies* rather than the number of births compared with the total number of women on the program.[3] This finding supports similar findings in a survey of IVF clinics in the US (Corea and Ince, 1987). Success is the repair of the malfunction – pregnancy – and not the effect desired by the patient – a child.

My survey also found that all IVF clinics in Israel will treat a woman who already has children from a previous marriage or from her present marriage who has since become infertile. Their reasoning is usually that infertility is a sickness that needs treatment. Even if this was an acceptable definition, it is clearly not true because this sickness has a social aspect. A single woman who is infertile is not 'sick' – if she was it would be the doctor's duty to 'cure' her. Yet 'cures' for infertility are available only for married women.

According to the doctors, infertility is a medical problem. Yet, quite astoundingly, doctors are willing to treat – give hormonal injections, do laparoscopies and operate – on perfectly healthy women. They do this quite openly and indeed according to the above-mentioned survey most of them saw this side of things expanding. The reason – male infertility. IVF is seen as a legitimate answer to male infertility.

Doctors claim that IVF is being done to help unfortunate women, desperate to control their reproduction. I have never heard this explanation given as a reason to grant abortion to rape victims or give artificial insemination to lesbians. It is clear that if doctors really cared about women and our health, IVF would be very low down on the scale of priorities. Instead, while the infertility clinics remain full to overflowing and have long waiting lists, every year new IVF clinics are opening up – clinics that are far more expensive, take far more 'man' power, and have very low rates of success, if we consider success in real terms (i.e. the number of babies born to the number of women attending the clinic).

The social attitude

Despite the fact that doctors are sure that infertility is purely a medical phenomenon, in most countries the use of medical procedures is backed by social and religious attitudes. In Israel, where many aspects of daily life are ruled by religion, one would think that this might have some dampening effect on the 'progress' of IVF. However, this is not the case, precisely because for the dominant religion – Judaism – the attitude towards infertility arises out of the first and supreme commandment in the Bible, to 'be fruitful and multiply'.

Despite the fact that only 30 per cent of the population are orthodox in faith, secular women are just as desperate as their religious counterparts to become pregnant. Fertility is not only a religious priority but also a national one. Children take on an almost holy aura for a people whose very existence was threatened during the holocaust and for a nation who feels its survival to be in constant danger. Thus both religious politicians and secular leaders call on women to answer the religious/national need for an increased Jewish/Arab birthrate.

Increased birthrates must be within the family framework and thus there are financial disincentives for single, childless women, such as higher income tax, no rights to a joint mortgage, less sick leave, and so on. To be married and voluntarily childless is seen as the height of selfishness, and I have yet to meet a young couple who would state openly, as can be heard so often by Western 'yuppies' – that 'we don't want children'.

I am not trying to say that infertility is *purely* a social problem. Many infertile women truly feel an overwhelming desire for a child. Yet leaving aside the question of whether there is an inherent motivation in some women to become mothers, the desperation of infertile women is undoubtedly exacerbated by social conditions and by certain lifestyles. Society, for its part, is happy to perpetuate the present patriarchal social order and thus does little to relieve women who may be the victims of it.

The feminist attitude

Until recently, infertility was not particularly an issue within feminist circles. Naomi Pfeffer (1985:50) describes the feminist reaction to infertility thus:

> Several years ago Anne and I made valiant attempts to set up workshops on infertility at women's health conferences and in our own homes. The response was nil. We had no preconceptions about how we wanted infertility discussed, we just wanted it to be put on the feminist agenda because we believed that we could find support from our sisters. Sadly our efforts failed. It has taken IVF and the more outrageous solutions to infertility such as womb-leasing to stir up feminist interest.

From personal experience and through conversations with other infertile women, I have found that the women's health groups know little about infertility and infertile women are likely to be told by feminist activists that motherhood should not be the central issue in life. All too often, our experiences are delegitimized and trivialized by women who would not dream of doing so in any other crisis situation such as rape. The only branch of feminism that has dealt with infertility is that dealing with reproductive technology. However, this aspect of feminist theory deals with infertility only very indirectly since it is aware that reproductive technology is a far broader issue than just infertility treatment. FINRRAGE – the Feminist International Network of Resistance to Reproductive and Genetic Engineering – believes that the 'externalization of conception and gestation facilitates manipulation and eugenic control', that reproductive technology uses biology to solve social and political problems created by exploitative conditions. IVF is seen as 'the division, fragmentation and separation of the female body into distinct parts for its scientific recombination', which leads to 'the take-over of our bodies for male use, for profit-making, population control, medical experimentation and misogynous science' to bring about 'a racist or fascist division of women into valuable women . . . who should have children' and 'inferior women . . . are forbidden to have children' (FINRRAGE resolution, 1985). FINRRAGE has exposed the fact that the use of reproductive technologies exploits women's suffering, but the feminist movement has not yet found a viable way to deal with that suffering. Some feminists say that in exposing the harm done by the reproductive technologies we do not ourselves have to find an alternative to them. For example, Pat Hynes (1987) deplored the fact that whenever feminists try to raise our voices against reproductive technology we have thrown back at us the question, 'but what is the alternative?' This line of argument then lays the responsibility on the critics and blames us for the situation that existed before the technologies. She suggested that in order for a problem to be recognized, an alternative solution does not have to be given. If society recognized that reproductive technology is *not* the best solution for infertile women, then it would be forced to look for better alternatives.[4]

Lene Koch and Janine Morgall (1987) have taken this one step further and given guidelines towards a feminist assessment of reproductive technology. They suggest that we should first ask basic questions such as, 'Do we need this technology?' 'What are the causes of infertility?' The answers to these questions lead clearly to the conclusion that reproductive technology is *not* addressing the needs of infertile women. 'The costs and benefits are calculated from the point of view of the scientist, sometimes articulated as the interests of the embryo' (p. 180).

Reproductive technology is clearly more than a treatment for infertility. It is actually providing 'wombs with a view', opening the door for advancement of genetic engineering as well as becoming a form of social control. Thus it is in society's interest *not* to examine reproductive technology in a certain way and *not* to come up with alternatives. This is why we feminists must come up with the alternatives. Feminist theory is most viable when it is put into practice. The setting up of rape crisis centers did not lead to an end to rape. However, it has resulted in the feminist assessment of rape being taught – to social workers, the police, and in certain schools of psychology – as if it was the obvious, 'objective' assessment of rape. This is an incredible achievement and was brought about solely by the implementation of feminist theory. We must bear this in mind when dealing with reproductive technology and infertility.

Infertility as crisis

While exposing the problems of the technologies, feminists often fail to differentiate between suffering caused by infertility and suffering caused by infertility treatment. Infertility is not a state that *only* becomes traumatic through its treatment, but is in itself a crisis that needs dealing with.

In using the word 'crisis', I intentionally bring to mind other crises such as rape crisis. As a rape crisis counselor, I have found many similarities in attitudes towards infertility and rape. These similarities can be seen in the following categories: (1) ignorance of the general population towards the crisis the victim goes through ('best to try and put it out of your mind dear'), (2) the stigma attached to the victim ('well, I don't like to ask her about it, it's not really something you talk about'), (3) feelings experienced in the aftermath or realization of the crisis (shock, denial, guilt, anger, depression, vulnerability, loss of (sexual) identity), (4) stereotyping of the victims of the crisis (see below), (5) reactions of women to a crisis situation (see below).

I am not drawing an analogy here between rape and infertility. The two are both major crises and any comparison is meaningless. Yet the feelings and emotions that arise out of these crises are very similar. This is because both crises are directly related to the essence of what being a woman may mean in a patriarchal world. Women are raped because they are women. Women's infertility relates to one of the most basic aspects of being a woman – the ability to reproduce. If it is claimed that the only difference between men and women is that women have the unique ability to bear children, we have to think about what this means to a woman who is unable to bear children.

Rachel Levy-Schiff (1986) states that in Israel the infertile woman is seen as physically disabled, a woman in mourning, a tragic figure. Pfeffer has also pointed out that the stereotype of the infertile woman is one so 'desperate' that she 'loses all personal control'. This stereotyping of the victim of infertility is very similar to the stereotype of the rape victim. Either she herself is guilty – infertile women are blamed for their infertility, either because they put off getting pregnant for so long, or they had previous abortions, or they have psychological problems that lead to unexplained infertility. Rape victims are blamed for provocative behaviour, getting into dangerous situations or subconsciously wanting to be raped. If they are not guilty, they are the tragic victims of circumstance and will probably never recover from this trauma. So too, it is assumed that infertile women can never lead truly happy lives without children. In fact, as Naomi Pfeffer (1985:50) points out:

> this common feature (infertility) does not mean that all women who experience infertility respond to it in the same way . . . Ignoring these very real differences between women serves further to alienate infertile women who are struggling to take control of a very negative experience and denies the mixed feelings, the pain and grief involved.

Although there are some situations that may be considered crisis-inducing for any individuals who experience them, an event that may be of crisis proportions for one person may have less effect on another. Crisis may be experienced differently and reactions to it may vary. However, it is generally accepted that a 'stressful life experience . . . (seriously) affecting the ability to cope' which often is or leads to a 'turning point' should certainly be treated as a crisis (Bard and Ellison, 1974:166) and this is surely so for infertility.

Characteristics of a crisis situation such as the suddenness of its occurrence, its unpredictability and arbitrariness are clearly present in infertility crisis. We tend to assume that we are fertile and, while the discovery of infertility may be gradual, the realization of its implications are usually sudden. The concept of 'family planning' becomes a mockery when you discover that you cannot, after all, plan your family. And, all too often, it seems to the infertile woman that she is the only one who is infertile – everyone has children don't they? Just as there is a rape trauma syndrome, so too Rachel Levy-Schiff describes an infertility crisis syndrome with six stages from denial through acceptance.

Reactions to the crisis situation

It is the infertile woman's reaction to the crisis situation of infertility that makes it important that she meets with a counselor – but a feminist-oriented one, not a member of the medical establishment. This is because in a crisis very often we become helpless and dependent on others and thus 'an otherwise mature and effective person behaves almost like a child in seeking support and nurturance, guidance and direction from those regarded as strong and dependable' (Bard and Ellison, 1974:167). In the case of infertility, that 'strong and dependable' person is all too often the doctor, who instead of giving complete information, suggesting alternatives, or giving counseling of any kind, assures the person with a fertility problem that she can solve all her problems if she just puts herself in his hands.

In instructing police on the treatment of rape victims, Bard and Ellison have the following to say: 'Individuals in crisis are extraordinarily open and suggestible. This provides a unique opportunity to affect long-term outcomes.' What a perfect situation for the doctor who finds himself sitting opposite a vulnerable and temporarily helpless woman. By the time she has come to grips with her infertility, the road forward is obvious. 'Being on the scene early allows us to take advantage of the period when the victim's defenses are down, when she is open and accessible to authoritative and knowledgeable intervention.' Furthermore, 'because professionals are expected to be competent, those seeking their services act in ways that will facilitate this competency; for example, people listen and follow directions' (1986:167).

I am not suggesting that women are weak and helpless, eternal victims. What I am suggesting is that if we recognize the infertile woman, about to embark on treatment, as *a woman in crisis*, it is easy to see that she can be manipulated because of her vulnerability. At some stage she will begin to come to terms with her infertility and then may begin to set limits on the treatments she is willing to undergo, but by then it is probably too late for her to make an objective assessment of her situation. I remember when I was in treatment talking with another patient who had undergone treatment for seven years. 'Why on earth don't you give it up?' I asked her. She looked at me as if I was mad. It was not a question she could ask herself at that stage. Similarly, an IVF counselor may help a woman in certain respects, but in order to get that far along the road of infertility treatment the woman must already be convinced that these forms of treatment are what she wants.

A feminist model for infertility crisis counseling

It would not have helped rape victims if the women's movement had listened to them and then repeated their stories without actually helping them and this is why we must start with infertility crisis counseling. Infertility is a crisis and must be dealt with by the feminist movement on two levels. The first is the personal level, to be with the woman where she is now, to accept her feelings and help her deal with them. The second level is the social level, to work towards a society where infertility is not a stigma and an infertile woman is not socially ostracized.

On the first level, we must recognize that infertility is a crisis to which every woman will have a unique reaction. However, if we recognize infertility as a crisis that may have a syndrome with clearly identifiable stages, we will be in a better situation to know how to help the woman. If she is at the denial stage, for example, telling a woman that 'you're not really infertile, we can fix you' or 'you're not a "failure" till you stop trying' (motto of the Tel

Aviv Sheba hospital IVF clinic, quoted in Anbal, 1984:16) is not the right way to help her. Instead, we can help her first of all to come to terms with the fact that she is, in fact, infertile in the sense that she will not have any (more) biological children. This is a very big step and is the main one in overcoming the crisis. Most women I have met have told me that they do not try to come to terms with their infertility because they believe it is only temporary. Denial is a natural reaction in crises such as rape and infertility. But it should be only a first stage and in order to come to terms with the crisis, the woman must face the fact that she won't have a biological child. Doctors who concentrate on 'curing' and 'fixing' do not help the large percentage of women who even after treatment will remain infertile.

If we recognize the social implications of being an infertile woman as well as the psychological ones, we will understand better the sources of infertile women's feelings of confusion and guilt, low self-esteem, anger, and distress. A feminist counselor must always accept the very real suffering of an infertile woman, however sure she may be that it is possible to live a full life without children. It is only by helping a woman where she is now that we can help her to move on from there. In rape counseling we listen to a woman, and deal with the problem as she sees it. We do not give her psychoanalytical explanations, nor do we tell her that while she may see the problem one way, in fact the cause of her problem is really something quite different. We listen to her, and we explore with her all the facets of her present situation and her present conflicts. In this way, we best help her to help herself in analysing her emotions and feelings. In doing this we empower the woman so that she makes her own decisions, instead of having to rely on the 'professionals' to do this for her.

Eventually we hope that she will be in a position to ask herself how she can use this crisis experience to actually benefit her in her life. For example, women find that the knowledge that they were utterly helpless and managed to overcome that helplessness gives them tremendous belief in their own strength. Women who never questioned many aspects of their lives as women find themselves with a new understanding of themselves. Women may feel better able to deal with challenges and difficulties that may enable them to want to change many aspects of their lives – sometimes even their whole lifestyle (Ben-Zvi and Solomon,

1986:4). I now believe that infertile women can accept their infertility and can use their experience to achieve not only a better understanding of themselves but also an increased motivation to advance and progress in their lives.

In addition to counseling, an infertility crisis center must be a source of information. In our rape crisis center, we have found that one of the primary reasons for turning to us is the lack of information concerning rape. The lack of information for the infertile woman is just as great. In both cases, women find themselves in a situation they never expected to be in and are thus not equipped to deal with it. Everywhere where there are infertility clinics there should be a crisis counselor on hand. This is because infertile women are powerless against their doctors – if they 'misbehave' they are out of the program/clinic. They are uninformed, or misinformed, and are thus unable to make real choices. I believe that in this social climate women still have very little choice, but the information must be made available. At the moment, there is nowhere for infertile women to get the real facts and figures as well as meaningful explanations about everything they are going through. Someone has to be there to tell the doctors what infertile women really want and how we feel; to explain to women what the full procedures are likely to be, what the risks are, and what the possible outcomes might be.

The aims of infertility crisis counseling are twofold. The first, as I have said, is individual counseling. The second is educating society. This is done by speaking out. Rape as a subject was surrounded by a web of silence. The myths that were generated about it encouraged women to think that it couldn't happen to them and if it did, they were at fault. Rape victims remained anonymous, isolated, and uninformed. In a similar way, infertile women are alone. Infertility, however, is an everyday reality for about 10 per cent of women. This fact must be broadcast, spoken about, and worked on.

There is a resistance to infertility education. In Israel, it has been claimed that if we educate young people about infertility they will not take contraception seriously.[5] It is this same distorted thinking that does not allow children to be taught about sexual abuse and it is clearly an attitude that must be changed.

Infertility crisis counseling centers should also act as pressure groups. They should expose the inhuman and misogynous aspects of current infertility treatment and demand a more holistic and caring approach. They should expose for whose benefit current treatments are being developed and they should help find more viable *alternatives* for infertility treatment. In addition, they should pressurize for more research to be done on the causes of infertility. If it is known that certain substances or certain environments may lead to infertility, infertility crisis centers should call for legislation leading to prevention of such substances. Preventative measures against infertility should deal with the problem before it exists, not after the damage is already done.

Finally, we must explode the myths surrounding infertility. Why, like rape victims, must infertile women remain anonymous? Why do our friends treat us with fear? Why is there such tremendous stigma about being infertile? Why do people look upon us with such pity when they hear we cannot have children (but immediately comment that 'it's quite lucky really' when they hear that we are divorced/single/lesbian/disabled . . .)? These are attitudes that have no basis other than a social one and they are ones it is possible to change. Infertility is a central issue in an increasing number of women's lives. The time has come for it to become a central issue in feminist theory and feminist practice too.

NOTES

1　Sephardi Jews living in Israel tend to originate from countries such as Iran, Iraq, Syria, Morocco, and India. They are largely a poorly educated and economically depressed sector of the community and may generally adhere to traditional values. Ashkenazi Jews are predominantly white Eastern European Jews with a more 'modern' attitude.

2　Throughout this article, doctors are referred to as male. This is because (1) most doctors working in IVF and the upper echelons of infertility treatment are indeed male and (2) women doctors have often absorbed the male medical mentality so that they may treat their women patients in a male (authoritative, patronizing) way.

3　If this difference seems trivial, it should be pointed out that using such a statistic totally falsifies the real success rate of IVF clinics. For example, one hospital in Tel Aviv had 350 patients, 54 pregnancies, and 6 births. It claimed a success rate of 26 per cent.

4 These points came up in discussion following the paper presented by Pat Hynes at the 1985 FINRRAGE emergency conference in Vallinge, Sweden, in 1985; see also Hynes (1987).
5 Dr R. Sharkshall made this comment at the 6th National Conference of the Israel Family Planning Association in 1986.

REFERENCES

Anbal, Leah. 1984. Who do you belong to, child? *Korteret Rashit* 28.11.84 (Hebrew): 16–18.

Bard, Morton and Ellison, Katherine. 1974. Crisis intervention and investigation of forcible rape. *The Police Chief*. May 1974: 166–171.

Ben-Zvi, Rina and Solomon, Alison. 1986. *Tel Aviv Centre for Victims of Sexual Assault. Annual Report* (Hebrew).

Corea, Gena and Ince, Susan. 1987. Survey of IVF clinics in the US. Paper given at FINRRAGE emergency conference, Vällinge, 1985. In Spallone, Patricia and Steinberg, Deborah Lynn (eds), *Made to Order: The Myth of Reproductive and Genetic Progress*. Pergamon, Oxford.

FINRRAGE Resolution. 1985. Women's Emergency Conference on the New Reproductive Technologies, Vällinge, Sweden. In Spallone, Patricia and Steinberg, Deborah Lynn (eds). 1987. *Made to Order: The Myth of Reproductive and Genetic Progress*. Pergamon, Oxford.

Hynes, Patricia. 1987. The road not taken. Environmental Protection in the US: A Paradigm for Regulation of the Biomedical Industry. Paper given at FINRRAGE emergency conference, Vällinge, 1985. In Spallone, Patricia and Steinberg, Deborah Lynn (eds), *Made to Order: The Myth of Reproductive and Genetic Progress*. Pergamon, Oxford.

Koch, Lene and Morgall, Janine. 1987. Towards a feminist assessment of reproductive technology. *Acta Sociologica* 30(2):173–191.

Laws, Sophie. 1983. The sexual politics of PMT. *Women's Studies International Forum* 6 (1):19–31.

Levy-Schiff, Rachel. 1986. Psychological and social aspects of infertility. Paper given at the 6th National Conference of the Israel Family Planning Association (Hebrew). At the same conference, comments by Dr R. Sharkshall.

Pfeffer, Naomi. 1985. Not so new technologies. *Trouble and Strife* 5:46–50.

Solomon, Alison. 1986. Survey of IVF clinics in Israel, undertaken under the auspices of Tel-Aviv University. Unpublished manuscript.

THE BARREN DESERT FLOURISHES IN MANY WAYS: FROM INFERTILITY TO IN-FERTILITY

■

LINDSEY NAPIER*

Australia

I was officially told in 1974 that I had a fertility problem. But there is a difference between when you are told and when you know yourself. I think I had fears about infertility ever since 1969. I let appendicitis get the better of me and didn't intervene in time. I ended up having an appendectomy but I think the tubal damage had been done.

I continued taking the pill; I ignored the fears despite the fact that three other women in my family were childless, too. In 1972, my partner and I came to Australia, travelling around the world, getting out of Britain. I had a secret plan, I thought I'd have a year out, come off the pill and be pregnant by the time we got back to England. I remember going to a Catholic GP soon after we arrived in Sydney who kept saying, 'Why don't you get on with it, you're twenty-what-ever-you-are?'! I was born in 1945, so I was twenty-seven.

We didn't go back to England which is another whole saga . . . probably quite relevant to my fertility history. As I had been off the pill without getting pregnant and I wasn't ovulating, or menstruating, I went to see a specialist. The verdict was the usual post-pill amenorrhoea and I was put on Clomid.

After taking Clomid for about a year, I began to menstruate but didn't became pregnant. I can hardly remember that year. I do remember being swapped around between doctors (in retro-

---

* The interview was conducted and edited by Renate Klein with final approval by Lindsey Napier.

spect it was pretty awful), and then getting a good one – Dr F
– whom I stuck with and who stuck with me. In my head I knew
the Clomid was not going to sort my system out. Very interesting
how one knows these things. . . . So they started investigating
me further – not my husband but me – and when I was about
thirty I had my first laparoscopy. I was depressed but this was
also to do with migration. I was also on an 'anorexic' trip. For
me that meant withholding all the good things, making sure I
could prove to the world that I didn't need anything to keep
going. On the outside I felt great; I loved my job as a social
worker in a hospital, but even in a good team-work situation
working with people who are sick and dying takes its toll. I
tended to play 'big sister' to many of my colleagues and deny my
own pain.

I remember walking out of Dr F's consulting room after he'd
told me that I had very badly blocked tubes, thinking, 'Right
lady, that's it, you're not going to have kids . . .' I felt totally
lost, after all I'd come to the end of the world – Australia – there
was nowhere else to go. I rode around on the buses all that day,
wondering where to put myself.

The best thing I did then was to give up paid work for a while.
I sat around, did patchwork, gathered my resources. Work had
always been my great passion and I wanted to figure out the next
step. I remember little about this time . . .

My husband was very supportive. I must have been in a pretty
bad way. I offered him all the things like 'why don't you go?',
'this is ridiculous, you're fertile', 'you've got relationships, you
can do it', 'why don't we split?', I'm bad for you.' I went through
all that and he simply said, 'Sorry, I'm staying'. Good man – he
gave me a lot of support.

At the end of that time I was ready for work again. I got a
demanding and exciting job in the Health Commission. For well
on five years I denied the fertility problem, it was extraordinary
really, the denial . . .

The context is that I actually never thought I wanted to have
children: I didn't want to be 'tied down'. Although we've never
talked about it, for my mother, I think, to have us, probably
stopped her life. My father was killed when I was born and she
had to be the full-time mother. To an extent I am my mother:
her old freedom and independence, that's what I am. So for me,

working, living, being a woman in the world, is what it is all about. I never thought I wanted to have kids, but obviously, on a deeper level I did want them . . . I wanted to have everything.

From 1975 to 1981 I worked at the Health Commission. I became a worker who operated around the clock. We worked night and day to establish new services, to help get social work and social policy onto the map of the health service here in our small way. It was a very exciting time. Community health services were being established and we were part of it.

Half-way through my time there I had worked myself up to the point of breakdown . . . I was fine on the outside but crumbling inside. It's all right working terribly hard if you're caring for yourself and nurturing youself and doing all those good things. But I wasn't doing that . . . It was a good proper breakdown! It was terrible. I was in the middle of organizing a National Conference. I wasn't actually able to go to the conference.

So I went to Europe for a month. I thought I'd get myself together while I saw my family. Then I came back to Australia and went into therapy with a woman. During that process I decided that I really did want a child. Very interesting, in retrospect, I mean who is to know what passes between two women! It was clear that a lot of the grieving I was doing was not to do with my childlessness. It was to do with a father being killed, leaving the land I loved, never having learned to trust anyone with the dangerous parts of myself . . . the whole lot. But I also began claiming things for myself and one of the things I decided I wanted to claim was the entitlement to be a mother. Though I had mothered all my life I wanted my 'own' child.

While all this was going on, we went back to see Dr F. He said, 'There's not much you can do, but there is microsurgery', and referred me to a specialist. I then became extraordinarily single-minded. I really don't quite understand the passion . . . I think the passion with which I went for microsurgery can be likened to the passion with which women invest energy in IVF. It's the whole thing about 'everything else falls by the wayside . . .' In retrospect I think that such intervention on the body is symbolic: it takes the place of personal reparation. The hope is that by repairing the body the whole person will be made 'whole' again. I saw the surgery as one part of my healing process. A colleague of mine talks about transforming the experience to give it meaning and in so doing making it manageable . . . For me doing work on the 'outer' me symbolized the 'inner' work of becoming whole again.

There's no conflict, you feel very purposeful. You enter into a totally different way of being – going into hospital and giving yourself over – that's the only way I can understand it. It's like moving out of one life into another. There is a ritual about to take place. The day before going into hospital – I remember thinking, 'Tomorrow I have to give my uterus over.' I think that's what you do. Looking back, when I went to see the surgeon for assessment he had said to me 'Well you've got about a 30 per cent chance, a very low chance, about 30 per cent'. But at that stage figures didn't mean anything. Not a thing. If he'd said 5 per cent I would have done it – it's a madness. That's what I meant about being single-minded. Quite extraordinary. I think it is beyond reason.

I don't remember the name of the surgeon who did the micro-surgery. I actually demanded to have a friend with me in pre-med. I had such fears of losing consciousness; I think it's about death. I have deep fears about 'giving myself over' at all levels. When I do decide to do it then it's the whole of me. But to actually see it as a technical act in which I'm not engaged, of which I can't be part – this is alien to me and very frightening.

I do remember that later the surgeon stood at the end of the bed and asked, 'When do you want to go home?' I remember the physical things. I remember the image that he actually gave me about my uterus. I had given away part of myself, and now he gave it back to me. He said to me, 'It's all right now.' And I thought, 'Thank you very much, now I can be whole again.' At one level it all makes total sense, at another it is a madness.

Experiencing all of this physical giving and taking of part of my body during tubal surgery was the reason why I did not go in for IVF. I remember my husband actually asking my gynaecologist, Dr F, 'What's this thing about IVF?' And this man, thank goodness, shook his head and said, 'I don't think that's what you want to be on about.' As far as I knew IVF was only happening in Melbourne then – and I thought, 'No way am I going to do this.' I felt very strongly that no one was going to take hold of my body ever again. With IVF I would never be able to actually feel any baby was mine, because you have to give your reproductive self away – a vital part of your self – and later have it put back. How do you make it belong to your self again? I understand when women say after they've had an embryo transfer and the transfer didn't 'take' that they can't relate to it. It must be extraordinarily difficult. For me, who finds 'attachment' difficult, that process would have been impossible. I think I would have felt that there was a foreign body inside me because I wasn't in charge of the procedure. I know, however, that other women have none of these fears and receive the 'gift' without trouble. After all the microsurgery I felt I needed to put boundaries around me. 'There's going to be no more invasion of my body', I thought . . . but unfortunately there was!

After the operation, I was told that if I was to get pregnant it would be most likely to happen within a year. Well I didn't. At one level I didn't expect it to happen, that's the madness. It's the deep knowledge that I as a woman have; that I wasn't going to bear a child and I think that that knowledge informed my acts. I think women often know things that we don't trust. And that we almost stop ourselves trusting in it. Certainly this is part of my biography. OK, you can have intercourse whenever. . . . On the outside, I did all the right things. But on the inside – it's the whole relationship of what's going on inside and what's going on outside and there are discrepancies – I knew it wouldn't work. I think my husband might have known it too. I think there is a lot of collusion; we both deluded ourselves.

In 1981 I left the Health Commission, I thought, 'I am going to leave and work out what I need in terms of my work and life.' Life, not children – life. My friend Susan had by that stage decided to adopt a child. We had lunch one day and she said to me 'You've been wanting to be a mother all your life. [It sounds so silly when you take it out of context!] Why don't you think of adopting?' And I sat back and thought, 'Why don't I think of adopting? There's no reason at all why.' It's about timing, it's about someone saying something to you at a particular time in your life. It's not to say that she didn't recognize that I had mothered all my life. One might well ask why I am doing social work . . . But I had always, before that, said I would never adopt. I felt there was absolutely no need to adopt. All I thought was 'Get on with your life.'

At lunch with Susan these feelings changed – instantaneously, that's all I can say. But it took a lot of work – intrapsychic work, because I started out thinking that adoption was the most outrageous thing that you could do. I thought it was wrong, it was taking another woman's child, it was theft, it was exploitation of other people. I took the whole of the western culpability on my shoulders and made myself responsible. And then decided that I wasn't, and that that was OK. I invested that shift of feeling with similar passion. Again I think I went through the adoption experience with a single-minded attitude. I was obsessed once more.

We moved house and put the adoption papers in. That was very symbolic. We had a beautiful house but we had one empty room that spoke to me of the barrenness of so many years. I wanted to put down some roots. I started my thesis on the rise of medical interest in infertility. and began to work at university. 1982 was a good year, though I was amazed at my obsessvie preoccupation with our adoption plans. We should have left for Sri Lanka on 3rd December to return with our child on Christmas Eve. On the last day of November I developed abdominal pain. I crawled to my GP who was unsure of the diagnosis – an ectopic pregnancy perhaps? After two days full of agony, he agreed to hospitalization: I shall never forget the relief of knowing that Dr F was 'on duty' and able to admit me immediately.

Surgery. Adhesions – they had wrapped themselves around the intestines. I went and read the medical textbooks afterwards, and, of course, adhesions follow every piece of surgery of which I had had quite a bit! It's horrendous to think of the information one ignores. There I was, working in the Health Service and I didn't know any of this! I am not saying this to blame myself. I certainly wasn't given any of this information. But all I had to do was to look up 'adhesions' in a medical dictionary – and there it all was – it's extraordinary the ignorance that one is prepared to live with.

One of the things I did during this period – which I call 'working-it-all-out' – was to found *Concern NSW*: a self-help group to support people with fertility problems. This is the only group in New South Wales which is independent of any clinic and is not purely an IVF group. Because I was a professional health worker at the time, I was permitted to attend the inaugural meeting of the Fertility Society of Australia in 1982. It wasn't because I was a consumer – I doubt if they would have let me in! I was amazed at how seriously they took themselves, marked by the founding of a learned college, the hallmark of specialization. I thought to myself, 'No woman should have to experience the loneliness, the guilt, the anxiety, the longing – all the stuff that not one of these "experts" has acknowledged.' At that meeting I talked to a couple of social workers and a psychologist who had a fertility problem herself. I said 'Come on you lot, we've got to do something!' And we did. But I now have very mixed feelings about that.

Concern has always been a very small self-help group – we are not like the IVF groups who I believe raise money – we do not take money from anyone, then you're not beholden to them. But the danger is that such groups become a place where people come in and get support to go straight into medical technologies! What I had wanted was to create a place where people – women – can come and be angry, and grieve and do all that is necessary to find ways of moving through infertility. But the pressures of the technologies, specifically IVF, are hard to keep at bay. Besides, the support needs are monumental. All the self-help groups provide a voluntary unpaid service – everyone is doing it at nights, on the weekend, many going through the mill themselves. The pressures to *give* people things to take away the pain are enormous; there is just no place for them to spend days working through a tiny little bit. I could afford good therapy twice a week for three years, other people can't get that. Women have so much to offer one another . . . but the problem is, the resources aren't there to do it. I am very concerned about that. In the meantime, reproductive technologies get advertised loudly. And women often only come to us after they've already been through years of medical treatments and are at the end of the line – the same moment when social workers are often called in. It's very difficult, in the face of so much despair, to stay away from technology at all. I was shocked when I heard myself saying, 'What kind of medication have you been on?', 'What kind of medical help have you received?', 'Do you plan to embark on another programme?' because I didn't have anything else equally powerful to offer. Medicine and technology are extremely powerful and we need equally powerful alternatives so that people feel they have a real choice.

I am not actively involved in *Concern* any longer. I still act as a contact and I'm involved at political and policy level. But I am also trying to *live* an alternative life; to provide an example that 'having a child' can be different. Now that I am a day-to-day mother of my 'own' child I want other women to have the fulfilment of the experience. Susan, my friend who has a daughter by adoption, and I decided we were going to break this whole nuclear number mainly because as 'older' mothers we'd better deal with our ignorance together! We started co-parenting – the children are moving in and out of each other's houses. I feel I really have two children – an amazing gift. Perhaps *living* an alternative works better than just saying it. At times at *Concern* – I blush when I think about it – I would say, 'Isn't it important that we all look at different ways of doing our parenting in the world?' But that's easy to say when one has opportunities – teaching, social work, moving in different circles. It's very different for someone who gets married, sets up home – and then there are no kids! I did sometimes say, 'Look, can't we really talk about the fact that there are, for instance, very damaged children in this place that we all live in?' I was trying to say there are different ways of doing things; we have to move beyond the need to have a child, which given my own actions *is* hypocrisy.

A woman I know who was refused IVF began to be involved in a birthing group and she now takes care of women throughout their pregnancy and birth. She says that for her the whole experience, not just the birth, has allowed her to become the closest she ever feels she could get to being a mother. This is just one example but I think we need lots and lots of examples of women doing those sorts of different things. Even Susan and I used to be regarded rather warily by other women who would say, 'How the hell could you do that, how could you share your child, how could you let your friend make decisions about your child?' I don't think it's very extraordinary at all. You need really good examples, where there are actually children involved, where you are saying, look, it is possible to share. No one can really take care of a child on her own, as we all know. It's possible but impossible. I think for many women there have to be concrete possibilities offered, say 'Have you thought of?', 'Let's explore.' You have to offer alternative experiences, so that they can *see* that there really are alternatives.

The question of 'Why children?', needs to be tackled again and again. For me being responsible for another being, a tiny person, who was actually making demands of me, needing me to be there, was part of it . . . that sounds extraordinarily stupid because I used to regard myself as somebody who moves around, never attaches herself, is never grounded, is never connected. For a child of course, especially a baby, you've got to be there. It's the grandeur of the mundane day-to-day living relationships that is the passion. Many women lack such passionate relationships in their lives with an adult partner, usually a man. That's the great deprivation for many, it's either through children or through other women that they may be enabled to have passion in their lives. That is often what women are looking for. It's not just nurturing or having a child, it's the intimacy which for so many women is never there and they crave it. I don't know how you say this to women but for some I think it is a really important part of the desire to have children. I'm lucky to have both!

The women's movement, too, has to change direction. If we don't want more and more women getting into invasive medicine at an earlier and earlier point in their (in)fertility history, we have to offer them something concrete. I think if there were deeply committed feminists who were prepared to begin to provide things and become known at women's health centres or community centres, if they started by doing things very slowly, very gradually, women would find that going to a women's group does not mean getting an ear full of preaching. I have personally felt under attack from some other feminists; I felt that because I'd made the decisions I had, I was deemed not to be 'conscious' enough – too much part of the dominant social construction, ideologically unsound . . . all those things. And that happened to *me* who actually had thought a lot about these things . . . I think we have to continue to say, 'Well, let's look at what that means, and why we feel so vulnerable to each other that I can't be allowed to say "that's how I feel".' To me feminism is in part feeling free to say, 'I think and feel', and then search – together with other women – for the analysis.

I still get quite a lot of phone calls from women. It's important to talk with them as early as possible, either at the point when the GP refers them to the specialist or when they meet the specialist for the first time. I could have been stopped in my tracks the day Dr F said to me, 'That's it.' But when the decision time came for me no feminists wanted to talk about infertility, not then in the early 1970s. So I tried to get out, away, avoid. Today, when women ask me about IVF, I tell them that I wouldn't do it. I explain that for me it was absolutely not on. I say why and I make sure I explain in detail what it involves – drugs and all the rest included.

But I also think that as concerned feminists, infertile and fertile women together – to use these thoroughly unsatisfactory terms – we need to do a whole lot of joint experiential work. How will we know what we can say to women who are desperate unless we kind of rehearse it? I think we could set up networks where women can teach each other lots. *Concern* has that potential. But many of my feminist friends – and some feminist researchers – don't really involve themselves. The world of fertile and infertile, the world of feminist and non-feminist is split. They don't even talk about their own fertility, what that means to them. That's why I often felt I was on a see-saw, I felt split for a long time. Fertility problems can be very overpowering. One woman I knew felt so threatened by me that I concluded she must have thought I was contagious.

(In)fertility problems have split women's groups. I feel very strongly about this because I am both concerned and a researcher. It's important that different women are involved in such groups. You can't talk about infertility without talking about fertility, that's number one, absolutely not, and the whole history of the medicalization of reproduction . . . And you can't talk about infertility unless you talk about being women in the world. And what attaches women to the world.

Infertility, the word, is meaningless; the old words were better. The barren desert flourishes in many ways, the desert can become the most lush place. It all depends on how you are in it. I felt in a barren state before I flourished, before I made the leap from infertility to in-fertility, before I became the woman that I am now: joyous and attached to the world.

A VOICE FOR INFERTILE WOMEN

.

ANN PAPPERT
Canada

Although the issues in new reproductive technology have broad implications that extend far beyond the personal, there is little doubt that the personal issues these technologies raise for infertile women have very special implications.

I am a feminist, a journalist who writes frequently on medical and health issues, and a woman with a fertility problem. Like many other infertile women, I initially looked upon reproductive technology as a beneficial option for infertile women, but after spending a year researching and writing on these technologies I have come to regard them as a highly destructive science that not only offers little benefit to women, but causes great harm. My own infertility problems were probably somewhat easier to deal with personally than for many other infertile women. As a long-time diabetic I had known since childhood that both getting pregnant and staying pregnant might prove difficult. Indeed, for many years I could not get pregnant, and later when getting pregnant was no longer a problem, I was never able to continue a pregnancy. In 1981 I adopted a child.

Barbara Katz Rothman (1984:26) has said, 'We thought that information would give us power. What we perhaps overlooked is that it is power which gives one control over both information and choice.' Nowhere is this truer than in the area of the new reproductive technologies, for the information to assess these technologies does not come easily.

The overwhelming public perception of new reproductive technologies is that they are amazing feats of science that give 'miracle babies' to infertile couples who previously had no hope of ever having a child. This has been the dominant image presented in the media and by *in vitro* practitioners since Louise Brown's birth in England in 1978.

The press has recorded each new birth as a milestone, whether it was the birth of the first child at a local IVF clinic, or the birth of the world's first frozen embryo baby. Since the media rarely, if ever, talks about the problems of IVF, and the doctors certainly never encourage any discussion, the image of IVF as a cure for infertility has been widely accepted.

Given this, infertile women can hardly be blamed for buying this image whole. After all, it is infertile women who have vested interests in believing in any procedure that holds out the promise of helping them to have a child.

Choice has been a central theme of feminism. All too often we have had the attitude that expanded choices can only benefit women. But as Ruth Hubbard (1982) has noted, 'as "choices" become available they all too rapidly become compulsions to "choose" the socially endorsed alternative.'

This question of whether increased choices really benefit women has particular meaning in the case of new reproductive technologies (nRTs). Any analysis which questions whether nRTs represent a real choice for women must address these points: do they give women more control rather than less; are they beneficial, how invasive are the methods employed and do they carry with them any additional risk of physical and psychological damage, do most women come away with a baby, is this technology women-centred in its approach and philosophy: and in whose interests is it being used? In the case of nRTs almost none of the conclusions made are positive.

Reproductive technology turns the desire of infertile women for children against us. Infertility, even when the infertile partner is not the woman but the man, becomes the woman's problem. Her body becomes the laboratory where the procedures of reproductive technology are carried out. If she fails to become pregnant, the failure is not perceived as a failure of science, but a failure of her body.

At the same time IVF practitioners are quick to claim all the credit in the few cases where the procedure is successful. The 'cure' for the woman's infertility is seen in the science, and in particular in the doctor who performed the procedure. The role of the woman, specifically the nine months she spends carrying the baby, is rarely acknowledged.

The language of the reproductive technologists is alienating, dehumanizing, and mechanical. Clinics rarely refer to their clients as women, preferring to use the term 'cycles' to keep track of IVF attempts. Doctors talk of 'success rates' for pregnancies or babies (rates that are frequently misleading) and miscarried or ectopic pregnancies become 'wastage rates'. Invariably women on IVF are called 'patients', thus labelling fertility problems as a disease.

Even if IVF worked, and produced babies more often than it failed, it would still be a technique that seeks medical control over reproduction, rather than giving more control to women. This separation of reproduction from the bodies of women to the laboratories of men, turning babies into products and women into breeding grounds for experimentation, amounts to expropriating women's bodies in the interests of science.

New reproductive technology exposes women to dangerous drugs and techniques. Infertile women often say that they will 'do anything for a baby', but the truth is that even for the most desperate woman there are limits.

I am certain that few women would knowingly choose *in vitro* and other reproductive technologies if they were aware of the potential long-term risks of the drugs used in hormone stimulation, for example; especially if they were told the risks might extend not just to themselves but to any baby they might have; that their child may, as recent studies (Gorwill, Steele and Sarda 1982:529–32) have suggested, have damaged reproductive systems or possibly increased risk of cancer.*

Nor would doing anything to have a baby include using techniques that expose women to the possibility of infections and damage from ultrasound and carry with them increased risk of miscarriage or ectopic pregnancy that may leave their fertility even more impaired. (Ashkenazi *et al*. 1987:316–8)

All of this is done in the name of helping women. Reproductive technologists assert that they are drawn to the science out of a genuine concern to help infertile couples have babies in whatever

---

* I have also interviewed many women whose fertility was further impaired by procedures used during *in vitro* attempts. Among the more common experiences, were ectopic pregnancies and burst cysts (which developed as a result of receiving Clomid), which in some cases blocked fallopian tubes.

way they can. Because of this, they rationalize the risks and benefits of the procedures by claiming that this is a new science that is improving its techniques and success rates every year, although the facts show these claims are untrue. In truth, reproductive technologies are more entranced by the solution than by the problem. The science is everything.

If reproductive technologists were truly concerned about infertility they would put greater effort into examining and eliminating the factors that cause the infertility of many of the women they see; conditions such as pelvic inflammatory disease, often associated with IUDs, and endometriosis.

For many women the expanded choices nRTs represent have a negative impact. The more positive exposure nRTs receive, the more publicly acceptable they become, the more pressure infertile women feel to try these technologies. nRTs have already become the socially endorsed alternative to which Ruth Hubbard refers. Barbara Katz Rothman (1984: 31–2) calls these expanded choices a new burden for infertile women; 'the burden of not trying hard enough'.

Before the development of nRTs infertile women eventually had to come to terms with their infertility. To find, each in her own way, but as part of a community of women (who often by sharing their own experiences helped the infertile woman find a direction for herself), a way of carrying on with her life and reaffirming her existence.

Infertility, to be sure, can be very painful. Even the strongest woman may find the experience of infertility emotionally devastating. But as hard as infertility is, surely it should not be a life-long burden – an endless road with no place to get off, the traumatic roller coaster of having to try again and again.

The new nRTs, however, try to seduce us with science. We live in an age where we are made to believe science can make all things possible. We are supposed to believe that nRTs will give us babies because we have been taught to believe in the promise of science. But the promises of new reproductive technology are false, and worse, they are cruel.

Women pay a high psychological price for this 'miracle' technology. Reproductive technology promotes a self-hating, self-blaming attitude in infertile women. Women feel compelled to try them simply because they are there. Even women with little faith in them admit that if they hadn't tried they would have felt they hadn't tried everything in their quest to have a baby.

Because reproductive technologists encourage the belief that each successive IVF attempt brings a woman closer to a viable pregnancy which by extension should mean a baby, quitting IVF is a far bigger issue for an infertile woman than accepting the fact that she has been unable to conceive naturally.

In an interview with me conducted in 1988, Canadian philosopher Christine Overall describes this as the 'lottery mentality'. Women are plagued by the thought that by quitting they will be seen as not having tried hard enough. The reality is that women in IVF programs have an elevated sense of failure. If science has all the answers, then surely their failure is their own, not a failure of science. It is their bodies they begin to hate, not the reproductive technologists who sold them false hopes.

When an infertile woman who has 'failed' to get pregnant stays with a programme, it is often because the reproductive technologists have persuaded her that what they may learn by 'trying' the technique on her may help other women later on. Thus she becomes nothing more than a laboratory experiment, an object of science, and this is done by appealing to her sense of altruism, difficult to escape for most women.

This double bind of reproductive technology makes it even more difficult for infertile women to begin to heal themselves psychologically, to re-establish their sense of value and self-worth and make positive connections to their place in the world; to find meaningful life beyond their infertility problems.

Infertility raises two important, but altogether separate, issues for women. The first issue is the infertility problem itself, the second issue is the desire to parent. I believe that one of the major issues in women's experience with infertility is confronting, and reconciling, what is seen by many infertile women as a betrayal of their body. For many it is the first time in their lives that they have felt and, indeed, are out of control of their lives and their bodies. The second point is the need to conceive a child versus the wish to parent. Although these two issues may seem to be connected, and reproductive technology has encouraged infertile women to view them as bound together, I believe it is a serious mistake for women to view them as one issue.

Having a baby is different from raising one. If all that mattered to most infertile women was giving birth, then we could say that after giving birth, most infertile women would have no problem giving their babies to other women (although I admit this is an exaggerated example). Parenting *begins* with birth, it does not end there. What most infertile women want is the experience of motherhood. If they could choose, obviously they want as much of that experience as possible, which includes experiencing childbirth. But few infertile women would forgo the opportunity to be a parent through adoption.

Because reproductive technology fixes on biological parenting as the only 'real' way to parent, it enforces the idea that the only child worth having is a child you give birth to. This fixation on biological procreation as the only acceptable method of parenting excludes a supportive view of other parenting options like adoption and a recognition of how many children are currently in need of parents. It is a philosophy profoundly anti-feminist which devalues both children and parenting.

Furthermore, I believe it makes a dangerous connection between not being physically able to conceive and give birth to a child and the act of parenting. Dangerous, because women who do not have a baby through the methods of reproductive technology are made to feel that the other options available for them to parent, like adoption, are less acceptable; that these children will never be more than second best. It increases their pain and turns even this attempt at overcoming infertility and becoming a parent into a defeat.

A voice for infertile women

It is extremely important for infertile women to examine the issues raised by reproductive technology. But it is equally important to examine the way in which, unfortunately, the debate over the nRTs has tended to divide women into 'infertile women' and 'feminists' – as if these were two mutually exclusive groups.

The current debate over reproductive technology would not exist if feminists had not initiated it. But if feminists have framed the debate on the nRTs, many have done so without including infertile women; put differently, the voices of infertile women have been largely absent. Often 'feminists' have alienated and pushed aside 'infertile women', instead of welcoming them as our natural partners in this debate.

That infertile women have been denied a role by reproductive technologists is hardly surprising – indeed allowing them a voice would have been the surprise. But infertile women *must* have a place in the feminist debate of these technologies – or else this debate is incomplete.

There are two especially worrying feminist positions on infertility and the nRTs which preclude any meaningful participation by infertile women. On the one hand, as I have experienced it, some feminists are loathe to take firm positions on reproductive technology, for fear that any criticism will be seen to be attacking not the technology, but infertile women who opt to use the technology. Thus we have the absurd situation where before these feminists criticise the nRTs they often feel compelled to explain that they are not attacking infertile women who use these technologies. When feminists, particularly feminist health activists, take this position they are giving implied support for the technology whether they realize it or not.

Another equally problematic position is to present the often desperate needs of infertile women for a child as a 'product of socialization'. This view is consistent with some early feminist analysis that motherhood was exploitative and not a condition to which women should aspire. Women who take this position seem to be saying to infertile women that what they really need to focus on is not how to get a child, but to realize that there are many other ways for women to live full lives. The overwhelming message is that all infertile women need is to 'get over' this desire for a child and their emotional trauma will be ended.

The hostility felt by many infertile women to this position often makes it impossible for them to accept any of the objections feminists raise to the new reproductive technologies. The result is that many feminists come to believe that infertile women in general are not open to review of nRTs, while infertile women believe that feminists in general see them as inferior by virtue of their desire for children.

These positions marginalize infertile women and further remove us from the debate. At worst, they are part of the belief that infertile women are unstable; emotional basket cases, whose obsessive desire for a child precludes any ability to contribute to the debate on these technologies. If feminists contribute to this view of infertile women, they add to the exploitation of their infertility.

A feminist critique of the new reproductive technologies without the voices of infertile women is incomplete. Feminist resistance to reproductive technology will be far more successful if infertile women join with feminists. We must do away with the splits between us, for, after all, any developments in reproductive technology will affect all women. Feminists involved in the debate over the nRTs must recognize that for many women the wish to be a parent is not simply a product of socialization but a true desire to be with children – for it is a unique, positive and wonderful experience – whether that child is by birth or adoption or other ways of social parenting.

What infertile women need is a woman-centred debate that addresses how we want to deal with our infertility – without being abused by exploitative technology. To put the power over what happens to our bodies, our health and our lives in our own hands, it is vital that infertile women speak out against the new reproductive technologies; about what is being done 'for their own good'. To do that infertile women need support. We need to be included in the information and research that details the problems and abuses of reproductive technology. This book contributes to this end. We need support that legitimizes our desire for children, and recognizes our pain about not having children – support that pulls women together, instead of pushing us apart.

In the end, I doubt whether women will be able to stop the proliferation of the nRTs; science seems far too fixated on these technologies to abandon them. But by exposing them as dangerous, exploitative and experimental techniques, and promoting a broad understanding of the personal and political issues they raise, an increasing number of women will realize that new reproductive technologies do *not* represent a true option for infertile women, but a new health and psychological hazard with a technological face. In realizing that, they will see these technologies not as a solution, but as part of the problem.

REFERENCES

Ashkenazi, Jack, et al. 1987. Abdominal Complications following Ultrasonically Guided Percutaneous Transvesical Collection of Oocytes for *In Vitro* Fertilization. *Journal of In Vitro Fertilization and Embryo Transfer*, 4(6):316-8.

Cunha, G. R., Taguchi, O. et al. 1987. Teratogenic Effects of Clomiphene, Tamoxifen, and Diethylstilbestrol on the Developing Human Female Genital Tract. *Human Pathology*, 18: 1132–3. Clomid package inset. Merrill Dow Pharmaceutical.

Gorwill, R. H., Steele, H. D., and Sarda, I. R. 1982. Heterotopic columnar epithelium and adenosis in the vagina of the mouse after neonatal treatment with clomiphene citrate. *American Journal of Obstetrics and Gynecology*, 144(5): 529–532.

Hubbard, Ruth. 1982. Some Legal and Policy Implications of Recent Advances in Prenatal Diagnosis and Fetal Therapy. *Women's Rights Law Reporter*.

Rothman, Barbara Katz. 1984. The Meaning of Choice in Reproductive Technology. *Test Tube Women: What Future for Motherhood*. Pandora Press, London.

OPTIONS FOR INVOLUNTARILY CHILDLESS WOMEN

·

UTE WINKLER & TRAUTE SCHÖNENBERG
West Germany

Three years ago an involuntarily childless woman[1] came for medical counseling to the Feminist Health Centre in Frankfurt (FFGZ). She met with very little understanding about her problem, as at that time the centre was geared exclusively towards the problems of pregnant women, abortion and contraception.[2] These are the problems with which the women's health movement has been concerned in the last two decades and they had come about through personal suffering and political intolerance. Female fertility had always been accepted as a matter of course and had never been questioned. Against this background, contraception, abortion and still later the question of the 'new maternity' could emerge as the new topics of emancipation and political programming.

Society has always accepted fecundity from women. This was – and is – connected with their social role, their 'biological destiny'. Inability to comply with this role continues to carry the stigma of biological impotence and it is this social norm which has made us blind to the fact that all women are 'fertile' as well as 'infertile' throughout phases of their lives.[3]

The development of the new reproductive technologies inevitably resulted in a political controversy about the new methods and their repercussions for women. Only recently did these discussions begin to include the sufferings of the women concerned. It was this new awareness which later led to the idea of counseling for involuntarily childless women. Since 1986 the FFGZ has offered such specialized counseling. At the same time a self-help group was formed.

General counseling

The starting point for discussing women's experiences with the new reproductive technologies within the group Women Against Genetic and Reproductive Technology[4] was the recognition that involuntarily childless women have no voice in the discussion of genetic and reproductive technologies and that their thoughts in the matter are trivialized or ignored. The women concerned with their individual case histories and what decisions to make stand alone between medical practitioners and promoters on one side, and the political opponents of these technologies on the other: the experiences and opinions of the women themselves are rarely reflected and discussed. On the contrary, for the promoters of these technologies, it is politically useful to either ignore their wishes or to overemphasize their situation. In other words, it is politically expedient for them to use women seeking IVF as battering rams to break down public taboos and thus to achieve the desired general consensus. In this way the conditions are created in which genetic research and its application is legitimized and advanced, regardless of its effects on women.

It is to avoid such abuses that we offer our counseling service. We would like to help women to clarify their conflicts and arguments concerning human fertility/infertility by providing them with time and space to reflect on their fertility problem which for many manifests itself as a life crisis.

Counseling is available for all women whose wish for a child cannot be fulfilled. It is for women who merely suspect that they are infertile, for women who have tried various forms of treatment, for women who have participated in IVF programmes and also for women who cannot see any chances in – or do not want to undergo – medical treatment. Our main emphasis lies on the discussion of the significance of involuntary childlessness, whether suspected or diagnosed, or whether in fact it is not the woman's but her partner's problem. We make space for emotions arising from an unfulfilled desire for a child, the disappointed hopes and wishes, the grieving and inner mourning as it affects the women. The discussions take place on a one-to-one basis, or in groups, just as the women prefer. The counseling is designed to air problems, to put them in words and make them public. For many women this is their first chance to come face to face with their innermost thoughts and fears. It enables them to express their own thoughts – often for the first time even to themselves – without having to fear criticism or trivialization.

Pregnancy, maternity and everything that has to do with getting and being pregnant has been surrounded by so many taboos and suffocating ideologies, that many women find it difficult to discuss the topic at all. There is no literature, no cultural institutions where these facts of life can be discussed critically. It is politically important therefore to create such a place where women have a chance to express their own thoughts about the whole complex of problems and to help them to develop these thoughts further.

This is a new way of empowerment and therefore extremely important and valuable for women. Together with the women seeking advice we try to work through the problems which have been expressed. The woman is at the centre of the discussion and determines what course it will take. The counselor's job is to support her in the formulation of her own thoughts, to assist her in seeing connections and to point out areas which have been consciously or unconsciously omitted in the discussion.

One of the principles of our counseling is the fact that infertility and involuntary childlessness need not be identical. As one woman put it:[5] 'Infertility and childlessness are two different things. Suffering caused by infertility is not necessarily the yearning for a child.' Infertility is also the loss of biological potency. This fact is often denied – especially by doctors. They make women believe that all that needs to be done is the curing of the symptom, as if involuntary childlessness could be equated with disease. In doing this they implicitly reduce women to the socially accepted image of mothers: the loss of potency gets defined as a loss of Self. As a consequence the woman's integrity as a person in her own right is violated. In our counseling we therefore refuse to emphasize involuntary childlessness, but rather place the whole woman as a complete person at the centre of our discussions.

Such counseling allows the involuntarily childless woman to confront her problem outside a medical context. This can lead to the formation of a self-help group or to contact with other women who can then exchange their experiences. It can also lead to psychological counseling and/or therapy. As a result women are discovering that they don't have to use any medical treatment, to which they often react very badly, and that it is all right for them to follow their own inclinations: respect their *feelings* and take them as seriously as their body which 'negates' a pregnancy.

Women often see their childlessness as a static process and thus feel their whole personality is sterile – an ideology all too often promoted by medical practitioners. As one woman put it:

> Physicians never say that 'you are biologically infertile', or that 'your reproductive system is limited'. They say *'you* are sterile'. They generalize and women accept the generalization. If one is in a bad phase one sees oneself as sterile – totally and completely.

Yet fertility and infertility ought to be seen as different expressions of a woman's relationship to her body in the specific context of her own life *and* her existence as a member of the social group 'women'. This concern was expressed as follows:

> I think that every person is in some form sterile and in some form fertile. There is always both. I think it is unfair to emphasize my restricted reproductive potency, to make it absolute, to declare it as my most outstanding characteristic. It is a part of myself, but other parts of myself may well be fertile, except that I don't see them as such.

Time and again women report that their physicians cannot find any medical reasons for unsuccessful attempts to get pregnant, but that despite this lack of evidence they insist on further treatment: 'The doctors never gave any concrete reason. They just fed me with generalities such as: "If you have been trying for three years without success, well then, you are sterile".' Unfortunately, due to our socialization which tells us to believe experts, women often have more trust in their doctors than in their own bodies. In our counseling sessions we ask why this might be so and we attempt to discuss the limits of medical knowledge – as well as the assumptions on which it is based. Very often women feel vindicated when we reassure them that they were right to instinctively distrust medical technology. Sometimes they feel comforted and relieved if they are assured that other women experience the same sense of futility about the value and usefulness of medical technologies.

All women who come to us have many thoughts and ideas of their own concerning their problems. Only very rarely are they accommodated by the medical practitioner. Worse, they are often found to be trivial and irrelevant.

The women's partners are rarely examined, or if they are, it is only much later than the woman; it seems that both the gynaecologists as well as the women 'protect' the partners. Some women say again and again that *they* cannot have children. Only after months of questioning one finds out that the problem is with their husband. In principle, the fault lies always with the woman.

In our capitalist-patriarchal society to be a woman is to be a mother and therefore it is the woman who must be the cause of the unwanted childlessness of the couple.[6] The new reproductive technologies are based on this assumption: they are conceived for and applied to women exclusively. Thus male sub-fertility is an indication for an IVF programme; *he* has the problem but *she* – a healthy woman – undergoes the dangerous and debilitating procedures. Men are usually not prepared to discuss and pursue their own desire for children and to take on social responsibility. As long as this is the case, the problems of infertility will remain a matter for women and it will be women who have to bear the tension to prove their feminine existence; the onus to be fertile will always remain with them.

In this context an essential part of our counseling is to question the assumption that the fertility problem is *her* responsibility. We support her in breaking down the normative categorization that the man is always potent and that it is the woman who is 'sick' and 'in need of treatment'.[7]

Men not only deny their collusion with these assumptions on all levels, as experts, partners and future fathers, they also refuse to enter the women's frame of reference; to try and understand the women and to participate in their thoughts and experiences. One woman said that after she had submitted to donor insemination her partner refused to have anything to do with her. He even assaulted her. It was impossible for her to tell him about her painful experiences during these inseminations. Since then he blocks every discussion about her wish for a child.

The lack of interest which stems from patriarchal premises is also to be found in the women's social environment. Women experience this phase as personal isolation. 'Friends, parents and acquaintances cannot be contacted and/or drawn into a discussion. On the contrary: these people continue to pressurize us and push us into a position of social outsiders.'

This attitude is often caused by uncertainty and insecurity: one does not know how to react to infertility/the desire for a child.[8] This insecurity has its origins in the fact that all topics concerning reproduction (yes or no to a baby), as well as female life plans and their realization become taboo. The topic of involuntary childlessness has been made public only recently. Previously it did not seem to exist. It was opened up only during the last few years by the discussion about new 'technological possibilities'; about success rates and consequent debates in traditional masculine domains such as law, ethics and economics. None of these clusters of problems, however, deal with the experimental situation of the women in question. Nor is it generally accepted that the new technologies have created a new reality for women: 'I am always asked to give reasons – why I don't avail myself of the new possibilities. "Why don't you do that? You can't be serious about a baby if you don't try this possibility . . ." '

Now women have to make decisions for or against a certain technology or for or against reproductive technologies in general. The greater the possibilities, the greater the woman's insecurity. As the technologies are available, a woman must submit to them, otherwise she has but herself to blame for her childlessness. Hence nobody needs to share her responsibility. 'Guilt' about and responsibility for her childlessness are fixed upon the individual and increase inner insecurity and also outer pressure on women. Yet it needs to be emphasized that society must accept a great deal of responsibility for infertility: it is often caused by medical technology, environmental influences and catastrophes like Chernobyl; in short, a number of imponderables brought about by the technological age in which we live. It is a general lack of familiarity with technology-related problems which sustains the illusion that technology could provide a solution for involuntary childlessness. Consequently, in deciding for or against the use of technology the choices are limited and in fact are becoming fewer and fewer. This is why it is important in the counseling sessions to discuss the possibility of resistance to these technologies and to support the women in taking a stand realizing that one *can* say no; that there *is* a choice, and that, above all, it is their right to *think* about the impact of involuntary childlessness on their lives and whether or not they want to try out any of the new technologies.

We now know that the new reproductive technologies are very damaging to women's bodies and souls. Often it is not only the technologies *per se* which are bad, but also how the women are treated. And, in addition, how women treat them/ourselves in that they allow themselves to be submitted to these procedures for such a long time. 'One is continually raping oneself or, rather, allowing others to rape one. Somehow one does feel this – but one does not want it to be true, does not want to admit it, cannot stop it.' In most instances, women are left completely alone in their decision-making when it comes to stopping the treatment or, rather, deciding not to submit to it in the first place. Such a decision is interpreted by society as a negation of the seriousness of their desire for a child. It also deviates from the common belief in technology. It is not only the individual's negation of a technological possibility which is relevant here, but also the woman's refusal to accept her socially appointed role. Behind this is an often unadmitted fear that society in general – and their husbands in particular – will abandon them if they refuse the technologies.

In deciding whether or not to have children, it is important to remember that women, by necessity, have to tackle the problem of two completely different life-plans: career/job versus housewife/mother. Of course it is possible for women to choose one of these avenues or to try and integrate them both into their lives. However, the social conditions and the expectations society has towards women – to become mothers – makes such a decision unrealistic from the very beginning. In our sessions we often meet professional women in good positions who long for a child. They are not aware of the fact that the fulfilment of their desire for children will have to result in giving up parts of their previous lives. Other women – once they have accepted that their desire for children will not be fulfilled – cannot regain the pleasures of living a self-determined life of their own.

Therefore, the most essential point of our counseling is the joint clarification of the motives behind the desire for children, without even asking the question whether such a desire is 'justified'. The wish for a child encompasses a multitude of phases and aspects: conception, pregnancy, birth, lactation, life with the child, her or his impact on the woman's future and her own death. In addition there are the expectations women have to live up to according to their socialization: to give life to other individuals, to live vicariously through others, to find sense and satisfaction solely through relationships with others. Wanting children, therefore, originates from a number of different desires.

For some women it is very important to share their lives with children. During counseling, however, it often emerges that it is the women's partner who wants his own biological child whereas she herself would be just as satisfied to adopt a baby: 'For women adoption is more of an alternative than for men. Men express the need for a child of their own body.' In such cases counseling initiates the possibility for a dialogue between the partners in order to work out their respective wishes and hopes for the future. In other cases, for example if a pregnancy would endanger her health or life, we assist the woman in her decision to adopt.

For other women the question of fertility is the central aspect. For them, infertility is perceived as a mutilation of their whole female being and 'potency'. Such feelings are a consequence of the relative scarceness of alternatives for women: even today it is not easy for most women to find a sense of Self as a proud and 'potent' woman outside maternity. Therefore, in the counseling, it is necessary to assist them in developing an appropriate life-plan *before* they can experience and express anger and resentment because of the public and private limits imposed on their lives. Often, such anger is healthy and releases unexpected psychic energies.

Other women want the bodily experiences which come with pregnancy, birth and, specifically, lactation: 'Imagining a child of my own always includes the bodily experiences.' Such a wish is reinforced by our society which attributes most value to what is visible and measurable. To express – and enjoy/validate – her own sexuality is hard for a woman connected as it is with organs partly hidden in our bodies. Pregnancy, on the other hand, enables a woman to express her desire for sensual/sexual experiences by making them physically visible in a socially acceptable way. Counseling encourages women to verbalize such bodily desires and to do so in the supportive company of other women.

Finally, the desire for a child can be the last remaining expression of people's wish for a more rewarding and satisfying love relationship. All these investigations of the possible *motives* for the desire for a child – jointly with a woman – does not mean that the wish for a baby should be negated or dissolved. But knowing more about the motives helps to locate it within its own specific context rather than having it take over a woman's whole life.

The self-help group

Counseling can provide an initial impetus for investigating the problem of involuntary childlessness by disentangling its various aspects. An even more intensive discussion can be achieved within the context of self-help groups for women with an unrealized desire for a child.

In such groups women have a chance to discuss their upsetting emotions: from hope to disappointment, grief to rage, envy and self-reproach; to verbalize their fading self-esteem, the tensions in the relationship with their partners, their difficulties in relation to their own sexuality and to their own bodies. Such a group can also provide a place for an exchange of medical experiences. The main aim, however, is to assist the women – through understanding and solidarity – in making decisions about how to deal with their unmet desire for a child and in developing new scenarios for the future.

Our self-help group began in April 1986 in the Feminist Health Centre. It was dissolved after about a year.[9] The group was completely autonomous; in other words discussion themes and scopes came from within the group.

Women were strongly motivated to participate, because they hoped for solidarity, a solidarity which they could not find anywhere else. As one woman put it:

Solidarity makes one feel good. It's an enormous relief

to not always feel 'deficient', to be able to say, well, we're obviously all 'like that' and if this is so then the desire for a child/infertility cannot be something *so* terrible, *so* deficient.

All participants expressed their feelings of isolation, of shame, of loss of dignity and voiced their need for active support:

> I think it is crucial that we encourage each other, that we help one another to be brave, to have courage so that we can do something for ourselves; so that we do not always need the expert who thinks he knows it all, that we can help ourselves.

To take part in a group and 'to help oneself' means among other things to question the competence of others, especially that of doctors.

All these women had their own history, their own experiences, and it was with these stories that we began our sessions. Experiences were compared, verified and worked through. This process was particularly important for the consolidating of the group. But other topics were also introduced, for instance: To what extent is the desire for a child an individual's desire? How much of it is imposed by society? Why is it that men deal with it differently?

Men's ignorance became evident and was discussed. There was one woman who had not mentioned the self-help group to her husband and only told him about it after several meetings. She had not dared to tell him before. In this way women reinforce the division between themselves and their partners. The women in the group discussed how they could support one another in informing their partners and demand more support from them.

However, the participants also voiced critical comments about their group. We believe it is important to make them public as it will further our understanding of the complex problem we are tackling here. For example, one of the negative consequences was the fact that for some women our weekly meetings increased their brooding . . . and the discussions in the group didn't help them to overcome this growing sense of desperation. In fact, some of these gloomy feelings can be explained through unexpressed tensions and differences between participants. Developing frictions and/or negative emotions were not expressed but rather directed towards themselves, thus leading to obsessive thinking which they were unable to voice at meetings.

The group did not succeed in exploring these depths. The women felt that this was a serious shortcoming and it contributed to the group's dissolution. One woman commented:

> If one wants to find a solution one has to take the risk and open up one's innermost core. Even if it hurts, because this is the only way to build up something new. And it does hurt, it hurts like hell. We all agreed that we wanted to do that, but none of us succeeded.

It seems that trust and confidence within the group had not been established sufficiently. Therefore, it *was not* possible to discuss the private demarcation lines between the women and to what extent it *was* possible to speak out without – unwillingly – risking new hurts and offences and yet still voice essential concerns: 'None of us wants to hurt the other, as we feel that we are all equal here.'

As a consequence, in the last group meeting the possibility of working with a group leader was discussed: 'In the end we all agreed that the group hadn't worked because we lacked a person with authority, who had the courage to say, for example, "What you are doing now is hiding behind some excuses . . .".' Such criticism does not deny the value of a self-help group. There is always the possibility for change; for instance, one or more women from the counseling group could be at the disposal of the self-help group members. If needed, she might be asked to help the group to get out of a possible impasse. However, the women themselves should be the ones to decide when to ask for 'help' as well as determine the content of their meetings.

In addition, the demand for an 'expert' has to be treated with caution. Of course it is absolutely legitimate to ask for help from others. But a self-help group is set up on the premise of mutual assistance. For this reason the 'cry' for authority should be discussed in depth when it is voiced for the first time. Sometimes, such an intensive discussion solves not only the need for outside assistance but, in fact, the very problem that caused this need to arise in the first place.

In our group the issue of 'help' from a competent woman has been fraught with difficulties. Our group was the second initiated by the woman we mentioned at the beginning of this article after she had come to the FFGZ and found no group to meet her needs. (After this experience she started a group outside the centre.) As the group proceeded she found herself in a role oscillating between being an involuntary childless woman and a group leader: a role which she had neither wanted nor anticipated. It was easy to see why she was caught in this position: because of discussions with some of the participants before the group began to meet and also because of her previous group experience, in which she had arrived at the decision to adopt a child.

We think that every woman sometimes wishes for help from other, perhaps more competent women. The wish for a child, equated as it is for women in our society with passivity, predestines women to exhibit passive attitudes. However, women also want to discover their own needs and feelings with the help of like-minded equals who share with them the experience of infertility/the desire to have children.

Based on our experience with the self-help group we now believe that this aim is easier to reach when all participants start the group with a comparable level of consciousness/insights into their situation. Because this was not the case in our group, it was difficult for the women to create a common base of mutual trust from which to discuss their personal hurts, deep grief and their sense of 'being different'. It speaks for the great flexibility of all the participants that it was possible to generate an atmosphere of solidarity in which the group could exist and work – at least for a limited period. Also, while it is easy to propose improvements, we must not forget that to find a 'solution' to the problem of infertility/the desire for children is tremendously difficult. As one woman said: 'There is just no solution. This is the conclusion we have reached. For this childlessness there is no solution; not for infertility.' Painful as it is, women have to accept this. At the very least there is no solution as it is offered and advertised by the promoters of reproductive technology: by focusing on parts of the problem only – the physical infertility – their 'solution', in fact, consists of 'dissolution' of the whole issue. We feel that a solution can only be understood in the sense that the problem of involuntary childlessness becomes integrated into our lives in such a way that the issue ceases to dominate our whole existence. Even if the infertility is 'solved' through a pregnancy, this does not present a solution to the whole problem of involuntary childlessness. As far as these women are concerned an essential part of their life story remains related to their infertility – a fact that cannot be ignored or erased.

The new reproductive technologies force women into the illusion that all their problems are solvable, provided that they trust the technodocs and hand themselves over to them. This bypasses reality. As a woman put it: 'The pain and the humiliation which have been in the past will always remain. They will remain even if and when I have a child.' Of course, there are ways to deal with this conflict. For instance, by living with children who are not one's own. Usually, women are much more inclined than their partners towards adopting, becoming foster parents, living with other women who have children, accepting sponsorship for children and so on. Alternatives such as these make having children in one's life possible. Nevertheless, the feelings of frustration and hurt which have been with the women for years because their bodies refused to give them what they wanted so badly persist. The remaining loss needs to be grieved for:

> One is forced to investigate what lifestyle one wants.
> To see how one can do without one's children. And
> what remains irreplaceable and needs to be grieved
> for. Because I don't believe that there will always be
> a substitute for an unfulfilled desire for a child.

Psychological counseling

Apart from counseling services and self-help groups the Feminist Women's Health Centre offers the possibility of psychological counseling/therapy. This is for women who would like to have a more intensive form of counseling with a therapist, or for women who either don't want to share their problems with others or are not interested in the experiences of other women in similar situations. By entering the process of psychological counseling these women allow the therapist to analyse their situation. Put differently, the therapist looks beyond specific questions and organizes what she is told within a psychotherapeutic framework. Through connecting her theoretical framework with the woman's specific reality the therapist should be able to offer her explanations to the woman seeking advice and discuss them with her.

On the one hand, we believe that it is important to offer psychotherapy to women who ask for it. Within the institutional framework of the FFGZ which is based on the principles of the Women's Movement, we try to bridge the chasm between 'client' and therapist. Furthermore, the professional knowledge of our therapist is structured in a different way from the knowledge of the conventional psychologist. It is influenced by solidarity with the women and incorporates specific knowledge about feminist scholarship on aspects of female development and socialization as well as an awareness of the oppression and exploitation of women in general.

Being different from conventional applications of 'clinical knowledge', such counseling is designed to ease the burden of infertility by widening the woman's understanding of the problem and enabling her to articulate her conflicts and protests. The main object of such counseling is to liberate the woman from her guilt feelings which are often intensified in order to exculpate medical and technological failures.

On the other hand, we believe very strongly that it is crucial to separate therapy from general counseling, informative discussions and self-help groups. A woman should only begin psychotherapy when she specifically asks for it and knows what to expect. Only then is a psychologist permitted to attempt interpretations of her situations. Every other form of therapy is tantamount to abuse and does more harm than good.

What follows are some examples of new insights we have gained from this form of counseling practice.[10] Given the difficulties of self-realization for women in our society, the wish for a child has become for many a permissible expression of their desire 'to give birth to themselves' with all the depth of feeling they are capable of. Women who come to our psychological counseling with this kind of (unconscious) background are desperate for help. The full depth of their despair becomes apparent only when we understand what such a woman gives up when she finally renounces her wish. She will not resign herself to living with grief for her unhad child or to fulfilling her wish through an artificially produced baby. Once the (unconscious) background has been explained, it becomes easier for her to decide what she might do next.

Another example of how psychological counseling may assist women in making decisions is shown in the following story. K, thirty-seven years old, runs her own business and is a perfect organizer. She does not want to join a self-help group, as she feels that other women's problems would only be a burden for her. In the first session the therapist recognizes that K has a lot of insights about her desire for a child. She is a woman who constantly gives to others, but rarely receives anything back. The therapist also realizes that everything which was said during the session was either already obvious to K or was totally unacceptable. K functioned well on her own but had not realized this positive fact. This was the reason why she tended to appear more ignorant than was actually the case. Her longing for a strong shoulder and for support intertwined with a great deal of fear and mistrust: she was afraid to appear weak. After she became consciously aware of these fears in her conversation with the therapist she was able to make a decision: she wanted to remain independent from husband and potential child and focus on developing positive feelings about her independence.

In another case the emotional togetherness of the partners seemed disturbed: deep gaps appeared within their emotional communication system. As in the previous example, in the sessions with the therapist the woman in question had to undergo a painful experiential process. Once she was able to acknowledge this lack of communication she remembered that her parents had always interpreted any form of anger as weakness: they had seen her tears, but did not realize that she was actually furious. It now seemed to her that in her marriage she was faced with a similar situation as in her childhood: How could a satisfactory togetherness develop if emotional signals were always misinterpreted by her partner? The discussion of involuntary childlessness thus led to a totally different source of pain, which, worked through, will hopefully open a new world for her.

Final remarks

The new reproductive technologies have created new taboos concerning the individual and the socially constructed desire for a child: as they promise technological 'fixes' they imply that it is not necessary – and in fact no longer *possible* – to discuss, explain or analyse the problem critically. In other words, these new taboos contribute heavily to the suffering of involuntarily childless women. Strong public pressures are brought to bear upon them in order to make them accept these new methods which, at best, cure only symptoms. In turn, however, they advance reproductive research and a burgeoning biotechnology industry. With the exception of feminists, nobody acknowledges the costs of these new methods for women. Instead, they are hailed as the solution to increasing infertility in Western countries.

We discover here the glaring contradiction between the wanton destruction of our biosphere and the ecological problems which threaten the continuation of the human species – especially in the rich countries of white western civilization. This process also contains a displacement of responsibility: it appears that the onus to find solutions for social and eco-political problems has been transferred to (involuntarily childless) women who are thus forced into performing their social role – which is to bear children at any price. As science celebrates the few individual 'successes' of the reproductive industry, the world can vicariously share the 'victory of technology over nature' where new life is created in a battle with nature, and society at large can heave a sigh of relief whilst watching the new parents' happiness. In the meantime the havoc that has been wrought on a woman's body and soul is conveniently forgotten.

The imagined dichotomy of 'nature' versus intellect/rationality/man [*sic*] has once again been resolved in favour of the latter: the technodocs are seen to be on the 'right' side, helping long-suffering humanity. This is an ideology based on the premise of an unreconcilable opposition of nature and human beings and on an eternal struggle between them. It is the ideology that produces a science which in turn creates the new reproductive technologies set forcefully in motion to destroy the environment, genetic diversity and reinforce the oppression and exploitation of women. And not only do the technodocs obtain their insights through experimenting on involuntarily childless women, their methods also represent a new degree of violence against women.[11]

It is not difficult to recognize already how these technologies are being developed not only for involuntarily childless women but for *all* women. In the last analysis they are intended to transform women worldwide into birth machines: to produce the perfect, genetically desirable, genetically screened and eventually genetically manipulated children and to produce them when and where the powers that be want this to happen.

We must break this vicious circle. One way is to recognize and obviate the social origins of infertility. The options offered at the Feminist Health Centre at Frankfurt together with political reflection and actions contribute towards this aim.

NOTES

1   We purposely avoid the term 'sterile women'. In the public – and medical – debates this expression refers to the whole woman and not only to her reproductive capacity. We regard this usage as extremely misogynist.

2   cf. the experiences of Andrea Belk-Schmehle in this book.

3   This is not to negate the increasing rate of infertility of women and men, for instance through environmental pollution as well as medical abuse (e.g. harmful contraceptives such as IUDs), or enforced sterilizations in the so-called Third World. A study of the causes of infertility is urgently needed. Instead of financing research into more and more variations of reproductive technologies and their perfectability, public funds should be made available for research projects which study the correlation of infertility and the environment. This is where social responsibility starts.

4   This group was founded in 1985 after the landmark Congress at Bonn, 'Women against Gene and Reproductive Technologies', in order to study the implications of the new technologies on a wider and deeper level. Since then counseling has become an essential component of our group, together with political and media work. An additional counseling group was formed to provide advice and reflect on its own work. Two counselors are present at each of the discussions and the sessions can be repeated if the participant(s) so desire(s). All the discussions are minuted in the form of discussion protocols which in turn are used to interrelate the woman's concrete situations with theoretical reflections. We would like to thank all

the women from both groups for their co-operation and their discussions which have enabled us to write this article.

5 The following is a collage of counseling experiences and interviews with infertile women and women of the self-help group.

6 According to statistics, 40 per cent of the women and 40 per cent of the men are 'the cause' of unwanted childlessness. In 20 per cent of the cases both of them are infertile or no diagnosis is possible.

7 Wouldn't it be great if all the men who are so enthusiastic about helping childless women to fulfil their desire for a child would apply the same energy, theoretically and practically, to persons of their own sex.

8 Relationships with families and friends are not further discussed in this paper. Andrea Belk-Schmehle does this in detail in her chapter in this book. We fully agree with her experiences.

9 Here we must add that some women from the group are still in private contact and support each other, especially when for one of them the negative feelings resurface during a certain life phase.

10 Not all counseling is meaningful and not every woman needs counseling. However, the insights gained through counseling seem to be valuable for many of them.

11 cf. Renate Klein: When Medicalisation Equals Experimentation and Creates Illness: The Impact of the New Reproductive Technologies on Women. Paper presented at the Forum International Sur Les Nouvelles Technologies de la Reproduction Humaine organisé par le Conseil du Statut de la Femme, Université Concordia, Montréal, Canada, 29–31 October 1987. In *Sortir la Maternité du Laboratoire*; Actes du Forum, Gouvernement de Québec, 1988.

PART FIVE

.

Resistance

Following the third ovum pick-up the gynaecologist told me my tubes were patent but my ovaries were bound by adhesions which prevented him from collecting the number of eggs which were there. He advised microsurgery via a laparoscopy which would increase my chances of a pregnancy and allow more access to my ovaries, if a further ovum pick-up was to be done. However I developed an ovarian abscess and septicaemia which meant three weeks in hospital – two further operations and removal of one ovary and tube and four different types of intravenous antibiotics. When I recovered I realized my health and time with my husband was far more important than an endless endeavour to conceive a baby. At this stage too, we were awaiting approval from the Welfare Department to adopt a child.

After IVF: I felt very depressed for weeks following the failure of my second attempt. Emotional, unable to cope. Very lethargic, tired. Headaches. Bloated stomach, irritated. Continued to superovulate for at least two or three months afterwards. PMT effects tripled. The worst was the continual *dizziness* – began on the second day of the injections and only gradually improved. Even now, three months later, I still feel dizzy if I overdo things. For the first two months it was terrible. Three months after my first attempt I bled for three weeks and was very ill as I developed a severe bronchitis at the same time. Now I have a rash – three months after my second attempt. The bleeding episode in June last year was very unusual for me – my GP said it was probably connected to the IVF treatment.

After attending hospital for two and a half hours one day, and being prodded and poked all that time, blood tests, ultrasound, needles, I eventually got off the table and said 'tell the doctor he can stick this up his jumper.' I knew weeks of that would be untenable, especially after having to get up at 5.00 am to travel two hours each way to hospital, *and probably no baby at the end. What a joke.* I feel so sorry for the women who have to use IVF.

BATTLEGROUND

.

SUSAN EISENBERG
USA

for Rita Arditti

Always anxious to rescue
damsels in distress

Knights of the Laboratory
design
   test tubes
      that will not suffer
      nausea or back pain
      hemorrhoids or edema;
   Petri dishes
      that will never
      blame miscarriages
      on their workplace,
      challenge the doctor's
      dominion in delivery
      or argue over alimony.

Only the womb
          with her mysteries
hold the Knights of Progress at bay,
their steeds trampling over centuries.

Thundering hooves: closer, closer.

RESISTANCE: FROM THE EXPLOITATION OF INFERTILITY TO AN EXPLORATION OF IN-FERTILITY

.

RENATE KLEIN

Women as experimental test-sites

Memories of pain, humiliation, dashed hopes and despair; of being poked and prodded, and statements such as 'I didn't know . . .', 'I was never told . . .' occur again and again in the women's stories in this book as they tell us about the medical malpractice and violence – indeed torture – as many say – they encountered during their medical journey in search of becoming a mother.

What is all too obvious from their stories is the medicalization of women's reproductive capacity – making infertility into a 'disease' that needs to be 'cured' or at least 'fixed up' – *and* the experimental nature of 'treatments' in reproductive medicine, be they of the 'conventional' type or a variation of the newer 'test-tube baby' method. Obvious, too, is the exploitative nature of reproductive medicine: women do what we are **all** told to do; we go to the doctor and trust his (sometimes her) professional expertise to solve our problems. In the case of infertility, the women who seek help to overcome their inability to conceive naturally – which can be experienced as a devastating life-crisis – are subjected to a host of dangerous experimental procedures and are used as guinea pigs in that grand international competition of baby-making in the laboratory. They also pay substantial sums for taking part in an *experiment* – for there is no such thing as a routine procedure, much less a 'routine IVF'. Even infertility specialists agree that they don't know why in some cases their operations or drug regimens work, and in others they do not.

Most of the women writing in this book do not in the end have their own biological child, but many of them are injured; some almost died. None of them can be sure that there won't be long-term effects from the drugs they have taken. The emotional toll that the years of trying to get pregnant has taken on their lives cannot be readily assessed: some of them have scars that will never heal. Alarmingly, these gruesome and enraging tales represent only the tip of the iceberg. Far from being 'exceptions', or cases of 'bad luck' (as no doubt some readers of this book will say in trying to trivialize or dismiss the women's experiences), I believe that their stories illustrate the thinking behind the development of reproductive medicine: what is claimed to be 'treatment' is, in fact, a process of trial and error, and women's bodies are the experimental test-sites.

These stories are not the exception: they are the norm. We don't hear very much about them because the medical establishment sees no need to inform the public of its doings: its power is (still) such that there is no shortage of clients. Also, of course, care is taken to cover up 'accidents'. The women themselves are often too hurt, too broken – or simply too fed up with it all: glad to have survived and gotten on with their lives, they don't want to speak out; they don't want to be 'dissected' once again: this time by the press hungry for some 'juicy' story – which the next day will be 'balanced' by a medical 'expert's' view saying that all of this is 'hysterical' or 'an unfortunate exception' and that doctors really do all they can, and they do it simply and honestly for the woman's own good!

As the contributors to this book have made very clear, there is also the tremendous social stigma of infertility to bear (many people still perceive a childless woman as a 'failure') and, above all, the power and authoritative voice of the medical establishment to confront. In the language of IVF doctors: 'the patient' was too old; she had 'bad' eggs; her womb – that 'hostile environment' – rejected the embryo: 'nature's best incubator' (an Irish IVF doctor's term) failed. The technology is never blamed for failing.

The woman who has 'failed', even with technology's help, is thrown by the way-side. She is only a 'bad statistic' – no longer of medical interest, she is left to her own devices. After years of traumatic ups and downs, often with her career abandoned, the relationship with her partner sometimes strained to breaking point and now too old to be considered for adoption, she finally has to come to grips with the fact that she might never have her own (or another) biological child. She must go through the process of upheaval and grieving this entails and get on with her life.

For the fertile women who became 'surrogate' mothers in order to fulfil the desire of others – usually a man who insists on having his own *genetically* related child – the end result is not very different: they *are* birth mothers but have lost their child. As the women say in this book, they are grieving too and often facing a severe crisis. Usually, however, they get little public sympathy. After all, they signed the contract, didn't they? Few people are prepared to challenge the contract itself or acknowledge that this new form of reproductive prostitution exploits women as living incubators – for a pittance in commercial surrogacy and for the 'free' labour of love in so-called sister-to-sister surrogacy.

Luckily, a few women survive the trials of reproductive medicine relatively unharmed. Some even have a child – though rarely in the case of *in vitro* fertilization (IVF) where roughly only five to ten out of 100 women (if not less) take a baby home. Others, however, pay with their lives but their stories never make the headlines. Zenaide Maria Bernardo in Brazil, Aliza Eisenberg in Israel, Andrea Dominquez in Spain, Lynette Maguire and an as yet unnamed woman in Perth, Australia, have died during or after egg collection via laparoscopy for IVF (Corea, 1988). In this book we have read of Rivi Ben-Ari in Israel who died after treatment with Pergonal (see pp. 46–50). How many people know that IVF can result in death? How many have heard these women's names, know that they died – not because they were sick but because they were told that technology could give them a child? Do we have to accept what Dr Trounson, a well-known Australian IVF scientist, said publicly on television: that, unfortunately, death from IVF is 'a terrible side-effect' (Special Broadcasting Service, May 2nd 1988). Why is it that we don't know of these deaths, yet are familiar with the names of famous 'test-tube fathers'? – national heroes pictured in white lab coats, broad smiles on their faces, one or more babies in their arms, while the woman who carried the child for nine months, gave birth to it and will look after it for many years to come, usually doesn't figure. Man made conception – women pay the price.

Women pay the price – but they are rarely told what the price will be. IVF success rates are a case in point. It seems an easy calculation to figure out how many of the women who go through an IVF 'treatment cycle' with egg stimulation, egg collection, embryo transfer and the nine-month pregnancy period finish by giving birth to a healthy live child at the end of this cycle: a live and well child is after all the only 'real' measure of success for a birth technology which purports to assist the production of children. However, IVF doctors worldwide, in order to cover the fact that IVF is a *failed* technology, prefer a much more complicated system. Some measure success by egg collection, others count biochemical pregnancies (a rise in β-human chorionic gonadotropin levels, falsely signalling a pregnancy), ectopic pregnancies (approximately 6 per cent), spontaneous abortions (approximately 11 per cent) and the onset of what they call a 'clinical pregnancy' (a misnomer: it means that the transferred embryo has successfully implanted itself in the woman's womb for at least five weeks of its nine-months-long growth period) – even though between 30 and 50 per cent of all such pregnancies in progress end with a miscarriage. Some clinics even count stillbirths (miscarriages after 20 weeks of pregnancy) as 'success'. What they do *not* count are what they call 'cancelled' cycles: that is attempts in which eggs do not mature, or can not be collected. This is a substantial number: according to one US study by Sung I. Roh et al. (1987), cancellations were as high as 41.6 per cent among one group of women who began IVF. In a survey in the US conducted in 1985, Gena Corea and Susan Ince reported that of the clinics who responded to their questionnaire (54 out of the then 108), 'half have never sent a woman home with a baby' (1987: 133). But even these clinics claimed 'success rates' – and they were as high as 18 and 25 per cent (p. 135).

Since then IVF clinics all over the world have become more circumspect with their figures. Reporting what they call 'crude live births', the British figures established by the Voluntary Licensing Authority (VLA) were 8.6 per cent for both 1985 and 1986 (VLA Report, 1988, p. 19). Australian estimates per treatment cycle for 1986/87 were similar: 8.8 per cent of live births (Batman, 1988b, p. 3; these include also ongoing pregnancies over 20 weeks). Not reflected in these numbers are the significantly increased number of children born prematurely (26.9 per cent for 1986, National Perinatal Statistics Unit, Australia, 1987) – who are most frequently delivered by caesarian section (43.9 per cent instead of 15–18 per cent for 'natural' pregnancies in Australia in 1986 (Stanley, 1988)) and therefore of low birth weight and in need of extra neonatal care – and the high proportion of multiple births: 24 per cent reported for England in 1988 (VLA Report, 1988, p. 21). The high proportion of children born with abnormalities is also a cause for serious concern. These are mostly neural-tube (spina bifida) and cardiac problems (transposition of the great vessels): 2.2 per cent compared with 1.5 per cent from 'natural' pregnancies for Australia. (Stanley, 1988, p. 425). Taking these cases into account (and the premature children needing intensive neonatal care), the Australian government report concludes that the success rate for an 'unproblematic live birth' is 4.8 per cent (Batman, 1988b, p. 3). That means that at least 95 out of 100 women will *not* have an unproblematic live birth!

The women who think of trying IVF are rarely informed about these statistics. More often they are deluded and told that with IVF, for example, pregnancy rates vary between 15 and 20 per cent, a statistic which is continually quoted in the media. I have not met a single woman who was told explicitly that she may risk giving birth to a child with a handicap. The question is which version of 'reality' should we trust? As the Australian government study says bluntly: 'The whole question of success in relation to IVF is confused and obscure' (Batman, 1988b, p. 2). There have been, supposedly, about 5,000 children born from IVF worldwide by 1988 but we know that there are thousands of women who have unsuccessfully tried this procedure. And the success rates do not go up: if anything, they come tumbling down because of the increasing supervision that IVF units experience as they are asked to report their figures to government committees, or, in the case of Britain, the VLA, a self-imposed watchdog (albeit one that is highly prejudiced in favour of the new reproductive technologies).

How small must success rates be before IVF is declared a failed technology and the programmes are closed down? How many women must be injured by reproductive medicine, how many must die, how many children must be born with abormalities or develop them as they grow older, before a halt is called? How much evidence is necessary to stop the abuse of women? How much value is attributed to women's health and psychological well being? The case of clomiphene citrate is a telling example.

Clomiphene citrate is a fertility drug which has been administered worldwide to thousands, if not millions, of women over the last 20 years, frequently under the brand name Clomid. Most of the women in this book did, at some point in their medical history, take Clomid in order to start ovulating, or, in the case of IVF, to superovulate (that is, to produce more than the normal one ripe egg per month). Many of the women, especially Titia Esser from Holland, reported alarming adverse effects. In my study of 40 Australian women who left IVF programmes without a child (Klein, 1988b), I came across women who developed ovarian cysts, enlarged ovaries, ovarian abscess and septicaemia. Some reported constant bleeding. Dizziness, nausea and generally feeling 'very ill' were 'side effects' regularly reported by women on clomiphene citrate. For some, these adverse effects do not stop when they abandon IVF: cysts continue to appear and need to be removed, the bleeding continues and the dizziness persists. Articles in the medical literature confirming the dangerous nature of clomiphene citrate begin to surface: there was a case in Bristol, England, in 1987 where a woman on an IVF programme who was administered clomiphene followed by hMG (Pergonal) and hCG developed multiple cysts in both ovaries. Her pelvic area was found to be filled by a tumour (Carter and Joyce, 1987). The cancer involved both ovaries and the tumour covered the uterus and the bladder. Loops of the small bowel and the appendix were adhered to the mass. She underwent massive surgery (a subtotal hysterectomy), bilateral salpingooophorectomy and chemotherapy. At the time of writing their paper, the authors commented that the woman was said to 'remain well'. They concluded: 'Although hormones may not directly initiate tumour formation, they can act as promoters in the process of carcinogenesis' (p. 127). One hypothesis is that incessant ovulation increases the risk of ovarian tumours by not allowing the ovaries to have rest periods. Discussing two previous cases who reported ovarian cancer following ovulation induction, Marian Carter and David Joyce noted: 'It is a matter of concern that in all three cases, the tumours developed with remarkable rapidity' (p. 128). Amazingly, however, they concluded that because of the 'rarity of cases reported despite the widespread use of clomiphene, Pergonal [hMG] and hCG it [is] unlikely that gonadotropin therapy directly initiates neoplastic growth' (p. 127).

The late Patrick Steptoe – one of the 'lab fathers' of Louise Brown, the world's first test-tube baby – dismissed the Bristol case as 'speculation, there is no proof whatsoever', and said 'I would think it's sheer chance . . . you've got to have hundreds of cases . . . there are no detailed cases . . . don't quote this paper, this is a single case' (from an interview for German television, given to Helga Dierichs for whom I acted as translator, September 1986). Hundreds of cases – did he mean hundreds of dead women? Similarly, when my Australian colleague Robyn Rowland published an article in the Melbourne *Herald* in October 1987 (Rowland, 1987b), discussing the adverse effects of Clomid on Titia Esser and other women, and drawing attention to the Bristol paper as well as the increasing suspicion that, because of its similar chemical structure to diethylstilbestrol, Clomid might lead to long-term adverse effects in both the women who take it and their children (see my introduction and Direcks and Holmes, 1986), Merrell Dow Pharmaceuticals threatened to sue the newspaper, and 'eminent endocrinologist' (described in these words by a journalist) Dr David Healy of the medical research centre at Prince Henry's Hospital in Melbourne, sent a letter to *The Herald*, stating:

> Clomid . . . is a medicine which has been used safely for more than 20 years for the treatment of infertility . . . The side effects which the Dutch and Geelong women claimed were due to Clomid such as depression, lethargy and impaired vision are **not** consistent with the side effects doctors would expect during or after the use of this drug . . . in fact the side effects are only minimal and are no more than hot flushes or mild sweats . . . the structure is **not** almost identical to DES. Medical practitioners and pharmacists are aware of this *fact*. Lastly, there is no evidence that super-ovulation increases the risk of ovarian cancer. Indeed, women who have had chil-

dren have less risk of ovarian cancer than childless women. Quite simply, helping infertile women have children decreases, not increases, their risk of ovarian cancer . . . it is concerning and unacceptable that these scientific errors continue to appear in print. (My emphasis)

The Herald chose not to print his letter (Healy nevertheless now distributes it to journalists making it seem as if it *had* been published), but the newspaper did publish a 'mild retraction' (their words) in response to Merrell Dow's legal threat.

There were glaring contradictions between our reading of the literature, and, more importantly, what we had heard from women themselves, and these experts' statements that all was well and we were wrong. This prompted Robyn Rowland and I to begin a study of what had been published about clomiphene citrate over the last twenty years (see Klein/Rowland, 1988, for more details including references). We were shocked by what we found. Firstly, contrary to our expectations, there *has* been a considerable debate in the medical literature over the last twenty years about clomiphene citrate: to this day, for instance, there is debate about how clomiphene citrate actually works. Originally, it was believed to *prevent* ovulation. Then it was seen to *induce* ovulation. It wasn't clear whether it acts as an estrogen or as an anti-estrogen. What seems accepted these days is, in the words of Canadian obstetrician and infertility specialist Hugh Gorwill (who also acknowledges that clomiphene citrate has a structural similarity to DES; 1982:529):

clomiphene citrate . . . is a mixture of two isomers of a compound that has a structural similarity to diethyl-stilbestrol. The biologic effect of clomiphene citrate depends upon *the system* in which it is studied. Both estrogenic and anti-estrogenic effects are seen.

One might have expected more clarity about a drug that is prescribed to thousands of women: a drug that 'some doctors are handing out like candies' as Dutch DES daughter and activist Anita Direcks very accurately points out (personal communication, February 1988). The literature confirmed our worst suspicions about the many dangers inherent in clomiphene citrate, administered to women alone or in 'hormonal cocktails' with hMG and hCG.

Health hazards for women, in addition to the already mentioned promotion of cancer through clomiphene, and a host of adverse reactions from weight gain to dizziness and nausea, include the possibility of multiple births and hyperstimulation of the ovaries which can lead to a dangerous swelling of the ovaries and/or the production of cysts. The formation of cysts can in fact lead to infertility as it did in the case of a Canadian woman whose superovulation for IVF resulted in a burst cyst (out of three) which then permanently blocked her one functioning fallopian tube (Pappert, 1988). Particularly disturbing are a number of studies published in medical journals about the development of breast cancer following treatment with clomiphene (one resulting in the death of the woman) (Bolton, 1977). These cases are most worrying. If it was indeed the drug which caused the cancer, then clomiphene itself could be seen as having a similar long-term effect on the women as DES. There are also indications that the drug may be detrimental to the follicle when the egg is released, thus leading to a corpus luteum which is inadequate, or an unreceptive environment for the foetus in the endometrium of the woman's womb. This might explain why, in IVF, approximately 80 per cent of all embryo transfers do not succeed.

The literature also revealed records of a number of abnormalities in children born after clomiphene-induced pregnancies. They include neural tube defects (spina bifida), visual symptoms, and a significant number of cases of anencephaly (which means that the head was too small for a brain to form). Worrying also is the possibility of long-term effects from the drug on the children. Studies in Canada by Gorwill et al. drew attention to similarities between clomiphene and DES. In 1984 Dr Hugh Gorwill is quoted as saying:

It raises the concern that potentially, Clomid-exposed daughters could be at risk for adenosis . . . which may have the effect on the [vaginal] tissue that somehow leads ultimately to cancer (in Lipovenko, 1984).

A 1987 study by Californian researchers grafting 54 foetal genital tracts of 4–19 week old foetuses for 1 to 2 months in host mice who were given clomiphene 'elicit changes in the human fetal vagina comparable with those of DES' (Cunha et al., 1987: 1137). During the study, the fallopian tube was also affected by clomiphene. However, Merrell Dow Pharmaceuticals argued that the doses used were not comparable to the doses of clomiphene given to women. Interestingly, since the considerable international stir his study caused, Gerald Cunha has apparently said that clomiphene is not dangerous for women (Pappert, 1988, personal communication).

Inconclusive and ambiguous as these findings are, they are serious cause for concern, especially in the light of research which indicates that clomiphene may remain in a woman's body for at least six weeks (as discussed by Ford and Little, 1981), when they recorded the case of a baby born with ovarian cysts to a mother who had been taking 'clomiphene immediately before conception' (p. 117). Although not mentioning the possibility of a prolonged life-span in the woman's body, Merrell Dow's analysis of Clomid in the *MIMS* (the book of drugs from which Australian doctors select those to prescribe) nevertheless recommends that Clomid should *not* be used in pregnancy. If clomiphene does remain in the woman's body for an as yet undetermined period – at least six weeks is suggested – this would mean that *any* woman who becomes pregnant in the same cycle in which she took clomiphene – be it on IVF or through conventional treatment – may inevitably expose the embryo/foetus to possible adverse effects from the drug! This in turn means that a large number of children may suffer from long-term adverse effects.

Other recent studies report chromosomal abnormalities in the developing egg cells collected from women in IVF programmes who were superovulated with clomiphene. Swedish researchers, in particular Hakan Wramsby et al. (1984, 1987), found that as many as half of these egg cells have abnormal chromosomal patterns. Instead of 23 chromosomes characteristic of human beings, they have between 5 and 25. This finding is another possible explanation for the low success rate of the embryo transfers in the IVF procedure because the egg cells were already too damaged to develop further; it might also explain abnormalities in the developing embryo/foetus which lead to miscarriages or even birth anomalies. There is, however, an interesting twist in interpreting chromosomal abnormalities in egg cells. Rather than naming clomiphene and other superovulatory drugs as possibly responsible for anomalies, it is the *women* on IVF programmes who are cited as the problem. As a French IVF research team writes (Plachot et al., 1986: 547):

> The high rate of chromosome anomalies can be explained by the nature of this *population of fertilisation failure*, the frequently advanced maternal age and the use of superovulation treatments. (my emphasis)

Calling women in conventional or IVF treatment 'a population of fertilization failure' demonstrates clearly the lack of respect with which women are confronted once they entrust themselves to reproductive medicine – an observation that the writers in this book have made so clearly. Furthermore, in many cases this term is a stark misnomer: many of the women are fertile and on IVF programmes because of their *male* partners' infertility problem. And those whose difficulty in conceiving is due to iatrogenic (doctor-induced) infertility (e.g. infections due to IUDs), could rightly be outraged at being called a 'fertilization failure'. This statement is indicative of 'blaming women', rather than the IVF procedure and the drugs associated with it. Asked to comment on the disturbing birth defects in children conceived by IVF, Dr John Yovich, President of the Australian Fertility Society and head of an IVF Programme in Perth, Western Australia, said that the problem could arise with laboratory techniques, but 'that it was more likely to be a factor in the women themselves' (in McIntosh, 1988).

Somehow, it seems, because it is all 'women's fault', this legitimizes the medical profession's use of women as test-sites for experimental procedures and fertility drugs. It was not only shocking to read through the medical literature concerning the dangers associated with clomiphene citrate; but also highly disturbing to notice that researchers continue to assure their readers that despite their discussion of a long list of serious health risks associated with the drug, there is nothing really wrong with it. If anything, they say what is needed is more research to find out if some of these 'inconclusive' findings (i.e. not enough women with cancer?) might indeed turn out to be statistically significant. Robyn Rowland and I arrived at quite a different conclusion: our study of the literature has confirmed what the women had told us. We believe that a drug that can lead to such serious adverse reactions and which has so many potential problems is **not** safe enough to be administered to **any** woman. Women used in this way become 'living laboratories' (Rowland, 1984). To us this is unethical medical malpractice. It is irresponsible. Clomiphene citrate should be withdrawn.

There is another lesson to learn from this story. If *we* could find the literature in the medical journals, so could the doctors and scientists. Do they not read their colleagues' work? Do they choose to ignore it? It seems as if both questions, unfortunately, must be answered in the affirmative. This was confirmed for us when we came across the official description of Clomid by the manufacturer Merrell Dow itself in the *MIMS*. A lot of the problems we were later to find in the scientific papers were in fact mentioned in an abbreviated (and in some cases understated) form in this text that every practitioner has at his or her fingertips. For example, the *MIMS* is straightforward on its recommendations with respect to the *dosage* of Clomid: women should be given 50 mg daily for 5 days, starting on the fifth day of the menstrual cycle. If ovulation, but not pregnancy occurs, 'subsequent courses for a total maximum of six cycles of Clomid treatment may be administered' (1987:373). They add that, if necessary, a second course of 100 mg per day for five days could be given.

In spite of these recommendations, however, in many of the papers we read in our research into clomiphene citrate, a great deal of 'flexibility' with regard to dosage is exerted by researchers in their experimental trials on women. In their review of the use of clomiphene citrate Yee and Vargyas say (1986:142) that 'the most widely used regimen in normally ovulating women undergoing IVF treatment cycle is 100 or 150 mg daily from cycle day 5 to cycle day 9'. The list of studies they quote to substantiate their claim is long: are these researchers aware that 100 mg should only be administered if 50 mg per day did not work and that 150 mg is definitely outside the drug manufacturer's recommendation?

A look at the practice, however, confirmed an even more worrying picture. Titia Esser's experience is a particularly blatant case (see pp. 59–64): from one tablet (50 mg) to two per day for six months. Next she was put on three tablets per day (150 mg) for six months. This induced ovulation but also terrible side effects. Her treatment was changed again, this time from one tablet on the first day, to two tablets on the second and up to five tablets (250 mg) a day. And there were many other abuses: in my Australian study there were several women who were given 150 mg daily and one woman was on 50 mg per day for a year. I also heard of a women who was on 50 mg of Clomid for the first five days of her cycle for *eight years*: an appalling disregard of the manufacturer's recommendation. Yet another woman was given Clomid with a typical 'let's see what happens if . . .' attitude. She remembers:

> I started with one tablet a day but when the ultra-sound check-up revealed that my eggs did not grow properly, I was told to increase the dosage to four tablets a day. The attempt had to be abandoned: my ovaries swelled considerably and despite injections to release ripe follicles no mature eggs were recovered.

We must therefore conclude that if doctors and scientists do indeed read the literature – of which we cannot be sure – malpractice seems built into their 'normal' science and clinical practice. And what about their peers? Where are the letters from other doctors and scientists voicing concern about this breach of recommended dosage, especially in the light of the shocking damage to health which has been reported, following the administration of clomiphene citrate? Is the evidence not gruesome enough yet? Must more women die, more children be born with or develop abnormalities?

A disturbing story from New Zealand may provide some clues: after almost thirty years of conducting an 'unfortunate experiment' (Coney, 1988) at Auckland's National Women's Hospital, which involved not telling women that they had abnormal cervical cells which might develop into cancer, but instead keeping them as living statistics, by routinely checking them and documenting the 'progress' of their cancerous cells, at least twelve women died. The scandal would not have become public had it not been for two feminist health activists – Phillida Bunkle and Sandra Coney – who put all the disturbing pieces together and presented them to the public. Their investigation ended with a public enquiry and a condemnation of Professor Herb Green's experimentation on women. But, instead of being thanked by the medical profession for ending this experimental trial on women and recalling women for treatment in case they had developed invasive cancer, Bunkle and Coney were criticized by other doctors for being too hard on this particular gynaecologist, and for maligning the hospital: 'Women don't want to come here now' . . . 'the morbidity you will have on your own conscience'. As Sandra Coney writes (1988:271):

> [t]he real victims were the good doctors who only had their patients' interest at heart. The baddies in the scenario were the feminists, myself and Phillida, who were able to use the inquiry process and the media as pawns in our overall master plan to bring down the male sex.

Another disturbing fact is that for more than twenty years whilst this 'unfortunate' experiment was being conducted, occasional complaints by other doctors to higher authorities – for instance to the superintendent-in-chief of the Auckland Hospital Board – were not followed up. Although in one such case the doctors put in several pages of documentation and 'included details of cases of serious mismanagements, involving two deaths', the superintendent said that 'there was "insufficient evidence" and an "absence of documentation"' (p. 63). Moreover, as Sandra Coney notes, 'he did not think it his role to call for more documentation' (p. 63), and thus enabled Herb Green to continue his experimentation on women for many more years to come.

Inquiries into the use of clomiphene citrate could easily suffer a similar fate. In the papers I cited earlier, the conclusion was often just that: more evidence is needed. If women's well-being – and indeed lives – are accorded so little respect, if their bodies are seen, above all, as convenient sites for experimentation, for gathering data, the medical establishment can continue to cover 'accidents'. As the Ministry of Women's Affairs, in their final submission to the cervical cancer inquiry in New Zealand in 1988, stated (Coney, p. 6): 'Ultimately the issues are about who controls medicine and how; about who benefits from it and who are its victims.' Fortunately, there are some indications that clomiphene citrate might gradually be used less frequently in IVF programmes. Not because of the adverse reactions it causes to women – nor due to Robyn Rowland's and my clomiphene study.*

The reason for the reduction of the use of clomiphene is, rather, that it may cause chromosomal damages in the eggs and hence be responsible for the small success rates in embryo transfers. This seems reason enough to abandon it and look for something new to ensure more eggs and higher pregnancy rates. Also, as some of these 'old' women on IVF in their thirties are such 'poor responders' (a scientific term for a woman whose egg production is not satisfactory to the IVF specialist), it was time to find better egg stimulants. What is important here is the success rates and prestige for the IVF doctors and scientists.

A new group of 'wonderdrugs' has been found; unfortunately, this is not good news for women. In fact, these new drugs may turn out to be as bad as or even worse than clomiphene citrate. Using chemically synthesized 'analogues of LH-RH' (luteinizing hormone releasing hormone) – sold under the trade names Buserelin, Decapeptyl, HOE 766, and Lucrin – and administered either intranasally every four hours during waking time for fourteen days or as subcutaneous injections for twenty-five days seems the secret to more eggs and more pregnancies in the late 1980s. For women, however, there are more uncontrollable 'side effects', such as extremely hyperstimulated ovaries. Buserelin and similar

---

* Upon presenting our paper at the Annual Meetings of the Australian and New Zealand Association for the Advancement of Science in Sydney, May 1988, our research was vilified by two other 'eminent' professors, Roger Pepperell and Henry Burger (again from the Prince Henry's Hospital in Melbourne), who asserted that our claims were false and that they were 'confident the drug [clomiphene] was being used safely and appropriately'. Interestingly though, they contradicted their colleague David Healy by stating, 'There is no doubt that clomiphene is similar in structure to stilboestrol . . .' (Voumard, 1988a; Pepperell and Burger, 1988:50).

LH-RH analogues represent the ultimate control of science over a woman's reproductive cycle: they work by de-sensitizing the pituitary (an important hormonal control centre in the brain), thus turning off hormone production and blocking ovulation. In other words they put women in what is called a reversible 'chemical menopause'. Once the hormone production has stopped, the women are then given fertility hormones, often Metrodin or Perganol (hMG). In this way a 'controlled' cycle of egg production can be started, or in the words of a French IVF doctor: 'The aim of the treatment is to reimpose a normal rhythm over a disordered one, to recover virgin soil' (in Françoise Laborie, 1988: 81, whose article provides an excellent review of LH-RH analogues).

Before blocking the hormone production, however, Buserelin and its relatives begin by inducing the opposite effect. Put differently, they 'stimulate the production of the LH-RH hormones through an unavoidable and very dangerous effect called "flare up" ' (Laborie, p. 81). This may lead to very strong overstimulation and the production of cysts on the ovaries. A French surgeon who was *not* an IVF specialist said he had never seen ovaries in such an abnormally enlarged state which he thought looked more like cysts (Laborie, p. 81). Furthermore, virtually no research has been conducted on this new group of drugs which are now used in IVF programmes in France, England, Holland, West Germany and recently in Australia, although they have been approved by the authorities only as treatment for uterine fibroids or endometriosis and prostatic cancer in men.

Clearly women now serve as guinea pigs to test just how bad, for instance, hyperstimulation of the ovaries can be. Thousands of them provide scientists with their life data in laboratories all around the world to be discussed at congresses and in scientific journals: 'Hyperstimulation was seen at each cycle' write French researchers Bernard Charbonnel et al. as they report 'successful treatment of infertile patients' and then go on to enumerate the hyperstimulation as abdominal discomfort, cysts, enlarged and painful ovaries (1987, p. 920), mentioning also that in five women who did get pregnant, a second hyperstimulation characterized by painful ovaries of more than 100 mm occurred ten days after administration of the egg releasing hormone (hCG). In other words, these women face the pain – and the danger – of hyper-stimulated ovaries twice in one cycle!

Nothing is known about possible long-term effects. Françoise Laborie quotes a French doctor expressing anxiety about Buserelin (p. 80): 'Aren't we risking with it the same problems we caused by prescribing DES? What are the results of animal tests?' It is more than worrying that Hoechst (the German manufacturer of the drug) countered this question by providing information of tests with approximately seventy-five rabbits and forty-five rats only in which they state: 'Extracted rat fetuses showed a retarded development and a urinary tract dilation'. Mind-boggling, after this research result, is their conclusion: '*no malformation was observed*', and the general conclusion of the report: 'Buserelin does not seem to produce teratogenic effects' [causing birth defects] (in Laborie, p. 80). The question needs to be asked if indeed it is responsible to use this dangerous drug on large numbers of women in IVF programmes.* One might also wonder how well *informed* these women are about the drugs they take. Which brings me to the question of consent. Out of the forty women in my Australian IVF study (Klein, 1989) – whose experiences are dispersed in quotes throughout this book – only nine said that there was a discussion of potential side effects from the hormones they were given. And even in these cases, information included the following limited assessments: 'Hormone levels will be affected' (1); 'Not a great deal of side effects' (1); 'Multiple births possible' (2); 'Lots of eggs will be produced' (1); 'Dizziness/nausea' (2); Weight increase (1). One woman was told 'not to worry'. Only one doctor discussed potential long-term

---

* This comment in no way means that I am endorsing animal experimentation. Cruelty to animals, torturing and killing them to test drugs and techniques before they are tried out on women is but another facet of the inhuman quest to 'cure' disease by killing other life first. Its latest shocking 'feat' is the production of a mouse with an inserted 'cancer gene' in order to provide the scientists with a continuously available stock of mice with cancer for their experiments. It is significant that a large number of the scientists now working on IVF programmes were animal embryologists and physiologists first. For a stirring exposé of science's exploitation of nature and the animal world see *Rape of the Wild* by Andrée Collard and Joyce Contrucci (1988).

side effects. He told the woman: 'It's a new science . . . we are not aware of potential long-term side effects'.

Not only were the women *not informed* about what is already known in the medical literature including the possibility of getting cancer and the danger of overstimulation, but, as some women say in this book, once on the treadmill of reproductive medicine, once again under pressure to 'perform', to not disappoint the expectant public – from husband to the doctors and families – to not, once more, 'fail', they close their eyes to dangers, humiliation and pain and go on and on. And, as the women's experiences in this book make very clear, very often they were not told that the drugs they were taking might be dangerous, or, in the case of Rivi Ben-Ari, lead to death. To play around, increase the dosage of drugs at will if there is no 'response' from, say, the ovaries, until too much follicle growth happens too quickly which for some women will lead to burst ovaries, is part and parcel of the experimental nature of medicine. To speak of 'informed consent' in such a situation is a farce. And to say 'but women want it . . .' is to add insult to injury. In my view the compliance, even in the face of failure after failure and dangerous accidents as we have heard from the contributors to this book, is not the women's problem, much less their 'fault'. It is their determination in wanting a technology to succeed which in the majority of cases *fails*. The tragedy lies in the women's co-operation with the experimenters. In so doing they allow the experimenters to make them both colluders *and* victims of their desire to control and conquer. In other words they are active *and* passive at the same time.

Clearly, as even a group of British IVF specialists admit: 'Nearly ten years after the first baby was born as a result of *in vitro* fertilization, this treatment is still largely unsuccessful' (Rutherford et al., 1988). For many other 'conventional' infertility treatments the assessment is the same; in fact there is some serious doubt whether treatment-independent pregnancies in people with a fertility problem are not as (in)frequent as among those who go through years of often horrendous medical interference. The question is whether all these attempts to 'bend' the female reproductive cycle into submission do in fact result in a substantial increase of children, as Canadian researcher John Collins and his colleagues doubt (Collins et al., 1983). Their research into 'conventional' infertility treatments shows that doctors are not getting any more pregnancies by treating infertility than they are without treatment (p. 1201) which seems to be supported by a leading article in the *British Medical Journal*. In 1987 Richard J. Lilford and Maureen E. Dalton wrote (pp. 155–6):

> [M]any doctors and lay people think that the great technical advances in the past 20 years in treating infertility have led to high success rates in treatment, but this is a myth.

So why aren't these attempts to 'trick nature' abandoned? Why isn't the money invested in research about the causes of infertility in order to prevent it? Why, above all, isn't the myth attacked at all levels of society (and in cultures around the world), that a woman has to have children to be a 'proper' woman, and that it is important that a couple must have their biologically and genetically own child to lead a happy life? And why aren't infertile people given more *real* support to help them cope with the choice they did not make: to remain without child?

Complex as the answers to these questions are, it is quite clear that it is *not* the concerns of people with fertility problems that matter most. Much higher priority is given to the concerns of those who invent, practise and promote the new technologies. An important motive is the opportunity which any infertility investigation provides to gather live data about people's, especially women's, reproductive biology; knowledge which can be turned into an industry promising fame and prestige as well as money and power for those involved: scientists, doctors and last – but not least – international pharmaceutical companies.

In countries like Australia, biotechnology, including human reproductive technology, is touted as a successful product for export – hence the establishment of *IVF Australia* in the USA in 1985: an expanding chain of IVF clinics, albeit with very little success. By March 1988 as few as 168 babies had been born. *Pivet Laboratory*, a Western Australia based group, exports Australian IVF 'know-how' to medical centres in Malaysia, Greece and Italy. In January 1988 it announced expansion to Singapore and plans to also establish IVF Clinics in the USA,

Hong Kong and Britain (Thorpe, 1988). It works on the principle of using the host country's medical staff, but sending Australian embryologists and doctors overseas to train support staff.

In the USA, despite the high failure rate of IVF, the infertility market is promoted as booming business; Dr Sher of Northern Nevada Center, an IVF clinic owned by a group of doctors, believes that eventually IVF could be a US$6 billion annual business (Blakeslee, 1987a). (In comparison, pornography in the USA brings in a revenue of $9 billion!) Serono, the Swiss based company with a US monopoly on Perganol – the fertility drug which seriously injured Maggie Humm and killed Rivi Ben-Ari in Israel (see pp. 36–45 and pp. 46–50) – is reported to have a record net income of US$35 million in 1987: a 65 per cent increase from the year before on sales of $327.6 million. In the first quarter of 1988 the surge continued. Worldwide sales rose by 48 per cent (Sanger, 1988).

The entrepreneurial aspect of the 'fertility business' (Sanger, 1988) is not to be underestimated. To a large part it is responsible for the rapid proliferation of new fertilization methods, drugs and instruments. The next section will give some details about the IVF enterprise – 'test-tube failure' as it might be called more appropriately.

Test-tube failure

In the pro-natalist industrial west (I will discuss the situation in the so-called 'Third World' later) if you are part of the dominant group (mainly white, middle class and heterosexual) – *how* to have children becomes increasingly prescribed. To choose *not* to have children becomes less and less of an option if it doesn't just happen 'naturally' in countries with a low birth rate. In a recent US book the author is frightened about the imminent 'Birth Dearth' (Wattenberg, 1987). The new procreation methods – advertised by the media in a misleadingly glamorous way – become almost compulsory: they have to be tried out. And as the women in this book describe so convincingly, once on the 'treadmill' of medicalized baby-making, it is hard to stop. As Kirsten Kozolanka puts it (p. 122), it is hard to be a 'quitter'. You have to try *everything* so that you are able to say 'I've done my best'. Yet with new methods being announced day after day, the word 'everything' stops making sense; reproductive medicine is in the process of creating addicts: customers who not only pay but who willingly become research material.

Gradually, the rationale that more and more people are in need of increased medical supervision and advice with regard to having babies gains ground. After pre-natal care and birth, it is now conception that is medicalized. Almost daily, the news is full of 'firsts' which suggest that you, too, can have your own baby, whatever the odds. Sensationalized new techniques combine various pieces of human raw material – eggs, sperm, embryos – in an increasingly alienating way for women who are reduced to 'womb-providers': living incubators to test whether the manufactured product 'embryo' might indeed develop into a live child. The 'reproductive supermarket' – Gena Corea's term – is expanding rapidly: from Australia, in 1983, came the birth of an IVF child from a donated egg, and in 1984 a birth from a frozen embryo as well as the first IVF quadruplets. 1983 also saw a US 'first': an IVF baby via 'lavage', meaning that the body of a woman was employed as a temporary breeder by artificially inseminating her and flushing out the embryo before it implanted itself in her womb and inserting it into the uterus of the sperm donor's wife. In 1985 we were told about the first pre-sexed IVF baby: a boy born in an IVF clinic in New Orleans. In 1986 news reached us about the first birth – twins – from frozen egg cells in Adelaide, a 'success' highly contested by rival medical teams around the world but followed up by another such birth in West Germany. In 1987 the media hailed the arrival of 'the frozen sister': a test-tube sister born to a British IVF child who in 1985 had been 'harvested' from the same 'egg-crop' – an Australian IVF doctor's term – as the first child, then frozen and thawed/implanted in her mother's womb 18 months later. In the same year we heard about the first woman in the world to give birth to her own grandchildren: a 47-year-old South African woman who had her daughter's fertilized eggs implanted – described as a 'host womb' (Reid, 1988) – which resulted in triplets born by caesarian section.

Particularly noticeable is the constant increase in transferring human material from one woman to another. Women without ovaries have eggs donated, fertilized with their partner's sperm and then inserted in their womb. Women without a womb insert their eggs in a 'surrogate' woman; in the case of a sister-to-sister surrogacy in Australia in 1988, the so-called surrogate mother was given an embryo which had been made out of her sister's egg plus an unknown donor's sperm (since her husband was infertile).

All these cases are nothing less than experimentation on live women. And for every 'success' there are hundreds of women for whom the technologies have failed. When we talk about egg donation, it means superovulation and then extraction of the eggs by various methods, which for some women has been fatal: in fact, Aliza Eisenberg who died in Israel was an egg donor. But the danger to women is not mentioned: egg donation is made to seem like sperm donation!

Often the women who give eggs before they undergo a hysterectomy are asked to perform an act of 'kindness' for an infertile woman. For others egg donation provides an income. In Austria, medical students are encouraged by private IVF clinics to sell their eggs. In 1987 the USA established the world's first 'egg bank' in Ohio, Cleveland. Egg donors are paid $900 to $1,200, the recipient women without ovaries who, according to the director of the programme Dr Martin M. Quigley, are 'as sterile as you can get', pay an estimated $5,000 per attempt. Quigley adds that 'A key part of the program . . . involves matching donors and recipients by physical appearance' but that 'technology does not exist to determine the gender of the fertilized egg'. However, he adds, 'These women will take anything' (Sheeran, 1988).

Not that egg donation is very successful. Originally announced in July 1987: 'Clinic to Provide Pool of Human Eggs' (*Boston Globe*, 15 July), a year later, only two women had become pregnant with a donated egg. Failure, however, seems to spur on the experimenters and, what's more, the new insights gained into the processes of human reproduction by means of all these trials on women need to be tested with yet other methods. DIPI (direct intraperitoneal insemination); POST (peritoneal oocyte and sperm transfer), and PROST (pro-nuclear stage tubal transfer) are all variations of a theme . . . mostly unsuccessful and dangerous to women's health. PROST, for instance, an Australian invention, necessitates egg collection on one day and reinsertion of the egg-sperm product before the nuclei of the two cells have merged the next day. This means that twice in a very short time a surgical procedure is performed on the woman (not to mention the previous hormonal stimulation), surely a considerable strain on her health – in addition to the psychological stress.

A method called 'Intravaginal Culture and Embryo Transfer', described as 'providing a simple, fast and inexpensive approach to the fertilization and culture of human oocytes' (*Ob. Gyn News*, 22 (12), 1987), is particularly dehumanizing. After superovulation, egg cell extraction and fertilization, the resulting embryos are put in a hermetically sealed tube and 'placed in the mother's vagina, held in place by a diaphragm, for an incubation of 44–50 hours'. As Dr Ranoux of the University Clinic in Paris said of his new technique (which, incidentally, earned him a prize):

> Intravaginal culture simplifies the laboratory manipulations needed for *in vitro* fertilization, since no incubator or carbon dioxide is needed.

'No incubator is needed. . . .'? It is difficult to envisage a more reductionist picture of a woman than a body whose vagina incubates her own future child in a test-tube.

Equally troubling, and raising fundamental questions about human dignity and the safety of a woman's life, is the substantially increased number of multiple births through conventional infertility treatments as well as IVF procedures. Five of the septuplets born to a British woman in 1987 after injections of FSH (follicle stimulating hormone) had died within a week of their birth, leaving the parents griefstricken. The only good thing to come out of this harrowing event was the beginning of a debate in the British media, questioning the ethics of such technological 'progress'. But instead of fundamentally revising the basic assumptions of reproductive medicine, which is to 'fix up' a defective *Mother Machine* (Corea, 1985, 1988), what was proposed as a safeguard against multiple births, both in Britain and the USA, was a *new* technique called 'pregnancy reduction' or 'selective abortion'. Should screening reveal too many foetuses in the woman's womb, potassium chloride (salt) will be selectively injected into the foetus' chest and thus cause the heart to stop. Eventually, the dead foetus is resorbed by the mother's body. Ian Craft, the British gynaecologist defending the use of the technology, especially in IVF where, he claimed, the insertion of up to thirteen embryos would ensure that at least some would 'take', only grudgingly stopped using the technique when the Voluntary Licensing Authority reprimanded him and public opinion seemed not to endorse his callous acts. Yet, at the third annual meeting of the European Society of Human Reproduction and Embryology in Cambridge in 1987, when a vote was taken on whether 'strict regulation' or 'flexible guidelines' should be aimed for, the majority of present IVF scientists and doctors indicated the latter (Burfoot, 1988:109). The greed for experimental guinea pigs is obvious. Contempt for women runs deep.

GIFT (Gamete Intrafallopian Transfer) is another case where 'myth' does not hold up to 'fact'. Euphemistically claiming to be a 'back to nature cure for infertile women' (Veitch, 1985), GIFT was originally developed by Ricardo Asch, an Argentinian living in Texas, and is now practised in the major infertility centres around the world. After hormonal stimulation and egg collection, usually two to three eggs and approximately 10,000 sperm are injected into each fallopian tube where – if it works – fertilization takes place. Success rates are said to be higher than with IVF (although long-term information on live birth is not available).

Even if the success rates for live babies were indeed somewhat higher, this could merely be a reflection of the fact that GIFT is increasingly used on women with irregular egg production but fully functioning fallopian tubes. In many cases they are fully fertile and it is their husbands who have a problem or, even more frequently, the infertility is 'unexplained'. It is termed 'idiopathic', and is said to be the case with at least a third of all couples seeking advice about the non-advent of a pregnancy, including a lot of people over thirty-five.

Needless to say, GIFT can be dangerous for women. The second Australian woman to die, in April 1988, attempted fertilization through the GIFT technique. She lapsed into a coma after a laparoscopy under general anaesthetic. At the time of writing (August 1988) the inquiry is still pending (Treweek, 1988). In another instance, a perfectly healthy woman who told me that her only 'fault' was to be forty (the 'quality' of her eggs was said to be 'lacking') tried GIFT three times in a London clinic. It did not work but she ended up with considerable pain and an infection. After the third laparoscopy she was told that egg collection 'had been very difficult' as she now had severe adhesions on her ovaries. This could have been due to the hormones she received for egg stimulation (Buserelin and Perganol), or to the three surgical egg extractions repeated within less than a year. The woman – a successful academic – was enormously upset: not only had she not been informed that GIFT was anything but a 'routine' procedure, but now that the damage had occurred, she was told that she *had* to remain on the programme. As it was, because of the adhesions, her 'old' ovaries would be even less likely to produce a ripe egg and through natural ovulation lead to a pregnancy. What was she to do? To continue and risk more damages to her health? To stop, knowing that she had fewer chances than before? She felt frustrated and bitter, in the knowledge that she had been cheated and had been had.

Using perfectly fertile women – to help boost the success rate – is an increasingly applied strategy. Importantly, it also expands the market for the many variations of IVF technologies. Originally developed for women *without* any fallopian tubes, they then expanded to women with two blocked fallopian tubes, but did not stop there. In a US study of IVF treatment-dependent versus independent pregnancies, Sung I. Roh et al. (1987) list the following indications for IVF in their clinic (Ohio, Columbus): 'idiopathic, male factor, cervical factor, endometriosis, pelvic adhesions, unilateral occlusion [meaning only one fallopian tube is blocked], immunologic, uterine, ovulatory dysfunction' (p. 984). French biologist Jacques Testart believes that as many as *half* of the women on IVF programmes should not be there (Laborie, personal communication, 1988), because sooner or later they might conceive 'naturally'. Roh et al.'s study points out that in a group of 151 women with at least one functioning fallopian tube, a total of 39 pregnancies resulted of which 21 (13.9 per cent) were treatment-dependent (i.e. a result of IVF) but as many as 18 pregnancies (11.9 per cent) were not. (In another study, treatment-independent pregnancy was as much as 25 per cent for women with at least one patent (functional) tube; Ben-Rafael et al., 1986.) Moreover, when it comes to live births resulting from both types of pregnancies, in the Roh et al. study the viable birth rate for the treatment-independent group was 61.1 per cent compared with 52.4 per cent for the treatment-dependent group. Although this difference is not statistically significant, I believe it to be indicative of the fact that there are far too many women who unnecessarily have to submit themselves to the test-tube peril! Roh and his colleagues appear to share this concern somewhat. In addition, they point out that, even in women with two blocked tubes, 'The possibility [of a pregnancy] is not completely excluded, because errors in diagnosis might occur' (p. 985). In the light of this statement one can only wonder how many of the children attributed to IVF treatment were in fact conceived 'naturally' (i.e. through sexual intercourse during the same time period as the IVF procedure): this might reduce the 'success rate' even further – to 1–2 per cent perhaps: an almost total failure!

Particularly disturbing is the practice of using fertile women as guinea pigs for 'microinjection': an experimental technique developed for men with what is called 'severe male factor infertility', that is, low or no sperm motility. A single sperm is *injected* into the extracted egg. If fertilization occurs, the embryo is then transferred to the woman's womb. Nothing is known about the chance of malformations. Professor Carl Wood, with Dr Alan Trouson one of the Australian inventors of this technique, said that results from mice studies showed normal foetuses born from microinjection. He suggests that most abnormal microinjection embryos would spontaneously abort after being transferred. The few that might continue to develop could be detected by repeated ultrasounds (another technique whose safety has never been proven) and could be aborted (Pirrie, 1988). As women who submit to the physical and emotional trauma of IVF are already pushed to the limit, this is an outrageously insensitive comment, to say the least. Also, many abnormalities might only be detected at birth or later. Only by putting the embryos into the womb of a woman who then carries it to term, gives birth to it and watches the child's development will anyone know if the technique 'worked'.

International competition has already produced many variations of this procedure: 'Zona drilling' is a process whereby acid solvents are used to make a small hole in the outer shell of the egg (the zona pellucida) through which 'up to 10 sperm are allowed to find their own way through the opening', as reported from New York Mt. Sinai Medical Center, USA (Downie, 1988). A similar method called 'Zona Opening', involving the use of two hooks to make a hole in the egg's outer shell, is practised at

Melbourne's Royal Women's Hospital, ironically praised by its 'pioneer' Ian Johnston as 'nature makes the choice' (Gluyas, 1988). Despite all these attempts to force a sperm's entry into an egg, no pregnancy has resulted, let alone a healthy child.

What is clear in all these experimental techniques is that an increasing number of women – fertile and infertile – are coerced into making their bodies available to have not just a child, but 'his' child at any price. As most IVF scientists are male, one might say that in fact it is 'boys helping boys to have boys' (since the sex of the sperm can easily be determined and it is well established that there is a world-wide preference for sons; see Williamson, 1976). What consequences will this have for the future of women? In a world where sperm banks with sperm from Nobel prize winners have been established and continue to produce 'bright children' (with beautiful mothers), what future could we expect should indeed the single sperm injection technology prove successful? Who will be chosen to have his [sic] genes transferred to the next generation? What woman – or women – will be deemed 'good enough' to provide the egg and carry the precious embryo? And, importantly, who will make the choice? In 1983, US writer Andrea Dworkin talked about the possibility of establishing farms where women could be kept as breeders. In 1988 we are a good deal closer. It is truly frightening.

From infertility to fertility control: global perspectives

Often, in the past six years whilst I was researching reproductive technologies, the image of the 'body snatchers' came to mind: virus-like creatures in a US film who – by means of growing bubbles in which they entrapped their victims – slowly but mercilessly suffocated all life. This is what I see happening with the new reproductive technologies which, ironically, are promoted as 'giving life'. More and more they are interfering with everybody's decision-making about having children, not only in the west, but also in the so-called 'Third World'. Because of the invested money which *will* have to be retrieved in one way or another, no matter how unsuccessful the technologies, the market needs to be constantly expanded: infertile women are not enough, the fertile population is increasingly targeted too.

Economic concerns are conveniently intertwined with the other crucial motive pervading the triumvirate science/reproductive medicine/pharmaceutical companies: the desire to *control* human reproduction: *To determine who produces what kind of life, in which part of the world, at which time and how.* Reproductive technology – intrinsically linked to genetic engineering – is not geared towards 'helping the infertile' and 'eliminating pain and suffering'. Reproductive technology and genetic engineering are geared towards the *global* production of the human species 'made to order', with less and less 'interference' from those who, until the advent of 'assisted procreation', were the only life-givers: women. These technologies will affect the lives of *all* people, especially *all* women in *all* parts of the world: this is the reason why they concern all of us, why none of us can afford to say 'that's nothing to do with me' and remain uninvolved.

In order to fully understand the implications of these technologies for humans, it is necessary to briefly describe 'advances' of genetic research on plants and animals. The last fifteen years have seen a rapidly accelerating process of identifying and manipulating smaller and smaller pieces of individual organisms. This development is the logical consequence of an increasingly compartmentalized, reductionist and mechanistic conception of life, intrinsic to patriarchal science, which has a deeply eugenicist basis. Eugenics is based on the premiss that 'someone' knows what is 'good': what is 'worthy' of living – and what must be eliminated. The aim is to control the cultivation of the 'best' crop, the breeding of the most profitable livestock, and the making of the 'perfect' human being in the lab. Since the advent of the recombinant DNA* method including cloning, in the early 1970s,

---

* The term recombinant DNA technology encompasses techniques for the insertion, replication and expression of gene pieces creating a hybrid DNA molecule which contains DNA (the molecule that encodes information for the reproduction and functioning of cells) from two or more sources. It is basically a simple process using 'scissors' (restriction enzymes) and 'glue' (ligase) to exchange bits of genes from one DNA piece to another. This does not mean, however, that it is completely understood: whilst it is possible to direct the gene insertion, there is no way of knowing where else in the genome (the full genetic information that characterizes an individual which is present in every cell) alterations might happen through the introduction of this foreign piece. It is precisely this impossibility of knowing what else might happen in the

no plant, animal or human being seems safe from being found 'deficient' – hence in need of genetic engineering to either screen (test) and eliminate it, or screen and then manipulate it: a procedure euphemistically entitled gene 'therapy' for humans!

By playing around with recombinant DNA technology – more elegantly called 'biotechnology' – international research teams financed by multinational chemical companies have produced a plethora of genetically engineered bacteria and viruses which they proclaim will create the 'gene revolution' (after the failed green revolution of the 1960s): oil eating bacteria, frost resisting bacteria, bacteria that will make plants resistant to insects and weeds and much more. They are all intended to improve harvests worldwide, but specifically in the 'Third World'. However, they are all newly created living organisms with the potential to reproduce, mutate, migrate and affect other plant (or animal) species. Once released into the open air, they cannot be recalled. Should they have deleterious effects – for instance on other 'non-targeted' plants or insects (and possibly animals and human beings) – they cannot be removed from the environment. They could also reduce the natural diversity of plants and drastically alter the composition of ecological systems. Moreover, they are bound to produce resistant strains in the hosts – which will then need yet another genetically engineered organism to counter the secondary effects. Worrying, too, is the increased economic dependence of 'Third World' farmers upon western biotechnology. Instead of eliminating 'world hunger', it will increase and further institutionalize the hegemony of the rich over the poor.

Inherent in the technology is the potential for biological warfare: the production of genetically engineered pathogenic organisms, for instance, to either destroy whole regions of cultivated crops or produce new strains of infectious diseases against which existing vaccines or the body's immune system is useless: research which is legitimately pursued for 'defence purposes' in

---

cell that constitutes the greatest danger in DNA technology. There is no space here to deal adequately with genetic engineering in plants and animals. For a useful, albeit pro-technology and non-feminist overview, see *Genetic Engineering. Catastrophe or Utopia* (Wheale and McNally, 1988).

the USA, the USSR, the UK – to name but a few nations (see Bullard, 1987; Wheale and McNally, 1988).

Then there are the transgenic animals: from the famous 'Geep' (a hybrid of goat and sheep) in Cambridge, UK, to transgenic pigs in Adelaide, Australia. Genetically manufactured bovine growth hormone in Austria is said to be of 'extraordinary economic significance with respect to its export to the Third World, specifically India' (GID, 1988). In the USA, Harvard scientists have produced 'the patented mouse'. Through microinjection they inserted a cloned piece of a human gene into a fertilized mouse egg, which was then transferred to the mouse's womb and brought to term. In so doing, they have produced a strain of mice with a supposed predisposition to breast cancer. (Many of the young mice died because the insertion of the foreign gene piece produced mutations that were fatal.) On 13 April 1988, the US Patent and Trademark Office issued the first patent for this genetically engineered mammal (Hubbard and Krimsky, 1988), thus legitimizing cruelty to animals not only in one generation but also in any further offspring! The same argument holds with respect to a genetically engineered AIDS mouse at the US National Institute of Health in 1987, potentially even more dangerous, given the additional security risk these animals create for their environment – the lab personnel and other people – should they escape.

With regard to human beings, the advent of an avalanche of 'powerful new drugs' – genetically engineered – to combat dwarfism, heart attacks, hypertension, heart failure, anaemia and even cancer and AIDS, is forecast. So far, however, there have been many more set-backs than successes, in fact it was reported that in the USA, in 1987, a mere *four* genetically engineered pharmaceuticals were on the market (human insulin, human growth hormone, alpha interferon and a hepatitis-B vaccine; Pollack, 1987). Furthermore, critics question whether they are necessary, and whether, in fact, they even work! But industry magnates remain optimistic and expect the profits to start rolling in by the early 1990s.

The 'Gene-Age' – which we seem to have entered – has also embarked on its race to establish a map of the human genome. Three billion US dollars over the next fifteen years will be invested into the mapping and sequencing of the over three billion nucleotide base pairs that make up the human genome: a multinational project supported by the governments of the USA, USSR, Japan and some European countries (Smith, 1988:577). The reason given for this gigantic undertaking sounds familiar: to identify the genes for what are believed to be 3,000 genetically inherited diseases so that, once identified, prenatal diagnosis can be intensified and 'defect' embryos can be eliminated – or 'therapeutically improved' by genetic engineering. This is where reproductive and genetic technology overlap and in fact become dependent upon one another. And this is why it is important to recognize the link between the women's stories in this book and the whole area of genetic engineering.

Genetic engineers such as Professor Baird from the University of British Columbia believe that 'genetics is as important as the environment in determining who will get diseases and when they will get them' and stress 'the importance of early genetic screening in identifying *those most at risk for every illness from hay fever to heart problems*' (my emphasis, in Miller, 1988a). This reductionist idea to say 'it's in our genes' is a resurrection of the theory and practice of eugenics as it came to scientific life over a century ago in the writings of Francis Galton (Darwin's cousin) in Britain in 1883. Since then, it has seen a number of horrific revivals through the passing of sterilization laws and restricted immigration in the USA, the UK and Germany in the first three decades of this century – to name just a few – to the Nazi genocide of Jewish people as well as the elimination, or at least involuntary sterilization, of Gypsies, 'people with schizophrenia, feeble-mindedness, manic depressive insanity, genetic epilepsy, Huntington's chorea, blindness, deafness, physical deformity, or alcoholism' in Germany from 1933 onwards (Ewing, 1988; Mies, 1987). Disturbingly, some of these same 'diseases' are said today to be genetically determined (e.g. manic depression and schizophrenia).

It is crucial to remember that doctors and medical scientists were the chief exponents behind this practice of 'racial hygiene' and that they promoted their actions as *Helfen und Heilen* (help and heal), whilst in reality they amounted to nothing less than *Auslese und Ausmerze* (selection and eradication). It is also crucial to know that much of the knowledge (e.g. on hormones) and many of the procedures used today in modern gene and reproductive technology were developed by Nazi scientists and doctors who performed cruel, often deadly, experiments on 'unworthy' women in concentration camps, and who did so, for instance, because they wanted to improve fertility for 'worthy' women (see Kaupen-Haas, 1988). Reproductive and genetic engineering has a history; what is new is only the refined technology which now makes it possible to select 'worthy' and eradicate future 'unworthy' human life at the time of conception.

Today, a very small percentage of children are born with severe abnormalities which are said to be genetically inherited. World-wide statistics are not established, but the figures usually quoted range from 2 to 3 per cent. According to British embryologist Dr Anne McLaren, only 'about 1 per cent of all babies born are affected by a severe genetic or chromosomal disability' (1987:42–47). Undoubtedly, having a disabled baby – or knowing that a genetically identified disease runs in the family – puts enormous strains on the decision of whether or not to have other children; and in most cases it is the woman who ends up looking after the baby in a society which is profoundly ablist and therefore treats disabled people and their carers as social outcasts, often plummeting them into poverty and making a life 'of her own' almost impossible for the woman.

But misconceptions abound. The risks of having a child with a disability are wildly exaggerated and this is what makes women so vulnerable: as more and more women say themselves, they become worried and frightened and often use prenatal tests because they believe they have to (Katz Rothman, 1986; Leu Zinger and Rambert, 1987/8). These technologies are said to 'reassure' the parents-to-be that they will have a healthy child. This is a gross misrepresentation when so much else can go wrong at a later stage of the pregnancy, or indeed once the child is born. Having children – in the same way as living – is a risk, it demands courage. No technological assurance can ever guarantee a healthy child. And of course the question must be asked: what *is* a healthy child and what will it mean for those people who will continue to be born with abnormalities – or become disabled throughout their lives – when even fewer provisions are made to integrate them into society, because, as will be said soon, many of them need not have been born? Will the disabled children of mothers who refuse the prenatal tests be barred from receiving social security? This is not a far-fetched possibility.

Much as the individual plight and hardship with disability can (but must not always) be devastating, 1 per cent, or even 2 to 3 per cent is a small figure. It should make us think why, all of a sudden, this is said to matter so much in a world in which thousands die of lack of food, economic security, clean drinking water and largely man-made ecological disasters; and where, in India, a woman 'must have between two and six children in order to have at least one surviving male child' (Patai, 1987a). Thus in a world overwhelmed by large numbers of women suffering from poverty, illiteracy and violence as well as femicide – and this includes poor women and women of the 'wrong' ethnicities in well-to-do countries – there is, all of a sudden, this supposedly heartfelt urge to eliminate the pain and suffering of a very small group of people, in the same way that test-tube technology is said to ease the heartache of involuntary childless couples in the west, while in the rest of the world women are sterilized or made sick by dangerous contraceptives. We must ask: what are the *real* motives behind these developments? who profits? and who pays the price?

Monetary factors are important. After the computer business, biotechnology is the biggest growth area worldwide, with billions invested in genetic manipulations of plants and animals. It is the hope of Big Business for the rest of the twentieth century, and it *must* succeed in order to avoid even larger world market chaos. Human reproductive technology and genetic engineering seem doubly lucrative: at one end, as has been discussed so far, the business of baby-making is attempted. At the other, the need for quality control of the offspring can be created. Both approaches need lots of drugs, instruments, machines and, importantly, diagnostic kits with 'genetic probes'. And because IVF is basically a failed technology, 'naturally' achieved pregnancies from fertile people, too, need to be controlled in order to boost the numbers of customers.

Abusing the fears about the worst kinds of disabilities both for the child and its parents there is an increasingly mandatory call to establish genetic counselling, genetic screening – and perhaps soon 'therapy' – at least for those 'at risk'. In fact, the demand for 'preconceptional care to be routine practice' in the US for all pregnant women has already been put forward (*Ob Gyn News*, 22(2), 1987). In the same way that the test-tube technology is increasingly becoming mandatory for infertile people, 'prenatal check-ups' are increasingly said to be necessary in order to have a healthy child. They have become what US medical writer Susan Ince called 'information-age rites of passage for pregnant women' (Ince, 1987:79). Two or three ultrasounds have become routine in any medically supervised pregnancy in the west. Amniocentesis, originally advocated for women over 35 at risk of bearing a child with Down's syndrome, is now discussed for women at age 30 (Crandall et al., 1986). Chorionic villus biopsy is becoming increasingly popular. Both tests allow for a check-up of some chromosomal abnormalities, with chorionic villus biopsy being carried out at about eight weeks of pregnancy whereas amniocentesis can only be performed from the sixteenth week onwards. But the latest method, due to be introduced in 1988 or 1989, assesses the 'product offspring' at an even earlier stage: *preimplantation diagnosis* purports to recognize 'defects' before the embryo actually implants itself in the woman's womb. And it is here where genetic engineers – and their industrial sponsors – see a future goldmine.

So what is preimplantation diagnosis? During the interval between fertilization and implantation, embryos can be checked out biochemically. That is, when grown *in vitro* in the lab, whether or not their metabolic activity is 'normal' can be diagnosed through an investigation of the effects the cell products have on the culture fluid. This method is a so-called 'non-invasive strategy'. More invasive is what is called *embryo biopsy*: one cell is taken from the 8–16 cell embryo (but possibly also later, at blastocyst stage, that is when the embryo has roughly 100 cells) and analysed for chromosomal abnormalities. The rest of the embryo can be frozen and, should the test-results be OK, put in the woman's womb. In other words the 'part'embryo has kept the potential of developing into a 'normal' foetus and then child. (This potential also means that cloning – the manufacturing of, say, eight embryos with the same genetic make-up from dividing one 8-cell embryo into eight parts and putting them into the wombs of eight host women – is technically absolutely feasible!)

It is on these isolated embryo cells that the biotechnology industry pins its hope; they provide the scientists with specific

DNA probes – 'short segments of DNA that signal the presence or absence of a gene of interest' (McLaren, 1987:43) – which are tagged with radioactivity and added to the isolated embryo cell. If the probe bonds to a piece of DNA, this means that a 'gene of interest' is present.

An even more promising extension of gene probes are 'marker genes': DNA pieces which will bond not to the 'real thing' but to a sequence on a gene that is *believed* to be in close proximity to the 'defect' part which has not (yet) been found. 1987 was a good year for discovering such marker genes: in the *New Scientist* in March 1987 it was reported that two possible marker genes were found for manic depression, in May for Alzheimer's disease and cystic fibrosis, in August for bowel cancer. In December 1987 we were first told about the discovery of the marker gene for lung cancer, next about genetic probes that recognized part of the Y chromosome, thus finding 'the gene that determines sex' (Joyce, 1987:29). But already in November, the story about the Alzheimer's disease had to be retracted: 'No extra genes in Alzheimer's disease' (Ferry, 1987:32). Thus similar to test-tube technology, people's hopes are raised – only to be dashed by unfulfilled promises.

But we can expect to hear many more such 'success stories'. After all, the investments of biotechnology companies must yield profit. To date there are only about fifteen marker gene probes available (plus approximately 100 tests using biotechnical methods). But one US company (*Collaborative Research*) has invested more than US$11 million since 1984 in developing genetic probes and has hired eminent researchers to develop its genetic screening kits. Its chairman notes that 'the big money will comes from probes that can determine an individual's predisposition to major illnesses, such as heart disease and cancer' (Joyce, 1987:46), and that the development of these gene probes is 'a piece of cake'.

It is often said that IVF and genetic engineering have nothing to do with one another. Yet the Second Report of the British Voluntary Licensing Authority (VLA 1987) states it quite clearly (p. 16):

> There are important research projects both to improve
> the present success rate for IVF and to develop tech-

niques such as the freezing of eggs and pre-embryos*
that may be used safely. *Recently some projects have
started that are related to the diagnosis of defects in the
pre-embryo.* The aim is to avoid replacing pre-embryos
with chromosomal or other abnormalities in the
uterus; a vital concern for couples who are at risk of
giving birth to children with severe inherited genetic
disorders. (my emphasis)

Preimplantation diagnosis in connection with IVF is thus openly
advocated in Britain. In West Germany, in its 1987 report, the
German Research Foundation (DFG) voiced strong support for
it too. Anne McLaren, at the 5th World Congress on *In-Vitro*
Fertilization and Embryo Transfer in Norfolk, USA, put it
clearly (1987:28):

Current *in-vitro* fertilization research is focused on
alleviating infertility, but future research is more
likely to be concerned with the early diagnosis and
prevention of genetic abnormalities.

Professor Robert Winston, well-known British IVF specialist,

---

* 'Pre-embryo' is a term invented by British scientists in 1985 to
describe an embryo younger than 14 days (Turney, 1985), in order to
appease people who see embryos already as 'unborn children' and for
these reasons are against embryo experimentation. But even people in
favour of embryo experimentation objected to 'the introduction of
cosmetic words' (David Davies, member of the Warnock Committee,
1986). As Gena Corea points out (Corea, 1988:326):

A linguistic trick was necessary to make people feel more
comfortable about experimentation on human embryos.
Many people feel there is something not quite right about
this; but they feel perfectly comfortable with the notion that
women will be experimented upon. There was no need to
invent a new term for women to justify pumping them full
of hormones and sucking out their eggs. To make people
feel better about their deaths, no one had to pretend that
Zenaide Maria Bernardo, Aliza Eisenberg, and Andrea
Dominquez were really 'pre-women'.

is quite specific about the connection between IVF and pre-implantations diagnosis. In an article he co-authored with other members of Hammersmith Hospital, London, applauding the improvement of IVF with Buserelin and hMG (see section 1, p. 243–5) they say (1988:1768):

> An important advantage of treatment with Buserelin is that large numbers of fertilisable eggs are produced during one cycle of treatment. This will allow the simultaneous screening of many zygotes [fertilised eggs] for single gene defects for preimplantation diagnosis, such that women at risk could embark on a healthy pregnancy.

The idea thus is to screen embryos not only for genetic diseases with which the future human beings will be born, but for *predispositions* that may – or may not – manifest themselves, often only when adulthood is reached: asthma, hayfever, psoriasis, diabetes, high blood pressure – the list of 'conditions' is endless. No wonder then, that internationally 'Biotechnic Firms Compete in Developing Gene Diagnosis' (*Science* 1986:1318). Robert First of White Plains, New York, predicts a human genetics market of US$48 million by 1990, and 'DNA tests are fast becoming a commodity traded in the medical market, much like pregnancy tests and insulin' (Joyce, 1987:45).

To test for predispositions that are likely to be at least as influenced by someone's environment and lifestyle as by their genes is disturbing to say the least. After the gene for manic depression and schizophrenia what is next? A gene for homosexuality, for feminism . . . the shadows on the wall grow longer, the parallels to the earlier mentioned 'illnesses' in Nazi Germany become all too obvious. Professor Carl Wood, famed Australian IVF pioneer, is an optimist. He predicts that we will have 'a much healthier, more long-lived race in the future' (quoted in *The Australian Women's Weekly*, 1988:76) and that:

> Emotional and physical problems often put down to stress, or to *menopause*, or something similar, *will also be diagnosed as genetic diseases*, and treated effectively with chemicals, or gene replacement. (my emphasis)

Professor Mark Ferguson of Manchester University (reported from the 149th Annual Meeting of the British Medical Association in Belfast, August 1987, in the *Guardian*, London) believes that:

> In 50 to 100 years every human will have his [*sic*] genes mapped at birth and stored on computer . . . Genetic defects and susceptibilities to diseases will be known. Prevention or treatment tailored to each individual could be started.

He also thinks that 'Individuals may choose to reproduce by IVF so as to have a bank of spare parts for their offspring when the latter begin to suffer from diseases or injuries' (*Guardian*, 1987:4). He is not the first to make such statements. In fact, as early as 1982 Robert Edwards, co-lab parent of the first test-tube baby in Britain, proposed to divide embryos, freeze half of them for use in later life and implant only half (*Nature*, 1982:383).

What they are saying then, is that IVF should be the preferred method of conception in order to have the embryo easily accessible for screening, discarding, or perhaps genetic manipulating. Or, as Dr Anne McLaren suggests (1987:46), in order to guarantee healthy babies, couples 'at risk' could use:

> hormonal stimulation, then normal *in vivo* [in the body] fertilization after intercourse, followed four or five days later by recovery [collection] of blastocysts [100 cell embryo] from the uterus by flushing (also known as lavage).

She concedes that at the moment the technique has certain hazards: 'the blastocyst may be damaged and there is a risk of causing an ectopic pregnancy, where the blastocyst implants outside the uterus'. However, she continues: 'The flushing procedure is no more stressful for the woman than the insertion of an IUD' (p. 46).

Dr Alan Trounson of Monash University, Melbourne, is equally confident that IVF will be widely available. He advocates gearing IVF to women under thirty-five, because, he says, they are more capable of successful pregnancies. He believes that 'low stress IVF [which he suggests might take place without superovulation, so that the women produce only their normal one egg a month] *would become like a dental appointment with the woman visiting the clinic each month for five months*' (Miller, 1988c; my emphasis). As we know, one of his areas of expertise is male infertility – microinjection (see p. 254) – is he thinking mainly of fertile women?

Dr Helmut Zeilmaker of Rotterdam envisages a future in which IVF will be the best mode of procreation because people could use genetically screened sperm and eggs for reproduction, which have been safely stored away in freezers deep underground to protect them from nuclear disasters (Vines, 1986)! And Professor Carl Wood in Australia describes artificial conception as superior to natural conception (McDonnell, 1988):

> Natural conception compares less favourably than artificial conception as it includes unwanted children, parents incapable of parenting, poverty-stricken parents and women with medical diseases or habits likely to adversely affect the child. The mother may harm the foetus by smoking or drinking or by not being immunized against rubella which may cause malformation.

I believe that in the light of these shocking statements about the increasing laboratory control of reproduction, the stories of the women in this book take on yet another dimension. Of course, the predictions of these 'experts' that IVF should – and will – become the 'natural' way of conception are based on the assumption that IVF is a success story – which I strongly dispute. At least for infertile women it does not work. But the only way to try to improve the success rates, using the medical model, about IVF *as well as* preimplantation diagnosis, embryo biopsy, genetic screening and 'therapy' is to do embryo experimentation – and to do it on a grand scale!

In other words, a constant supply of eggs and embryos is needed. And where do they come from? They come from women. Women who have been superovulated to produce ripe eggs, either in IVF programmes or as egg donors and who are asked to donate their 'spare' body parts for research (see Rowland, 1987a). *It is here that the crucial link between IVF and embryo research – and in extension genetic engineering – becomes evident: a link that so few people want to acknowledge, let alone see.* The stories the women tell in this book take on a *global* dimension; they reveal the crucial role women play as members of the social group women: by using IVF they are making raw material available for a science which, ultimately, in connection with the criteria applied to embryo screening and 'therapy', could produce, in the words of Erwin Chargaff, biochemistry professor and Nazi victim, the 'engineering of a molecular nightmare . . . a molecular Auschwitz' (Chargaff, 1987:200).

Most of this book describes the developments in the west. This is because so far it has been mainly white, well-to-do middle-class women whose – or their partners' – desire for a child serves as the justification for the use of women's bodies as experimental test-sites in IVF programmes. On the one hand this is not surprising. Within a capitalist/technopatriarchal logic, the development of a birth technology for the control of women's reproduction in countries where birth rates are declining steadily (Wattenberg, 1987) makes sense. This same cruel logic targets women's fertility in the 'Third World' as the main factor of population control and has led to deaths from Dalkon shields and other IUDs as well as mass sterilization (often executed under appalling sanitary conditions). On the other hand, the use of relatively privileged western women as medical subjects in reproductive medicine *is* a change from the well-known history of abusing poor women in Puerto Rico when the contraceptive pill was developed; from administering Depo-Provera to West Indian and Asian women in Britain, Aboriginal women in Australia, Maori women in New Zealand, women in Thailand, the Philippines, India, and many other 'southern' countries (Bunkle, 1984); from the continuing testing of the two-month injectable contraceptive Net-Oen on Indian women; from experimenting with the contraceptive implant Norplant, the 'morning after pill' and anti-pregnancy vaccines on women in Bangladesh, Thailand, Ecuador, Indonesia, Brazil. These are just a few of the medical crimes against poor women of 'undesirable' ethnic backgrounds in the west, and the majority of women in the so-called 'Third World' all of which have led – and still do – to severe ill health and often death. In addition they impose total control over women's decisions about whether or not to have children.

I believe that this will change, that in fact it *is* already changing. Reproductive and genetic engineering in the west is only the prelude – some preliminary testing, so to speak – to the technological take-over of the reproduction of those millions of people in parts of Asia, Africa, South America, China and the USSR, whose 'reckless breeding' it is feared will interfere with the continuation of white western dominance. In the words of German sociologist Maria Mies (1987:336): 'The myth of over-population in the poor countries serves as justification for the development of ever more anti-fertility technology.' Thus technologies allegedly created to alleviate sterility 'as a disease' could easily turn into population control. In theory, the scenario is quite simple. You sterilize most of the (female) population; then, by means of technology in the lab – IVF – you choose a few 'worthy ones' to have children. Genetic testing will further insure that only 'quality products', whatever the specific demands – boys, for instance, rather than girls – are born.

There are indications that such thinking is not science fiction; sex selection is a case in point. As early as 1973, John Postgate, a respected scientist at the University of Sussex in England, urged the development of a 'manchild' pill which would eventually eliminate women who will not, or cannot, stop breeding (Postgate, 1973). Today, amniocentesis is used specifically for eliminating female foetuses in India (and among Asian groups in many other countries, e.g. Britain and Australia). The test is cheap (500 Indian Rupees) and it is estimated that between 1978 and 1983 78,000 female foetuses were aborted in India (Patel, 1987a). This prenatal femicide has been successful in disturbing the female/male sex ratio. In one study of 1000 amniocenteses in Bombay no pregnancy was terminated when the foetus was male, whereas 97 per cent of all female foetuses were aborted (Ravindra, 1986).

Sex selection is also practised by means of selecting male bearing (Y) sperm. The US inventor of an X and Y separating technology – Ronald Ericsson – has a chain of clinics that use his method which, he claims, is 70–80 per cent accurate. Not surprisingly, the clinics are in India, Egypt, Jordan, Pakistan, Malaysia, Singapore, Taiwan – as well as in the USA (the most famous one being *Gametrics Inc*, California). In one of his leaflets

Ericsson states that out of 263 couples who approached him, 248 selected boys and 15 selected girls (Patel, 1987b:73).

Sex-determination with a DNA probe might be even more accurate. In 1987 this was achieved in Britain. Significantly, the various tests are all developed to recognize the *male*-determining Y chromosome. This, we are told, is because of sex-linked diseases. John West, a member of the Edinburgh medical team, emphasized that it wouldn't be ethical to use the DNA probe test for sex predetermination of babies, but, he admits, 'we couldn't prevent the technique from being used in that way' (Johnston, 1987:547).

The DNA probe to identify the male Y chromosome is commercially available. Pre-sexing embryos on a routine basis could become an important tool of population control programmes. Of course, sex-determination of embryos demands access to embryos, four to eight days old, in the lab. In other words, in order to use preimplantation diagnosis, IVF programmes must exist. This prerequisite is already fulfilled: the number of IVF clinics in India, China, Singapore, Brazil, Malaysia and Indonesia is growing steadily.

In India, the first test-tube baby was born in 1986 and there are at least seven IVF clinics – both public and private – in operation. After the first birth *India Today* reported that 'all indications are that there could soon be a test-tube baby boom', and that the waiting room at the KEM Hospital in Bombay 'spills over with women clutching medical reports, their faces mirroring a mixture of hope and desperation' (1986:78). Other reports confirm that the clinics are snowed under with requests from well-to-do middle- and upper-class women for whom the stigma of infertility *or* the inability of producing *a son* often equals divorce, the loss of their home, and sometimes even death. (Before the opening of IVF clinics in India, women from India – as well as from Arab countries – made up a significant number of well-paying clients at Patrick Steptoe's and Robert Edwards' Bourn Hall Clinic in Britain, and Robert Winston's private practice in London.) 'Infertility inflicts 110 million' was the headline of a newspaper report in the *Indian Express* (Bombay, 1985) which listed 'improper medical care and sexually transmitted diseases as its leading causes'.

The link to population control is openly made too. On the occasion of the third IVF birth, Dr Indira Hinduja, the IVF specialist, and Dr T. C. Ananda Kumar, Director of the Institute for Research in Reproduction in Bombay, both said that the test-tube baby technology signified a 'promotive effect in the country's family planning programme *as it showed the successful reversal of sterilisation techniques*' (my emphasis): couples who wanted a child after sterilization, could undergo IVF (*Times of India*, 1987). We can be sure, however, that in the same way as in the west only 'respectable' women gain access to IVF, sterilization reversal for the poor landless peasant woman will not become a priority. But of course poor, uneducated women might be experimented on as 'volunteers', as in the case of other medical experimentation mentioned earlier.

Given the economic hardship for many women in the so-called 'Third World' and the ingrained social stigma of infertility that affects poor women even more than rich ones, it is highly likely that they will become the experimental subjects for procedures that are harder to perform in countries like Australia, where at least some ethical committees act as 'watchdogs'. We should not forget that the West Australian IVF company *Pivet* has already established IVF clinics in Malaysia, Indonesia, India and plans to expand further. Who will be able to control their research?

Also, since 1987, Professor Christopher Chen, renowned for the first successful IVF birth from frozen eggs in Adelaide, Australia, in 1986, moved to Singapore where he now has his own IVF clinic. He also plans research into microinjection to 'treat' male infertility and is in the process of establishing the world's first egg bank where 'a woman could have her eggs stored when she is young and healthy . . . to be implanted later when the eggs she produces deteriorate' (*The Economist*, 1988:126). His work in prosperous Singapore, where the college-educated women don't have enough children, will be of great importance to the national leaders who, like their counterparts in some western countries (e.g. West Germany), are worried about the low birth rate of 'proper' women.

To conclude these thoughts on the *global* perspective of reproductive and genetic engineering, I believe that with a growing number of IVF centres in 'Third World' countries – many of which are directed, or at least financed, by western IVF companies and the pharmaceutical industry (and perhaps population control groups?), we are witnessing the infiltration of

'conventional' population control programmes by the whole
gamut of reproductive technologies. In many cases, only living
women who carry a manipulated embryo to term will be 'proof'
that the technology works. This applies to many new variations of
IVF, particularly microinjection. It also applies to the enormous
project of gene 'therapy': the insertion or extraction of gene pieces
– be it in body cells (somatic therapy) or egg or sperm cells (germ
line therapy). Undoubtedly, pharmaceutical companies will also
think of genetically engineered contraceptive vaccines. And drugs
used in IVF – such as the LHRH analogues (Buserelin and
others, see pp. 243–5) are also tried out as new contraceptives.
It must be feared that in countries which have a significant
number of poor women and a strong preference for boys attached
to the sometimes deadly stigma of infertility, it will be possible
to carry out human trials without too much public outcry. Ultimately, it could lead to the final control over the production of
all human life in the hands of a few.

This is why the individual stories of the women in this book
are of such crucial importance: they are a warning as to what
further inroads IVF and genetic engineering might make on
women's freedom. This is why I believe that *no one* can afford
to ignore these technological developments and say 'they have
nothing to do with me . . . they are just about a few privileged
white women in the west'. This is why we have to build an
international resistance movement before yet more women are
abused, humiliated, get sick and die. The future of women looks
bleak if we don't. The latest developments in reproductive technology illustrate this point.

Maturing immature eggs, in vitro *wombs and neomorts: the ultimate
feat*

Gena Corea once said that in order to know what will happen to
humans tomorrow, one has to look at what is happening in cattle
farming today. In 1989, her words seem more true than ever
before.

'I would have been content if only human eggs had come my
way more freely', Robert Edwards said in 1980, recalling his
frustrating years before Louise Brown of having to work with
the eggs of cows, sheep and monkeys instead of women (Corea,

1984:42). 'Seven research embryos only . . .', complained IVF specialist Alan Trounson in 1987, deploring the restriction Victoria [the Australian state of which Melbourne is the capital] had put on his team's forays into microinjection (Bartels, 1988). Research embryos are indeed precious: women in IVF programmes – even when under considerable emotional pressure to help other infertile women – are hesitant to donate their spare eggs or embryos for research purposes (Rowland, 1987a; Klein, 1989). In addition, newly established bodies like ethics committees, who raise some questions about the ethics of the new reproductive technologies and genetic engineering, focus their concerns on the *embryo*. (What is happening to *women*, unfortunately, does not figure much in their deliberations!) This means that tampering with embryos cannot be done as freely as the scientists would like it to be.

This could soon change, however. Emulating research on cattle, one solution to the problem is to take *immature* eggs from a woman's ovary, mature them in the lab, fertilize them with sperm (which is not difficult to get) – and you have all the research embryos you could possibly wish for. Any woman would do, young or old – because we have about 400,000 immature egg cells in our ovaries of which only about 350 to 400 ripen. At a further stage, one could even implant such artificially matured eggs in surrogate mothers – again any woman would do.

Reporting work on cattle by Ian Gordon's team at the University College of Dublin, Ireland, in collaboration with Masstock, an international farming company, in the *New Scientist* in August 1987, Gail Vines says (1987a:53):

> He harvests immature eggs from the ovaries of cattle carcasses in slaughterhouses and matures the eggs in the laboratory. He has fertilized the eggs and matured them in the laboratory to the morula stage when the embryo is a solid mass of cells.

Another group in Britain, *Animal Biotechnology in Cambridge* (ABC), is also working on perfecting IVF in cattle (they also try to freeze pig eggs; 'there is a lot of money in pigs'). Edward Friend of ABC explains the cattle experiments (Vines, 1987a: 53):

> We are looking for a cheap and more reliable source
> of embryos in cattle. . . . *Then breeders wouldn't need*
> *to keep animals just to produce embryos.* (my emphasis)

By September 1987, Gail Vines reports that it has worked:
'Gordon has just produced the truly [*sic*] "test-tube" calves'
(1987b: 42). By December the *New Scientist* provides us with a
picture of one such calf: 'Calves a la Carte' from Ireland (Vines,
1987c: 23):

> Scientists collect ova (immature eggs) from slaugh-
> tered cows, nurture them in the laboratory to full
> maturity and fertilize and freeze them as seven-day-
> old embryos. The scientists then transfer these to
> recipient cows.

By March 1988, ABC at Cambridge is setting up the service:
'egg delivery'. Dr Robert Moor, who developed the technique,
said (the *Independent*, UK):

> We get about 20 eggs from one ovary at present but
> we are working on methods which will enable us to
> grow up to half a million eggs from a single ovary.

What does the future hold for women? In 1983, a committee
of the *Royal Society* in Britain wrote (p. 5):

> Recent progress in maturing eggs from rodents and
> other mammals *in vitro* raises the possibility that
> human ovarian tissue *obtained from cadavers or removed*
> *during surgery undertaken for other purposes*, might
> provide an alternative source of material. *This would*
> *considerably enhance the scope for research on human*
> *fertilization and embryology.* (my emphasis)

In 1985, a US scientist, Dr Lucinda Vek from the North
Virginia IVF team, predicted that one day it will be possible to
cut a wedge out of the human ovary with hundreds of eggs in it
(Kramer, 1985):

By maturing the immature eggs one would recover from such a wedge, and then by freezing them, the woman could become pregnant whenever she chose, simply by transferring a fertilized, mature egg into her uterus.

In 1988 Ditta Bartels reported that 'the three most prominent IVF research groups in Britain are actively working on the human system' (Bartels, 1988: 144). As documented in the 2nd Report of the *Voluntary Licensing Authority* in 1987 (VLA Report, 1987), these are the research teams of Patrick Steptoe and Robert Edwards at Bourn Hall, Cambridge; the IVF centre of Professor Templeton at the University of Aberdeen; and the IVF unit at the University of Edinburgh under the direction of Professor David Baird. In September 1986 the late Patrick Steptoe confirmed research into the maturation of immature eggs in an interview given to German Television (see p. 235). Asked where the immature eggs came from he said:

> From patients. We often recover 15–20 eggs per patient . . . we know many of them will be immature. . . . Women who are sterilized also volunteer eggs.

By mid–1988, the 'egg fever' makes news in Australia: 'Scientists set to "ripen" human eggs in millions' (Miller, 1988d). A scientist who has worked with IVF programmes in the UK and been successful with egg maturation in sheep and pigs has now as his brief 'to perfect the procedure for human eggs' at the Centre for Early Human Development at Monash University – better known as the 'Carl Wood–Alan Trounson' territory. Calvin Miller reports that by using egg maturation techniques, Dr Jeremy Osborn 'predicts that the poor survival rates of fertilized eggs – less than 4 per cent for IVF procedures' – an admission which is made rarely in the IVF context – 'will improve to match nature's 30 per cent survival rate'.

Dr Max Brinsmead, a reproductive physiologist at the University of Newcastle, New South Wales, Australia, also believes in the potential of maturing immature eggs to improve the success rates of IVF. Like Osborn, he is forthcoming with figures one usually does not hear from IVF specialists, such as 'about 95 per cent of 4-celled or 8-celled human embryos returned to the uterus fail to implant' – which is precisely what feminists have been saying for a long time (Miller, 1988e). According to Brinsmead, this low figure would be substantially increased if immature eggs could be collected and then matured *in vitro*. In his words (Miller, 1988e):

> Instead of stimulating the woman at the beginning of her cycle and collecting five or six eggs, we may be able to excise a small part of an ovary containing several hundred primordial follicles. We could then grow the follices to maturity and harvest the eggs as they're needed.

This procedure, Brinsmead suggests, would result 'in a healthier patient and more receptive uterus at the time of the embryo transfer and could lead to a greater rate of successful pregnancies'.

While this is, of course, only a theoretical assumption, the idea of maturing immature eggs would, as Australian geneticist Dr Ditta Bartels rightly said (in Miller, 1988d):

> lead to a sudden surplus of literally millions of eggs . . . it will be like winning Tattslotto. All their dreams will come true . . . human embryos will become available for research.

Together with the method of freezing eggs – as previously discussed – the maturation of immature eggs would represent yet another giant step in the control and take-over of women's decision to have – or not to have – children, as well as their control over the circumstances and the time in their lives that they would like to have children.

Not only would human embryos be plentiful to allow for experimentation, but as has already been suggested with regard to the possibility of freezing eggs, a woman might be coerced to have her eggs frozen at an early age when they are still 'good'. In other words, before the adverse effects of a polluted environment including hazardous work conditions, cancerous chemicals, possible dangers from VDU units* have deteriorated the 'quality' of her eggs.

It is not the prevention of health hazards at the workplace that is targeted; it is the prevention of 'living a normal life' that is sought; a life-hating philosophy which places little importance on the well-being of its *living* population – women and men – and is instead only concerned with the controlled survival of the human species – of molecule-machines – whatever the price.

Seen in this light, Dr Brinsmead's statement that the successful technique of maturing immature eggs may be applied to extracting egg follicles – from a *foetus* – may not be that surprising: 'A foetus which is not even born could ultimately have children', he says, and explains (in Miller, 1988e):

> By the 14th week a foetus contains its full complement of 100 million oocytes surviving in the neonate [newborn]. Thus, terminated foetuses or non-surviving neonates could theoretically become egg donors.

We have to seriously ask when this roulette with parts of human bodies – female bodies – will stop. Sadly, it should not really come as a surprise that in 1988 bioethicist and reader in medico-legal studies at the University of Queensland, Dr Paul Gerber, suggested that brain-dead 'neomorts' [newly deads] could first be used as surrogate mothers and then for organ transplants to make better use of the 'living corpses': 'I can't see anything wrong with it', Gerber said in an interview (Miller, 1988b). A specialist in reproductive physiology at Monash University 'who preferred to be unknown' backed his idea: 'I can't see any reason why the pregnancy shouldn't go ahead normally, as long as the female incubator is receiving the appropriate nutrients and care.'

In fact this has already happened. Michele was the name of the child who was born in the USA in 1987, seven weeks after

---

* In December 1987 the Australian Public Service Association said that radiation from visual display units could cause genetic changes in men and women and lead to birth defects in their children. They issued a warning against using VDUs if they – women and men – wanted to become parents (Wainwright, 1987).

her mother was declared dead from a brain tumour but kept alive on life-support until the girl's birth (*Boston Globe*, 1987). We also heard about the case of the baby girl without a brain (an anencephalic child) who was carried to term by her mother, kept alive artificially and was flown from Canada to California to have her heart donated to a new-born boy with a heart problem (Blakeslee, 1987b). And we have heard a German neurologist predict that since IVF technology exists to produce embryos *in vitro*, they might be manipulated in a way as to develop as anencephali and then be implanted into a 'surrogate' mother's womb – and poor women in the 'Third World' came to his mind immediately – and their organs sold to sick people: the ultimate use of women as living incubators. (*Der Spiegel*, 1987.)

The use of foetal cells is another case in point. Do we really want women to get pregnant and then abort their foetuses for use in some adult's tissues – be it to try and correct Parkinson's or Alzheimer's disease? Whatever happened to people's dignity – and is it an accident that we are only talking about *women* 'performing' this service – because, of course, men cannot (yet?) conceive and give birth?

Maturing immature eggs, the use of neomorts – this is not all. In June 1988 the highly reputed US journal *Fertility and Sterility* reported the first case of ectogenesis: the artificial womb. But it was a case with a twist. It wasn't the plastic incubator into which an embryo was placed in order to grow 'in man's image' – it was wombs taken from three *living women* – apparently cancer patients who had hysterectomies – into which spare IVF embryos were placed, one of which then began its 'normal' development within its 52-hour life span. The uteri themselves were connected to so-called perfusion machines which provided them with oxygen and the necessary nutrients and hormones mimicking early pregnancy. The experiment taking place at the Reproductive Medicine Unit at the Department of Obstetrics and Gynecology, the University of Bologna, Italy, 'was undertaken to obtain the first early pregnancy *in vitro* because future complete ectogenesis should not be ruled out' (Bulletti et al., 1987:991). Carlo Bulletti and his colleagues also reported that 'The experimental design used in this project was previously approved by the Ethical Review Board' (p. 993).

So this is where we have, at last, arrived: talking about using foetuses as future 'mothers' and sticking embryos into uteri removed from women's bodies. And women taking part in IVF programmes probably do not realize that, unwittingly, they contribute to this sick scenario of interfering with human reproduction. Nor do they realize that their great individual pain and sorrow are grossly exploited as propaganda for continuing IVF. For they have it in their power to withdraw their bodies and minds: to stop this crazy technology by saying *no*.

On 21 September 1988 several hundred cattle breeders, soberly dressed, met in the ballroom of the Southern Cross Hotel in Melbourne – plush scarlet carpet, ornate chandeliers – under the flickering lights of eight television screens for an embryo auction: a multi-million dollar event, the seventh of its kind in Australia, reported as, 'Stock breeders choose a ritzy setting to flush out embryo buyers' (Flanagan, 1988). Cattle 'conceived and immaculately unconceived . . . netted $A270,000, with embryos selling for an average $A6,137'. The strong links between Australia and the USA became evident: at least 50 per cent of the stock had a North American progenitor. The sale was relayed to Sydney, Adelaide, Perth and Brisbane and lots were bought by these markets. Don Anderson of Queensland's Inverary stud believes that 'the stud cattle industry has accepted the challenge to market their produce, not just offer it for sale'. After the auction, the audience, wearing bow ties, sat down to eat beef.

Resistance

The rapid growth of the technologies is alarming and resistance is urgently needed. The technologies don't work, but we are led to believe that they do; they are *anti*-woman, but we are told that they are *for* women; they are dangerous and dehumanising in their theory *and* application. Given their intricate relationship with genetic engineering they have a very real potential to become an instrument of population control to 'curb' fertility in the 'Third World' as well as breeding the 'best' people in the west. These technologies exploit and profit is made out of a very vulnerable group of people: women with a fertility problem. The technologies promise hope where there is only more pain. They promise life where there may be death. And in most cases no baby at the end. We have read the women's painful stories in this book and many more remain untold.

There is very little new in the overall ideology of reproductive and genetic engineering – much as its specific technology has broken some new ground (Klein, 1985). The age-old ingredients of patriarchal dominance are all present: it is a woman-hating and inherently eugenic, profit- and fame-seeking 'science'.* The machine logic of dissection and commodification runs at full speed, as does its propaganda machine that coerces infertile people into trying the 'miracle fix-up' and fertile people into getting a 'quality-child', thereby making heaps of money for the pharmaceutical companies, doctors and scientists involved.

It is for these reasons that women have been mounting an opposition to these technologies since 1980. This feminist organizing has led to international and national conferences in the USA, England, Holland, Sweden, Belgium, Austria, Australia, Spain and most notably in Germany.† At the historical Congress 'Frauen gegen Gentechnik und Reproduktionstechnik' in 1985, over 2000 women from all parts of West Germany as well as other European countries and India gathered together: the largest ever event anywhere in the world where women officially recognized the threat of these technologies to women's present and future lives. It was also the first time that reproductive and genetic engineering were discussed jointly and their many tech-

---

* Given all the tampering around with producing embryos in the lab, in theory, a man could have a baby. In 1985 this thought became very fashionable and there were a number of articles and TV programmes around the world discussing this possibility. In the 1970s, a woman without a womb (she had had a hysterectomy) from New Zealand had given birth to a child. The fertilized egg had attached itself to her bowels in the abdomen where it received sufficient nutrients to develop a placenta and mature. With IVF technology an embryo could be inserted into a man's abdominal cavity; there is a place called 'omentum': a fatty tissue loaded with blood vessels. Hormone treatment might sustain the pregnancy, and delivery could be by caesarian.

† For a detailed account of the international feminist resistance since 1980 and its achievements see my chapter in Jocelynne Scutt's *The Baby Machine. Commercialisation of Motherhood* (1988). For the full range of feminist publications including the journal *Reproductive and Genetic Engineering* see FURTHER READING.

nical, ideological and financial interconnections exposed. It is significant that this first strong national reaction took place in Germany; opposition to the technologies has been mounting constantly, culminating in a second national conference which will be held in October 1988. As one of the conference organisers put it: 'German women are so clear on where all this leads; we feel we have a special responsibility to stop it'.

As part of the feminist opposition, an international network was established in 1984: FINNRET, renamed FINRRAGE in 1985 in order to express more clearly that this is not just a network 'on' the technologies, but in fact 'against' them (FINRRAGE stands for *Feminist International Network of Resistance to Reproductive and Genetic Engineering*). From the very beginning it was important to emphasize the crucial connections between infertility-as-disease control in the west and fertility-as-disease control in the so-called 'Third World'. In 1989 FINRRAGE will be holding a conference in Bangladesh co-ordinated by Farida Akhter with the explicit aim of finding common strategies to resist the dumping of harmful contraceptives in one part of the world and the experimentation on women's bodies in another.

Feminist opposition has also had some impact on national politics. Undoubtedly, the German Women's Congress Resolution in 1985 influenced policy recommendations by the Green and Socialist Parties; Robyn Rowland's courage to take a public stand against the technologies in Victoria 1984 has made her a recognized voice in Australia and internationally. Gena Corea's work and political activism together with Janice Raymond's and other women's efforts has been the main force behind establishing, in 1987 in the USA, *The National Coalition against Surrogacy*. And there are many more women in other countries who have been active forces publicly and behind the scenes, among them also a number of heads of Offices for the Status of Women such as State Secretary Johanna Dohnal in Austria, who convened a 'Gene-Hearing' with women experts in June 1987, and the late Francine McKenzie, president of the Conseil du Statut de la Femme who organized a major conference on the new reproductive technologies and genetic engineering in Montreal, Quebec, Canada, in October 1987.

Not surprisingly, there is not much to commend the various

government reports issued so far. The *Warnock Report* in England (1984); the *Ontario Law Reform Commission Report* in Canada (1985); the *Benda Report* in West Germany (1985); the *Senate Select Committee on the Human Embryo Experimentation Bill* in Australia (1986) and a proposal for a law currently pending in Spain have one thing in common: the glaring omission of a discussion of the effects these technologies have on women as human beings in their own right. This is not surprising given the composition of these committees: worthy 'experts' (mostly men) of science, medicine, law, ethics – plus the one or two token community representatives. Whilst these reports may differ in detail, they are all foetus-centred as well as in pursuit of the protection of that most important bastion of patriarchy: the nuclear family. Hence, when women appear in the reports at all, they are discussed as part of 'the couple' which is heterosexual, preferably married, in stable economic circumstances and part of the dominant group of society. In addition to their disregard for women the reports also share the belief that the scientists and doctors developing these techologies 'mean well' and act with integrity: hence they should be entrusted with their own regulation.

Interestingly though, these reports have not yet led to inclusive *national* laws although this may happen in Spain in 1988 and the British Parliament is set to decide on the recommended law based on the Warnock Report in its second legislature period in 1988. In West Germany, opposition to the draft law based on the Benda report and suitably entitled 'Embryo Protection Law' remains fierce and debate lively after the presentation of a government paper in early 1988. An exception to this general slowness (undoubtedly industry and science working behind the scenes to bargain for as much freedom as they can) remains the quick introduction of a law criminalizing commercial surrogacy in Britain in 1985 (such a law is also pending in West Germany).

One notable exception to all these documents which make women invisible should be mentioned. In April 1988, the Commonwealth Department of Community Services and Health in Australia published a report, 'In vitro Fertilisation in Australia' (Batman, 1988 and b) with the main intent of discussing government funding of IVF. The report is critical of IVF, has calculated its success rate for 1986/87 as 8.8 per cent (4.8 per cent for a *total unproblematic live birth*), mentions its experimental nature, questions the safety of the drugs used for women, looks into the increased rates of abnormalities in children born from IVF and asks whether the high expenditure – $A17 million or $A40,500 per baby with a cost to government of $A22,680 – can be expected to be paid by the taxpayer, especially when funding for the National AIDS program was only $A10.1 million and $A32.9 million for the National Community Health Program during the same period. Not surprisingly, the report has been fiercely attacked by doctors and scientists and it remains to be seen whether its criticism will be rejected in proposed policies. Similarly, time will show whether the *National Bioethics Consultative Committee*, established in 1988 (which has some feminist members), also housed in the Department of Community Services and Health, will issue equally critical material.

On a state level, in a number of countries, there have been some moves. In Switzerland, in the Kanton [state] Zurich, there is a moratorium on gene technology, whilst the Kanton St Gallen has prohibited IVF and in the Kanton Basel, legislation is still pending. A number of feminists in influential positions must be credited with these advances.* In the USA, not least because of the efforts of *The Coalition Against Surrogacy*, beginning with New Jersey, a steadily growing number of states is making surrogacy illegal in 1988. In Australia, the state of Victoria (in 1984) and more recently South Australia (1988) have issued laws which are geared towards preventing misuse of the technologies. Unfortunately, they too do not question IVF fundamentally. In 1985 a committee was established under the Victorian Act to administer it – the Standing Review and Advisory Committee chaired by Law Professor Louis Waller. It has been a constant thorn in the side of IVF experts such as Carl Wood and Alan Trounson

---

* However, opponents have appealed to the Federal Court and it remains undecided whether such prohibitions are not, in fact, unconstitutional. Also, a so-called 'public initiative' (submitted by the liberal newspaper *Beobachter*, Zürich, in 1987) which gathered over 120,000 signatures asking the Swiss government to issue laws with regard to gene technology will be discussed in late 1988 or 1989. Unfortunately, the text of the initiative did not consider the effects of these technologies on women.

who have to submit their research proposals and who claim that stringent controls are jeopardizing their leading role in the international scene.

How little they can be trusted, however, and of how negligible importance watchdog committees seem to be, is exemplified by the following tale. In late 1986 the members of the Standing Review and Advisory Committee in Victoria could not reach agreement over the (unanswerable) question 'when does life begin?', prompted by a research proposal submitted by Dr Trounson's team to investigate the effects of microinjection – the injection of one sperm into an egg cell (see Section 2, p. 254) – on human embryos. To place microinjected embryos in the woman's womb without such research, the scientists posited, would be 'ethically irresponsible'. Noble words. Followed by heated debates in the newspapers and a public information day. As a result an amendment to the 1984 Victoria Infertility (Medical Procedures) Act was passed in Parliament in October 1987 allowing embryo experimentation up to 22 hours* – much less than what the scientists wanted: a limit of at least 14 days. This amendment was to be enacted in July 1988.

In April 1988, however, an unidentified 'source' at the Monash University Medical Centre leaked a story to the public. It became known that microinjection *had* been performed and the so created embryos *were* transferred to one or more women's wombs. Forgotten were the noble words about unethical experimentation on humans. Professor Wood now claimed that 'mice studies showed normal foetuses born from microinjection' (Pirrie, 1988a). The Waller Committee had not been informed; it learned indirectly that this work had begun and was 'surprised and

---

* In order to justify this and not another moment as 'the beginning of life' the term 'syngamy', meaning the fusion of the pre-nuclei from the sperm and the egg, was invoked. Not too dissimilar from the invention of the use of 'pre-embryo' in Britain, the term syngamy, supposedly, is to alleviate worries from some conservative circles about 'unborn children'. The same moment has also been chosen by the German lawmakers, but there is a little twist: 'syngamy' as a term is not mentioned; what is mentioned is the first gene product after the fusion of the two pro-nuclei (a molecule called β-Galaktosidase) of – surprise – the *sperm*. No doubt, patriarchy is alive and well (Satzinger, 1988:18).

disconcerted' according to chairman Louis Waller (Voumard, 1988b). The Health Minister then ordered IVF scientists to stop using this technique. With the exception of FINRRAGE-Melbourne members, no one pointed out that this was grossly unethical experimentation on women. And no one pointed out that transferring a microinjected embryo stood in stark contrast to the scientists' own statements of a year ago (September 1987) that evidence from mice was not sufficient to justify direct applications to humans.

But that is not the end of the story. Came July 1988 and the proclamation of the amendment with its 'green light' for embryo experimentation up to 22 hours. 'All-clear for research on 80 embryos' read the headline in Melbourne's *Age* on 14 July (Pirrie, 1988b). But Alan Trounson had already found a way: at a Medical Update Conference in Bangkok a member of a Sydney IVF team announced that Dr Trounson and his team had set up a microinjection laboratory in their Sydney offices: the state of New South Wales has no restrictions on embryo experiments . . . (Downie and Allender, 1988).

The moral of this story is that whatever the loopholes in the legislation, the scientists will find and use them. This is why no *regulatory* legislation will ever guarantee that the fiddling around with women's bodies will end. *Nothing less than legislation to stop IVF and to end the availability of embryos for genetic screening and 'therapy' experimentation will do*.

Rather than relying on ethics committees and national laws to stop the experimentation on women on IVF programmes as well as the invasion of our minds which suggests that we all – fertile and infertile – need any of this technology, we must continue the movement begun by feminists and make it even stronger. By distributing information about what *really* happens in IVF programmes, about what genetic screening *really* entails and about the technologies' long-term consequences for people who do not belong to the dominant group – whatever that means in different countries – we should be able to reach out to a much larger group of people and touch the 'grass roots': those many women in the population at large who will in the future be most affected by such medical 'advances' because, unless informed differently, they will be told that the technologies are all for 'their own good' and that they have to use them.

Most importantly, as Alison Solomon, Lindsey Napier and Ann Pappert stress, it is crucial that women with a fertility problem who have undergone one of the treatments become involved in the fight against reproductive technologies. To this end, this collection is an enormous step forward. For the first time, women who have actually undergone some of the medical procedures – be they of the conventional or the more 'high-tech' variety – have talked about their experiences. And some of the fertile women who have been abused through surrogacy told their stories. I hope their courage will motivate other women to speak out too.

There are no better spokeswomen against these technologies than women who have actually gone through the procedures – and survived. At first this may seem a horrendous idea – haven't they suffered enough? Why put more pressure on them? But 50 years ago, if someone had suggested that women who were raped or sexually harassed speak out against rape (or even more so against rape in marriage), she would have been lectured that such a proposal did not respect the ordeal the raped women had already undergone. Rape victims would have been advised to keep quiet – in their best interest. And yet, it is only thanks to the courageous women who disregarded the advice to 'suffer and be still' but spoke their anger and pain passionately and without fear of ridicule or threats, that gradually a greater recognition of male violence against women and with it some changes in attitudes and laws have occurred.

In that tradition women might speak out like for instance Elizabeth Kane who is one of the co-founders of the US *National Coalition against Surrogacy* and who is now engaged in tremendously important work to dissuade other women from becoming so-called surrogates and to help those who like herself have done it, cope with their pain. As suggested at a FINRRAGE conference, there should also be an *International Tribunal of Medical Crimes Against Women* where global medical violence against women from the 'old' (contraceptives, sterilisation), as well as the 'new' reproductive technologies could be exposed.* Women

---

* Such a tribunal could be modelled on the *International Tribunal of Crimes Against Women* which took place in Brussels in 1976 (organized by Diana Russell; Russell and Van de Ven, 1976) and which contributed greatly to a wider recognition of the many forms of violence against women.

might even take legal action by suing public patriarchy (that is, for instance, IVF programmes) for violence against a woman's basic human right to bodily integrity and dignity. Although the law generally is unsympathetic to women's interests, it may perhaps be possible to devise new laws for prevention, rather than those of protection or prohibition. A lawsuit by IVF patients against their doctors for failing to give them truthful information about the technologies and their long-term effects would shift the terms of the debate: from *our* having to prove to them that these technologies are harmful, to *their* having to prove to us that they are not. Such a suit could perhaps be filed with the United Nations or the European Court at Strasbourg and might contribute to public favour – including funding sources – being turned away from invasive fertility treatments, thus forcing the technodocs to close their clinics and end their research into the manufacturing of future life.

The conceptualization of a different kind of science is crucial: a life-affirming undertaking that assesses a person as a whole and not just as an assembly of parts; that looks at infertility not as a disease, or – worse – a curse, but, as Lindsey Napier put it so well, seeks to understand the many stages of being 'in-fertile', how they often change over time, and sometimes depending on the person one is with. Little is known about the causes of infertility – and what could be done to prevent it (but as many women said in this book, we *do* know that much of it is due to another technological fix – harmful contraceptives – and must make sure that such abuse stops).

In the face of all the pro-technology hype it is often hard to be firm and advise women not to use the technologies. After all, it *might* work . . . there *might* not be serious adverse effects . . . the genetic test *could* spare misery . . . these are difficult decisions. Above all, there is the hesitancy about telling someone else what to do. But in valuing our friends and all women we owe it to them to inform them as best as we can. If we keep quiet, we too are in collusion with the promoters of reproductive technologies.* To decide in favour of the technologies on an

---

* Some people say that to speak out against reproductive and genetic engineering – in particular embryo experimentation – on the one hand, and, on the other, to defend a woman's right to her own decision about

individual level alone and neglect their larger impact on women as a social group is to opt for a dangerously short-sighted option: let us never forget that what operates here is POWER in a variety of forms!

No matter how clear the dangers of the technologies, this alone may not be enough to convince women who think they must 'try everything' not to use them. In addition to warnings against the technologies, what we must also provide are *visions* for a different kind of life: a life without one's own biological children perhaps, a life in which a woman is valued for herself, a life in which women value themselves. This entails nothing less than working towards a society that cherishes a woman's full humanity as an invaluable part of the community; that sees her as a whole person and not as a female incubator destined to give birth. Fertile and infertile, we can all help to de-stigmatize infertility, to remove those feelings of shame, worthlessness and despair of which we have heard many times in these pages.

One of the most important things is to take *seriously* the pain and suffering of women and their partners when their desire for a child of their own cannot be fulfilled. As Traute Schönenberg and Ute Winkler suggest, many varieties of support offered by (feminist) Health and Community Centres may be of immense help. As for any ardent wish that must remain unfulfilled, time is needed to mourn, time is needed to envisage the world anew, time is needed to gather strength to go on – differently. If a strong network of people exists from whom women and men in distress over their un-realized child could seek support till they

---

whether to have – or not to have – an abortion, is a contradiction. This is clearly not so if one's focus is on the *woman's* well-being, rather than on the embryo/foetus. The aim of an abortion is to end a pregnancy that is unwanted; that is, the woman decides to stop her body from functioning in a particular way (i.e. from developing the embryo as part of her body). The aim of reproductive and genetic engineering is to firstly artificially extract parts of women's bodies (eggs or embryos), then manipulate (e.g. screen or perhaps soon engineer) them in the lab and then reinsert them in the woman's body. Abortion and embryo experimentation are two completely different processes and can only be mixed up by people with an embryo-centred perspective in which the focus is on the embryo as an 'unborn child' rather than on the woman as a living human being.

are back on their feet ready to face life again, this would quickly diminish the queues at the Ob. Gyn and IVF clinics and would deprive the technologists of their experimental material. Importantly, these support people might include those who have gone through the life crisis of infertility themselves, survived it – and thrived, as Alison Solomon would add – *without* using the technologies, particularly the various forms of IVF. Role models are important; people who demonstrate with their very existence that a child'free' life can be happy, creative, exciting, and that it allows for plenty of 'giving' and 'nurturing' (in a positive rather than a destructive sense) can make the difference between deciding to let go and be without child – or entering the emotional and physical trauma of years of poking and probing. Thus counseling OUT of technology is what is needed, *not* counseling for a woman once she is on the IVF programme which amounts to counseling *to stay on* IVF, whatever the odds.

There is still time to stop the technopatriarchal clock that races towards a future of people 'made to order' – an un-humanness of an unprecedented degree. It is not too late. Immature eggs cannot yet be matured . . . the artificial womb is not yet perfected. Living women still play the most important role in the technological set-up. May the voices of the women in this book increase a movement with a strong basis in international feminist solidarity that resists the technologies and says *no* with passion.

REFERENCES

Bartels, Ditta. 1988. Built-in obsolescence: Women, embryo production and genetic engineering. *Reproductive and Genetic Engineering: Journal of International Feminist Analysis* 1(2): 141–152.

Batman, Gail. 1988a. *In-vitro fertilisation in Australia*. Commonwealth Department of Community Services and Health, Canberra, Australia.

Batman, Gail. 1988b. *Commonwealth Perspectives on IVF Funding*. A Discussion Paper. Commonwealth Department of Community Services and Health, Canberra, Australia.

Ben-Rafael, Z. et al. 1986. Treatment-independent pregnancy after *in vitro* fertilization and embryo transfer. *Fertility and Sterility 45*: 564.

Blakeslee, Sandra. 1987a. Trying to Make Money Making 'Test-Tube'. *The New York Times*, Sunday, May 17.

Blakeslee, Sandra. 1987b. A baby born without her brain is kept alive to donate her heart. *The New York Times*. October 19: 4.

Bolton, P. M. 1977. Bilateral Breast Cancer Associated with Clomiphene. *The Lancet*, December 3: 1176.

Boston Globe. 1987. Clinic to provide pool of human eggs. July 15.

Bullard, Linda. 1987. Killing Us Softly. Towards a Feminist Analysis of Genetic Engineering. In *Made to Order. The Myth of Reproductive and Genetic Progress*, eds Patricia Spallone and Deborah L. Steinberg, Athene Series, Pergamon Press, Oxford and New York: 110–119.

Bulletti, Carlo et al. 1988. Early human pregnancy in vitro utilizing an artificially perfused uterus. *Fertility and Sterility 49* (6): 991–996.

Bunkle, Phillida. 1984. Calling the Shots? The international politics of depo-provera. In *Test-Tube Women. What Future for Motherhood?*, edited by Rita Arditti et al., Pandora Press, London and Boston: 165–187.

Burfoot, Annette. 1988. A Review of the Third Annual Meeting of the European Society of Human Reproduction and Embryology. *Reproductive and Genetic Engineering: Journal of International Feminist Analysis 1* (1):107–111.

Carter, Marian E. and David Joyce, 1987. Ovarian Carcinoma in a Patient Hyperstimulated by Gonadotropin Therapy for In Vitro Fertilisation: A Case Report. *Journal of In Vitro Fertilisation and Embryo Transfer 4* (2): 126–128.

Charbonnel, Bernard et al. 1987. Induction of Ovulation in Polycystic Ovary Syndrome with a Combination of a Luteinizing Hormone-Releasing Hormone Analog and Exogenous Gonadotropins. *Fertility and Sterility 47*:920.

Chargaff, Erwin. 1987. Engineering a molecular nightmare. *Nature 327:* 199–200.

Collard, Andrée and Joyce Contrucci. 1988. *The Rape of the Wild*. The Women's Press, London.

Collins, John A. et al. 1983. Treatment-independent pregnancy among infertile couples. *New England Journal of Medicine 309* (20), 17 November: 1201–1206.

Coney, Sandra. 1988. *The Unfortunate Experiment. The Full Story Behind the Inquiry into Cervical Cancer Treatment*. Penguin Books, Melbourne.

Corea, Gena. 1984. Egg snatchers. In *Test-Tube Women. What Future for Motherhood?* edited by Rita Arditti et al., Pandora Press, London and Boston: 37–51.

Corea, Gena. 1985. *The Mother Machine. Reproductive Technologies from Artificial Insemination to Artificial Wombs*. Harper and Row, New York; The Women's Press, London, UK, 1988.

Corea, Gena and Susan Ince. 1987. Report of a Survey of IVF Clinics in the USA. In *Made to Order. The Myth of Reproductive and Genetic*

Progress edited by Patricia Spallone and Deborah L. Steinberg. Pergamon Press, Oxford and New York: 110–119.

Crandall, B. F. et al. 1986. Maternal age and amniocentesis: should this be lowered to 30 years? *Prenatal Diagnosis 6*: 237–242.

Cunha, G. R. et al., 1987. Teratogenic Effects of Clomiphene, Tamoxifen, and Diethylstilbestrol on the Developing Human Female Genital Tract. *Human Pathology 18*: 1132–43.

Davies, David. 1986. Embryo Research. *Nature 320*:208, March 20.

Der Spiegel. 1987. Einen atmenden Leichnam begraben. *52*, December 21:163.

Deutsche Forschungsgesellschaft. 1987. *Stellungnahme zu dem Diskussionsentwurf eines Embryonenschutzgesetzes*. Bonn, March 9.

Direcks, Anita and Holmes, Helen Bequaert. 1986. Miracle Drug, Miracle Baby. *New Scientist*. November 6:53–55.

Downie, Sue. 1988. Is microinjection down for the count? *The Australian*, Australian Woman, July 11.

Downie, Sue and Jackie Allender. 1988. IVF man takes embryo work to NSW. *The Australian*. July 8.

Dworkin, Andrea. 1983. *Right-Wing Women. The Politics of Domesticated Females*. Perigree Books, New York/The Women's Press, London.

Ewing, Christine. 1988. Tailored Genes: IVF, Genetic Engineering and Eugenics in *Reproductive and Genetic Engineering: Journal of International Feminist Analysis 1*(1): 31–40.

Ferry, Georgina. 1987. No extra genes in Alzheimer's disease. *New Scientist*, November 19: 32.

Flanagan, Josephine. Stock breeders choose a ritzy setting to flush out embryo buyers. *The Herald*, Melbourne, September 21:5.

Ford, W. D. A. and K. E. T. Little. 1981. Fetal Ovarian Dysplasia Possibly Associated with Clomiphene. *The Lancet*, November 14: 1107.

Gen-Ethischer Informationsdienst (GID). 1988. Meldung: Oesterreich foerdert Hormon-Produktion. No. 33, June 12.

Gorwill, Hugh et al. 1982. Heterotopic Columnar Epithelium and Adenosis in the Vagina of the Mouse after Neonatal Treatment with Clomiphene Citrate. *American Journal of Obstetrics and Gynecology 144* (5): 529–32.

Gluyas, Richard. 1988. Nature makes choice in chosen IVF technique. *The Australian*, April 4.

Hubbard, Ruth and Sheldon Krimsky. 1988. The Patented Mouse. *Gene WATCH 5* (1):6–7.

Ince, Susan. 1987. High-Tech Pregnancy. *Savvy*. June: 79–81.

Indian Express (Bombay). 1985. Infertility afflicts 110 million. June 9.

India Today. 1986. Test-Tube Babies Made in India. July 15: 78–80.

Johnston, Kathy. 1987. Sex of new embryos known. *Nature 327*:547.

Joyce, Christopher. 1987. Genes reach the medical market. *New Scientist* 16. July: 45–46.

Joyce, Christopher. 1987. Geneticists find the gene that determines sex. *New Scientist* 24/31 December: 29.

Kaupen-Haas, Heidrun. 1988. Experimental Obstetrics and National Socialism: The Conceptual Basis of Reproductive Technology. *Reproductive and Genetic Engineering: Journal of International Feminist Analysis 1*(2): 127–132.

Klein, Renate. 1985. What's 'New' about the 'New' Reproductive Technologies? In *Man-Made Women*, Gena Corea et al., Hutchinson Press, London; Indiana University Press, 1987.

Klein, Renate. 1988a. Segen oder Fluch? Reproduktions- und Gentechnologie aus feministischer Sicht. In *Kinder machen. Strategien der Kontrolle weiblicher Fruchtbarkeit*, by Gertrude Pauritsch et al. Wiener Frauenverlag, Austria.

Klein, Renate. 1988b. *The Exploitation of a Desire: Women's Experiences with IVF*. An Exploratory Survey, Women's Studies, Deakin University.

Klein, Renate. 1988c. Biotechnology and the Future of Humanity. *Women's Worlds. ISIS-Wicce*. March (Part I) and June (Part II).

Klein, Renate. 1988d. Genetic and Reproductive Engineering: The Global View. In *The Baby Machine, Commercialization of Motherhood*, edited by Jocelynne Scutt, McCulloch, Melbourne.

Klein, Renate/Robyn Rowland. 1988. Women as Test-Sites for Fertility Drugs: Clomiphene Citrate and Hormonal Cocktails. *Reproductive and Genetic Engineering: Journal of International Feminist Analysis 1* (3).

Kramer, Michael. 1985. Last chance babies: the wonders of in vitro fertilization. *New York Magazine:* 34–42.

Laborie, Françoise. 1988. New reproductive technologies. News from France and elsewhere. *Reproductive and Genetic Engineering. Journal of International Feminist Analysis 1* (1): 77–86.

Leuzinger, Monika and Bigna Rambert. 1987. 'Ich spuer' es – mein Kind ist gesund' in *Genzeit*, by Claudia Roth, Limmatverlag, Zürich; 1988 'I Can Feel It – My Baby Is Healthy'. *Reproductive and Genetic Engineering: Journal of International Feminist Analysis 1* (3):239–49.

Lilford, Richard J. and Maureen E. Dalton. 1987. Effectiveness of Treatment for Infertility. *British Medical Journal 295* (July 18): 155–6.

Lipovenko, Dorothy. 1984. Fertility Drug Causes Tissue Changes in Mice, MD says. *The Globe and Mail*, Toronto, May 14: 3.

McDonnell, Dan. 1988. IVF professor blasts critics. *The Sun*, Melbourne, June 8.

McLaren, Anne. 1987. Can we diagnose genetic disease in pre-embryos? *New Scientist*, December 10: 42–47.

McIntosh, Philip. 1988. Birth defects claim fuels campaign against IVF. *The Age*, Melbourne, January 8.

Mies, Maria. 1987. Sexist and Racist Implications of New Reproductive Technologies. *Alternatives XII*: 323–342.

Miller, Calvin. 1988a. Disease and Genes. Medical File, *The Herald*, Melbourne, September 15.

Miller, Calvin. 1988b. The brain-dead could be surrogates, say scientists. *The Herald*, Melbourne, June 26.

Miller, Calvin. 1988c. Gear IVF to under 35s – expert. *The Herald*, Melbourne, August 22.

Miller, Calvin. 1988d. Scientists set to 'ripen' human eggs in millions. *The Herald*, Melbourne, June 29.

Miller, Calvin. 1988e. When a foetus is a mother. *Australian Doctor*. May 27.

MIMS Annual, 1984. 1987. MIMS Publishing, New South Wales, Australia.

National Perinatal Statistics Unit and the Fertility Society of Australia. 1987. IVF and GIFT Pregnancies, Australia and New Zealand 1986. National Perinatal Statistics Unit, Sydney.

Nature. 1982. New UK row on embryo research. September 30, *299*:383.

Ob. Gyn News. 1987. Wants Preconceptional Care to Be Routine Practice. *22* (9), May 1–14.

Ob. Gyn News. 1987. Intravaginal Culture, Embryo Transfer Could Reduce Cost of IVF. *22* (12), August 1–14:30.

Ob. Gyn. News. 1987. Shift to Prevention of Genetic Anomalies Predicted for IVF Research. *22* (2), August 1–14:28.

Pappert, Ann. 1988. Critics Worry Women Not Told of Fertilisation Program Risks. *The Globe and Mail*, Toronto, February 6: 14.

Patel, Vibhuti. 1987a. Eliminate Inequality, Not Women. *Connexions 25*, Winter 1987:2–3.

Patel, Vibhuti. 1987b. Campaign against Amniocentesis. In *In Search of Our Bodies. A Feminist Look at Women, Health and Reproduction in India*, by Kamakshi Bhate et al., Shakti Publishing Company, Bombay: 70–74.

Pepperell, Roger and Henry Burger. 1988. Clomiphene. Letter to the Editor. *The Medical Journal of Australia, 149*, July 4:50.

Pirrie, Michael. 1988a. New IVF treatment stopped. *The Age*, Melbourne, April 2.

Pirrie, Michael. 1988b. All clear for research on 80 embryos. *The Age*, Melbourne, July 14.

Plachot, Michelle et al. 1986. Chromosome Investigations in Early Life. I. Human Oocytes Recovered in an IVF Programme. *Human Reproduction 1* (8): 547–551.

Pollack, Andrew. 1987. Gene-Splicing Payoff is Near. *Business Day*, June 10: S1, D6.

Postgate, John. 1973. Bat's chance in hell. *New Scientist 5*: 11–16.

Ravindra, R. P. 1986. *The Scarcer Half*. Counterfact No. 9; Centre for Education and Documentation, Bombay.

Reid, Sue. Labour of Love. *The Story of the World's First Surrogate Grandmother*. The Bodley Head, London.

Roh, Sung, I. et al. 1987. In vitro fertilization and embryo transfer: treatment-dependent versus -independent pregnancies. *Fertility and Sterility 48* (6), December 1987: 982–986.

Rothman, Barbara Katz. 1986. *The Tentative Pregnancy. Prenatal Diagnosis and the Future of Motherhood*. Viking Penguin Inc., New York; Pandora Press, London, 1988.

Rowland, Robyn. 1984. Reproductive Technologies: The Final Solution to the Woman Question? In Arditti et al. (eds), *Test-Tube Women. What Future for Motherhood?* Pandora Press, London and Boston: 356–370.

Rowland, Robyn. 1987a. Making Women Visible in the Embryo Experimentation Debate. *Bioethics* 1(2): 179–188.

Rowland, Robyn. 1987b. Women – the Silent Victims of IVF Research. *The Herald*, Melbourne, October 2.

Royal Society. 1983. *Human Fertilisation and Embryology*. London.

Russell, Diana and Nicole Van de Ven. 1976. *Crimes Against Women*, Les Femmes; rpt. 1984, Frog in the Well, Oakland, CA.

Rutherford, A. J. et al. 1988. Improvement of in vitro fertilisation after treatment with buserelin, an agonist of luteinising hormone releasing hormone. *British Medical Journal 296*, June 25: 1765–1768.

Sanger, Elizabeth. 1988. A Fertile Line of Work. *City Business, New York Newsday*, May 9.

Satzinger, Helga. 1988. Wider die Ermordung der Nachtigall. Zur Ethik-Debatte in der Embryonenforschung. *Wechselwirkung 37*, May: 15–19.

Sheeran, Thomas J. 1988. Donor Egg Program Results in Two Pregnancies. *Associated Press*, July 17.

Smith, Richard. 1988. The race for the human genome. *British Medical Journal 297*: 577.

Stanley, Fiona J. 1988. In vitro fertilization – a gift for the infertile or a cycle of despair? *The Medical Journal of Australia 148* (May 2): 425–426.

The Australian Women's Weekly. 1988. The Next 200 Years, January: 75–77.

The Economist. 1988. Human egg banks. Frozen to life. May 14: 126.

The Guardian (London). 1987. Prenatal test could eliminate hare lip. August 27:4.

The Independent (London). 1988. Test-Tube for dairy farmers. March 23.

The Voluntary Licensing Authority for Human In Vitro Fertilisation and Embryology (VLA). 1988. *Third Report*. London, UK.

Thorpe, Deryn. 1988. IVF expertise now exported worldwide. *The Australian*. January 18.

Times of India. 1987. Tube baby will boost FP schemes. May 6.

Treweek, Ann. 1988. Coroner investigates IVF patient deaths. *Australian Dr Weekly*, May 5.

Turney, John. 1985. Embryo Guidelines set out. *The Times Higher Education Supplement*, England, June 14.

Veitch, Andrew. 1985. 'Back to Nature Cure' for Infertile Women. *The Guardian*, London, November 24.

Vines, Gail. 1986. Whose baby is it anyway? *New Scientist* III: 26–27.

Vines, Gail. 1987a. Better Ways of Breeding. *New Scientist*. August 13: 51–54.

Vines, Gail. 1987b. Choosing sex to beef up cattle farming. *New Scientist*, September 17:42.

Vines, Gail, 1987c. Calves a la carte. *New Scientist*. December 3: 23.

Voumard, Sonja. 1988a. Fertility drug defended against cancer charges. *The Age*, Melbourne, June 20.

Voumard, Sonja. 1988b. Surprise at move to apply IUF techniques. *The Age*, Melbourne, April 4.

Wainwright, Robert. 1987. Union raises VDU fears. *The West Australian*, December 22:5.

Wattenberg, Ben. 1987. *The Birth Dearth*. Pharos Books, New York.

Wheale, Peter and Ruth McNally. 1988. Genetic Engineering. *Catastrophe or Utopia?* Harvester, Wheatshelf, England/St. Martin's Press, New York.

Williamson, Nancy. 1976. *Sons or daughters. A cross-cultural survey of parental preferences*. Sage, London.

Wramsby, Hakan and P. Liedholm. 1984. A Gradual Fixation Method for Chromosomal Preparations of Human Oocytes. *Fertility and Sterility 41*: 736–738.

Wramsby, Hakan et al. 1987. Chromosome Analysis of Human Oocytes Recovered From Preovulatory Follicles in Stimulated Cycles. *New England Journal of Medicine 316* (3): 121–124.

Yee, Billy and Vargyas, Joyce M. 1986. Multiple Follicle Development Utilising Combinations of Clomiphene Citrate and Human Menopausal Gonadotropins. *Clinical Obstetrics and Gynecology 29* (1): 141–47.

GLOSSARY

.

adenosis A disease of glandular tissue, especially one involving abnormal proliferation or occurrence of glandular tissue (e.g. vaginal adenosis).

adhesions Scar tissue resulting from infection, surgery or bleeding which can distort or cause dysfunction of bodily organs.

amenorrhoea in women Absence of menstruation. Amenorrhoea can result from the use of chemical (hormonal) contraceptives. See **post-pill amenorrhoea**.

amniocentesis A pre-natal diagnostic test performed on a woman after the fourteenth week (usually not before the sixteenth week) of her pregnancy. It is used to diagnose certain 'foetal abnormalities' (such as **spina bifida**). The procedure carries risks, and errors in diagnosis may occur. The pregnant woman is given a local anaesthetic and a needle is inserted through her abdominal wall and into her womb. A sample of her amniotic fluid is withdrawn, cultured and analysed to detect 'abnormalities' which have been associated by scientists with certain genes and biochemical conditions. Chromosome analysis also detects foetal sex. See **sex predetermination**.

analogue (chemical) A chemical compound structurally similar to another but differing often by a single element of the same valence and group of the periodic table as the element it replaces.

artificial insemination A simple procedure by which sperm is deposited in a woman's vagina as close to her cervix as possible. Although this procedure is performed on women in clinical or hospital settings by medical practitioners, it can easily be performed by a woman herself.

basal body temperature The temperature of the person's body at rest. Women chart changes in their body temperature in order to monitor their menstrual cycles, especially to locate their time of ovulation (e.g. the temperature method of birth control). Doctors use these charts to interpret women's menstrual hormonal cycles, often in order to intervene and alter them with drugs. In the **in vitro fertilization treatment**, women are asked to chart their temperature (or it is done for them by hospital staff) to enable doctors to monitor women's (chemically induced) ovulation (**superovulation**) and time the egg collection procedure.

cervical mucus test An analysis of a man's semen which requires intervention on women. A sample of a woman's cervical mucus is used as a medium into which semen is placed in order to assess sperm motility (movement) and speed. Also called the cervical mucus penetration test.

cervical smear A specimen of cellular material is scraped from the neck (**cervix**) of a woman's womb and examined under a microscope in order to determine whether abnormal cells or cancer are present.

cervix A ring of flexible muscle at the base of a woman's uterus which extends into her vagina.

chlamydia A sexually transmitted disease which, if not diagnosed and treated in time, can lead to **pelvic inflammatory disease** and fertility problems in women. Women who have chlamydia often experience no symptoms. At present preventive screening seems to be the best way of minimizing the incidence of chlamydia and the secondary infections which can seriously damage women's internal organs.

choriohic villi sampling (CVS) A **pre-natal diagnostic** procedure for analysis of a woman's foetal tissue. A small amount of chorion tissue surrounding her foetus is removed through her cervix. It is performed at eight to fourteen weeks of pregnancy, and results can be evaluated overnight. Preliminary studies show it poses a greater risk to women of miscarriage than **amniocentesis**. Other attendant risks have yet to be determined. There has been variable success in obtaining women's villi for analysis, and a greater risk of error in diagnosis.

chromosomes Thread-like structures in the nucleus of a cell where genes are located.

Clomid A trade name for **clomiphene citrate**.

clomiphene citrate A synthetic **oestrogen** which, in chemical structure, resembles DES. It is administered to induce women's ovulation, presumably by interfering with the oestrogen receptors in her brain. The drug has many adverse effects, including **hyperstimulation** (over-stimulation) and enlargement of a woman's ovaries with the risk of rupture. Other effects include nausea, hot flushes and visual blurring. It is used in **in vitro fertilization** treatment to induce women to **superovulate**.

cloning The laboratory production of genetically identical organisms.

corpus luteum The yellow 'body' which develops from a woman's follicle after she ovulates and which produces **progesterone** and **oestrogen**.

DES (diethylstilbestrol) A synthetic oestrogen which was frequently given to pregnant women from the 1940s to 1950s in the belief that it prevented miscarriage. It was never proven effective in preventing miscarriage and has been found to cause cancer and other severe problems both in the women who were given the drug and their offspring – in particular their daughters. It is still used as a 'morning after' (contraceptive) pill.

ectogenesis A 'pregnancy' which in theory will begin and continue until 'birth' outside a woman's body in an 'artificial womb'.

ectopic pregnancy A woman's pregnancy which occurs in her **fallopian tube** rather than her uterus. An ectopic pregnancy can never come to term. It is a dangerous condition and always requires surgical intervention to save the woman's life. She will nevertheless almost always lose her fallopian tube.

egg collection A name given to procedures used by doctors when treating women with **in vitro fertilization**. After women are **superovulated** practitioners surgically remove women's eggs from their bodies so that they can be fertilized in a petri dish. Other names for the procedure include 'egg pick-up' and 'egg retrieval'. See **laparoscopic egg collection** and **ultrasound scanning**.

embryo flushing The procedure of 'washing out' a woman's fertilized egg from her womb before implanting it in another woman's womb. This procedure can also be used to remove a woman's fertilized egg for diagnostic assessment (genetic and biochemical screening) before reimplanting it back in her womb. Also called surrogate embryo transfer.

embryo replacement (ER) A procedure used in conjunction with **in vitro fertilization** treatment on women in which a doctor inserts a catheter into a woman's vagina, through her cervix and into her womb. The doctor then transfers the eggs (which have been fertilized *in vitro*) into the womb. This is the final phase of *in vitro* fertilization. Also called **embryo transfer** when the woman receiving treatment is not the same woman who provided the (fertilized) egg(s).

endometrial biopsy A procedure used on women to diagnose ovarian dysfunction and as a screening test for carcinoma (cancer) of the uterus. It is performed by doctors with either a cutting instrument or by passing a hollow curet through a woman's vagina, into her womb. Using suction, fragments of her endometrium (the lining of her uterus) are aspirated into the curet. The procedure is painful for women and doctors are advised to take as few strokes of the curet as possible.

endometriosis A painful condition of the female reproductive system in which the lining of a woman's womb sticks to other organs in her body. It often leads to fertility problems (of varying degrees) and can cause a woman very painful periods and pain during intercourse.

estrogen See **oestrogen**.

fallopian tubes Two tubes which lead from the top of a woman's uterus and end with fine finger-like projections near her ovaries.

fibroids Uterine tumours which are composed primarily of smooth muscle. Hence the term 'fibroid', which means fibrous tissue, is a misnomer. Doctors consider the correct name for this condition to be **myomas**. This condition is common, usually without symptoms and usually benign (non-cancerous). While they can occur as isolated microscopic growths, they are more commonly multiple and may (uncommonly) grow to enormous proportions. In most instances, myomas do not require treatment, particularly if there are no symptoms. Countless women with insignificant myomas have been subjected to unnecessary hysterectomies.

follicle An enclosing cluster of cells that protects and nourishes a structure within. Follicles in the ovaries surround the developing eggs. The follicular fluid, which encases the developing egg within the follicle, is an often-used component in **in vitro fertilization** research and treatment.

frozen embryos Early embryos, removed from women with **in vitro fertilization** procedures and then placed in a serum and other chemicals to minimize damage at low temperatures, which can be frozen in liquid nitrogen at a temperature of $-196°F$. A technique now exists for freezing women's eggs (with markedly less success). The long-term effects of the freezing procedures on the women in whom these frozen embryos and gametes are reimplanted and on their offspring are unknown.

gamete intrafallopian tube transfer (GIFT) A variation of **in vitro fertilization** in which eggs collected from a woman (with the same procedures as in the original *in vitro* fertilization treatment regime) and sperm are injected into the woman's **fallopian tube** so that fertilization can take place there instead of in the laboratory dish.

genetic counseling An advice service offered by medical scientists which fosters the (eugenic) philosophy of selective breeding, which aims to both increase the propagation of 'desirable' human traits and decrease the propagation of 'undesirable' types. Counselors take the medical history of a man and woman who wish to reproduce together in order to determine an 'inheritance pattern' of traits which are socially and/or medically defined to be undesirable. Based on this medical pedigree, counsellors assess the statistical probability of producing 'genetically damaged' offspring.

gonadotrophin releasing hormone (GnRH) In a woman: a hormone produced in her **hypothalamus** which causes her to release follicle stimulating hormone (FSH) and luteinizing hormone (LH) from her **pituitary gland**. All three hormones play an important role in a woman's menstrual cycle, particularly in the maturation of her **follicles** and ovulation. They are also part of a woman's overall endocrine (hormone) system.

haemorrhage Bleeding. The escape of blood from a ruptured vessel internally or externally. Rupture of a major blood vessel can lead to the loss of several litres of blood in a few minutes, resulting in shock, collapse and death, if untreated.

'hormone cocktail' A mixture (cocktail) of hormone drugs. These hormone drug mixtures are often administered to women as part of both conventional infertility treatments and **in vitro fertilization**. Both the short- and long-term effects of such drug mixtures on women and their offspring are virtually unknown.

human chorionic gonadotrophin (HCG) A hormone used as a

drug in infertility treatments and in **in vitro fertilization** treatment, usually in conjunction with other drugs such as **Clomid** and **Pergonal** to induce women to **superovulate**. It is extracted from the urine of pregnant women. HCG is sold under the trade name **Pregnyl**.

human menopausal gonadotrophin (HMG) A commercial preparation of two hormones (FSH and LH, follicle-stimulation hormone and luteinizing hormone) which are part of a woman's menstrual cycle. It is extracted from the urine of newly menopausal women. HMG stimulates women's **follicle** development. It is extremely powerful and the risks include **hyperstimulation** (overstimulation) and enlargement of a woman's ovaries, with a serious risk of rupture. It is administered to women in both conventional infertility treatments (posing a serious risk of multiple pregnancy) and **in vitro fertilization**. HMG is sold under the trade name **Pergonal**.

hypothalamus The gland at the base of the brain which influences the release of hormones from the **pituitary gland**.

hyperstimulation Overstimulation of a woman's ovaries as a result of the administration of hormone drugs to induce **superovulation**. Hyperstimulation can lead to ovarian enlargement or rupture of a woman's ovary(ies). See 'hormone cocktail', **human chorionic gonadotrophin, human menopausal gonadotrophin**, and **superovulation**.

hysterectomy (subtotal) The surgical removal of a woman's womb, leaving her cervix intact in her body. In a total hysterectomy, a woman's womb and cervix are removed.

hysterosalpinogram X-ray examination of a woman's uterus and fallopian tubes using a radio-opaque dye (liquid radiographic contrast medium) injected into her uterus under pressure. This technique is performed on women without general anaesthetic, in order to detect anatomical abnormalities. Results are misinterpreted in 25 per cent of cases.

iatrogenic infertility A condition of physiological infertility that has resulted from medical intervention. This condition is sometimes known as 'doctor induced' infertility and is most common in women. Common causes of iatrogenic infertility in women include failure to prevent (through preventive screening for diseases such as **chlamydia**), diagnose or properly treat **pelvic inflammatory disease**. Other causes include septic (usually illegal) abortions, and infection following abdominal surgery.

idiopathic infertility Unexplained infertility. No physiological cause, after examination by a doctor, can be found to explain why a woman (with or without the same male partner) has not become pregnant, usually after a year or more of trying.

illiac veins The veins draining most of the blood from a person's lower limbs and pelvic region.

intravascular thrombosis The formation of a blood clot within a blood vessel.

IUD (copper IUD) Intra-uterine device. A contraceptive device which is inserted into a woman's uterus to inhibit conception. IUDs frequently cause a great damage to a woman's womb and other internal organs (usually by causing infections such as **pelvic inflammatory disease**) and can lead to **iatrogenic infertility**.

IVF (*in vitro*) fertilization 'Test-tube baby' technique. The Latin phrase '*in vitro* fertilization' means literally 'fertilization in glass'. As such the term conceals more than it describes. What is referred to as IVF actually entails a long series of procedures performed on women at great risk to their health and that of their offspring. In the first phase of IVF treatment, a series of hormone drugs is administered to induce them to **superovulate**. In the second phase of treatment, women's (chemically matured) eggs are surgically removed from their bodies with one of several **egg collection** procedures. In the third phase of treatment, the eggs are fertilized by IVF practitioners in a laboratory dish. Finally, women's fertilized eggs are reimplanted into their bodies (**embryo replacement**). IVF treatment is almost always unsuccessful; women undergoing treatment will often have to repeat some or all of the treatment phases several times and will very rarely end up having a baby. The risks posed as a result of treatment to women's health (and that of their offspring) are largely unknown, though evidence suggests that they are likely to be very serious, perhaps immeasurably so.

laparoscopic egg collection A procedure in which women's eggs are removed during laparoscopy by the insertion of a laparoscope, a suction device and forceps for grasping a woman's ovary. It requires three incisions in a woman's abdomen, general anaesthesia and distension of her abdomen with carbon dioxide gas mixture. Laparoscopic egg collection is one method of **egg collection** used on women undergoing **in vitro fertilization** treatment.

laparoscopy Visual examination of women's ovaries (or other abdominal organs) by insertion of a laparoscope (light guide) through a small incision in a woman's abdominal wall.

micro-surgery (tubal) See **tubal surgery**.

neoplastic growth A tumour.

oestrogen A collective term for a group of naturally occurring hormones with a variety of functions; for example oestrogen is necessary to complete the development (maturing) of women's eggs during her menstrual cycle. Synthetic oestrogens are drugs produced in laboratories which are similar in chemical structure to naturally occurring oestrogens, but not identical. Their function is to alter or interfere with the natural production of various hormones in women's menstrual cycle.

pelvic inflammatory disease (PID) In women, any infection and inflammation of their pelvic organs which is caused by bacteria or viruses. The infection often localizes in a woman's **fallopian tubes** and can cause irreparable damage from scarring. This scarring is a cause of fertility problems. PID is often a secondary infection most commonly following un/mis-diagnosed or un/mis-treated sexually transmitted diseases, the most common of which is **chlamydia**. PID is often iatrogenic (doctor induced), either resulting from medical negligence or malpractice in the treatment of conditions (like chlamydia), or following as a complication from poorly performed abdominal surgery or botched abortions (usually illegal). By extension, fertility problems for women which result from PID can also be said to be iatrogenic. See **iatrogenic infertility**.

Pergonal A trade name for **human menopausal gonadotrophin**.

pituitary gland A hormone producing gland in the brain.

pleural effusion A condition in which fluid is trapped between the membrane covering a person's chest wall (parietal pleura) and the membrane covering their lungs (visceral pleura).

post-coital test Examination by doctors of a woman's cervical mucus, after she has had intercourse, in order to assess her male partner's sperm quality.

post-pill amenorrhoea A condition in women where their menstruation does not return after they cease taking contraceptive drugs. Post-pill amenorrhoea is a common adverse effect of contraceptive pills.

Pregnyl A trade name for **human chorionic gonadotrophin**.

prenatal diagnosis Diagnostic techniques for assessing the condition of a pregnant woman's foetus. See **amniocentesis**.

Primolut-Depot Hexanoate A synthetic progestational steroid hormone which has actions similar to those of **progesterone**. It is administered to women, by intramuscular injection, to prevent miscarriage and to treat uterine disorders and **amenorrhoea**. Primulut-Depot Hexanoate is a trade name for Hydroxyprogesterone.

Primolut N. A synthetic progestational steroid hormone which is administered in pill form to women, generally in conjunction with oestrogens, to inhibit women's ovulation (as a contraceptive drug). It is also used in the treatment of **amenorrhoea** to bring on withdrawal bleeding and for the opposite effect, to delay or prevent women's menstruation. It is used to treat premenstrual tension, to relieve dysmenorrhoea (painful periods) and to treat **endometriosis**. Adverse effects include: headaches, tension, depression, nausea, vomiting, breast engorgement, fluid retention, weight gain, a state of pseudo (false) pregnancy, aggravation of pre-menstrual tension, breakthrough bleeding, hirsutism (excessive hairiness), skin rashes (acne), deepening of the voice and virilization of a female foetus. Prolonged use can lead to liver impairment. Regular use of progestational oral contraceptives combined with oestrogens increases risk of **intravascular thrombosis**. Progesterone-only contraceptives may cause **ectopic pregnancies** and may not prevent conception. Primulut N. is a trade name for norethisterone. Another trade name is Noriday.

progesterone A hormone produced in a woman's ovaries after ovulation, and by her placenta during her pregnancy. Synthetic progesterones were first developed for use as contraceptives. They work by interfering with the processes necessary for ovulation, egg movement, development of her uterine lining and cervical mucus production. They have immediate adverse effects, such as irregular bleeding. Little is known of the longterm effects, and risks may include loss of fertility and alterations in the immunological system. They are also prescribed to treat pre-menstrual tension and fertility problems – for example to prevent miscarriage.

retroverted uterus When a woman's womb is tipped back so that the cervix (the neck of her womb) points toward the pubic symphysis (the bone under the pubic hair).

salpingoophorectomy The surgical removal of a woman's **fallopian tube** and ovary. In a bilateral salpingoophorectomy, both fallopian tubes and both ovaries are removed from a woman's body.

secondary infertility The diagnostic term used by doctors to describe the situation where women, who have had previous pregnancies and/or children, have not, by the time they seek medical consultation, become pregnant again (usually after a year or more of trying).

septicaemia Widespread destruction of tissues due to absorption of disease-causing bacteria or their toxins from the bloodstream. Blood poisoning.

sex predetermination A term which refers to either (i) the identification of the sex of an already existing embryo (e.g. during **amniocentesis** or pre-implantation screening of an *in vitro* embryo) for the purpose of, or effectively facilitating, selection (by abortion, or selective reimplanation) of a 'desired' sex of offspring; or (ii) the engineering of the sex of an embryo before fertilization occurs (e.g. by selecting sperm according to the gender which they are coded for). Also called sex pre-selection.

sperm count A laboratory investigation of a sample of a man's semen to ascertain the number of sperm. Other sperm tests include those to determine the shape (morphology), size and ability to move (motility).

spina bifida A developmental defect in which a newborn baby has part of its spinal chord and its coverings exposed through a gap in its backbone. Spina bifida is associated with high levels of alpha-feto-protein in a woman's amniotic fluid. See **amniocentesis**.

superovulation The process whereby a woman is administered a regimen of fertility drugs and hormones to induce her to mature and ovulate more than one egg at a single menstrual cycle. In **in vitro fertilization**, women are superovulated so that several of their eggs can be surgically removed from their bodies (**egg collection**) at one time and then fertilized in a laboratory dish. Women's surgically removed eggs can also be used for 'egg or embryo donation', for egg or embryo freezing, for experimentation, or for other procedures such as **gamete intrafallopian transfer**. The risks to the women from the use of superovulatory drugs include **hyperstimulation** of their ovaries and the formation of cysts, both of which can be serious conditions and can adversely affect fertility, jeopardize general health and even cause death (e.g. from rupture of ovaries). The long-term risks of superovulation regimens has not been actively investigated by those who have developed and used these drugs on women. However, it has been noted that some of the drugs used are chemically similar to known carcinogens such as **DES**.

surrogacy An arrangement (often by commercial contract) whereby a woman becomes pregnant and carries a child for another person or couple. She may be artificially inseminated or she may receive **superovulation** drugs (irrespective of the fact that she has no diagnosed fertility problems) or undergo **in vitro fertilization**. She may also receive another woman's IVF embryo, or flushed embryo (**embryo flushing**). Women who bear children under these conditions have been referred to as 'surrogate mothers'. The term 'surrogate' means substitute and is therefore incorrect. A woman who bears a child (whether for herself or otherwise) is a mother.

thrombophlebitis A blood clot (thrombosis) in a vein which may be associated with inflammation.

tubal surgery Micro-surgical attempt to repair a woman's damaged (scarred) fallopian tubes in order to restore a clear passage for her egg to pass down from her ovaries to her womb. This form of infertility treatment has extremely low success rates.

ultrasound scanning (**vaginal ultrasound**) The use of high frequency sound waves to show visual outlines of internal body structures. The picture (or scan) is shown on a television screen. In obstetrics it has been used since the 1960s to visualize the inside of a pregnant woman's abdominal cavity and womb. It is used to diagnose 'abnormalities' in a woman's pregnancy (foetus), to estimate gestational age and to determine the sex of her foetus. Ultrasound also enables doctors to carry out other obstetrical interventions on pregnant women, such as **amniocentesis**. In **in vitro fertilization** treatment, vaginal ultrasound is used to monitor a woman's ovulation and as a method of **egg collection**. Ultrasound is now widely used on pregnant women for antenatal diagnosis, although no long-term studies on its effects on women (or their offspring) have as yet been reported. Also called sonogram.

zona pellucida The membrane covering women's eggs.

zytogenetic testing See **pre-natal diagnosis**.

NOTES ON CONTRIBUTORS

Andrea Belk-Schmehle is the mother of two (adopted) daughters aged three and one and a half years. Previously she worked as a freelance journalist and founded two women's self-experience groups for infertility.

Charlotte Böhm is a German journalist who lives in Hamburg. Since 1985 she has written many critical articles about the new reproductive technologies and genetic engineering. She has also published short stories and plans to write a novel.

Gena Corea is an investigative journalist whose articles have appeared in such publications as *The New York Times, Commonweal, The New Republic Feature Syndicate, Omni,* and *Mother Jones.* In 1977, she published *The Hidden Malpractice: How American Medicine Mistreats Women.* For the past eight years, she has been researching the new reproductive technologies. Her research in this area has appeared in her book *The Mother Machine,* and in chapters in several books including *Test-Tube Women, Made to Order, Birth Control and Controlling Birth, Man-Made Women, Reproductive Technology and Women's Lives.* She is co-chair of the National Coalition Against Surrogacy in the United States.

Christine Crowe is currently researching the development of IVF and embryo research in the United Kingdom and Australia. She has published articles in *Women's Studies International Forum; Made to Order: The Myth of Reproductive and Genetic Progress; The Baby Machines: Commercialisation of Motherhood* (1988); and *The Social Dimensions of Reproductive Technologies* (1989).

Susan Eisenberg, writer, electrician and mother of two, is the author of the poetry book *It's a Good Thing I'm Not Macho*. She has maintained an interest in feminist health issues since working for a collectively-run free clinic for women in the early 1970s.

Titia Esser is a part-time teacher at a secondary school, and a full-time wife and mother of an only child.

Anita Goldman is a Swedish writer and journalist, living in Jerusalem, Israel. She has recently published two books in Sweden *Vara Bibliska Mödrar – Our Biblical Mothers*, a feminist analysis of the Old Testament, and *Den Sista Kvinnan Från Ur – The Last Women from Ur*; a novel on biblical Sarah. Both books deal extensively with the theme of infertility.

Maggie Humm is Dan's mother and Co-ordinator of Women's Studies, North East London Polytechnic. She is the author of *Feminist Criticism* and *An Annotated Bibliography of Feminist Criticism*.

Peter Humm is Dan's father and also the Head of Literary and Cultural Studies at Thames Polytechnic. He has edited two books – *Popular Fictions* and *Dialogue and Difference: English Now and For the Nineties*.

Elizabeth Kane is the pseudonym of the USA's first so-called 'surrogate mother'. In 1980 she gave birth to a baby boy and actively promoted surrogacy out of altruistic motives. She has since revised her position and co-founded the Coalition Against Surrogacy in 1987. With the help of the Massachusetts-based Institute on Women and Technology, Elizabeth Kane has formed a support group for women who have been injured by the surrogate industry. She can be reached at: P.O. Box 311, Appleton, Wisconsin 54912, USA. Her book, *Birthmother*, was published by Harcourt Brace and Jovanovich in 1988.

Lene Koch has recently completed the first Danish survey of the experiences of women on Danish IVF programmes. The survey will be published in 1989. She has an MA in History and Anglosaxon Literature and is the director of KVINFO, Centre for interdisciplinary information on Women's Studies in Copenhagen.

Kirsten Kozolanka is a freelance journalist and writer living in Ottawa. She has just completed a Master of Journalism thesis called 'No Choice in the Matter: The Experience of Infertility'. She has worked as a political press aide and as an editor of a human rights magazine.

Lindsey Napier is a founding member of *Concern*, New South Wales, Australia, the mother of a six-year-old son and a lecturer in the Department of Social Work and Social Policy at Sydney University.

Brigitte Oberauer studies medicine and sociology, and writes for feminist publications.

Ann Pappert is a Canadian journalist, specialising in health issues. She is a frequent contributor to the *Toronto Globe and Mail* and has produced documentaries for the Canadian Broadcasting Corporation. In 1988 she became the first recipient of the Atkinson Fellowship in Public Policy, Canada's largest fellowship for journalists. It was awarded to enable her to research public policy issues in reproductive technologies.

Traute Schönenberg studied chemistry and psychology. Since 1981 she has been working as a therapist at the Feminist Health Centre in Frankfurt. She specializes in feminist therapy and counseling, groups for involuntarily childless women and women who experienced sexual abuse.

Alison Solomon is currently the assistant coordinator of the Tel Aviv Crisis Center for Victims of Sexual Assault in Israel. She is an activist on various women's issues, the most central being reproductive technology. She is the Israeli representative of FINRRAGE. Her aim is to engage in further study in order to achieve her goal of a combined career of counseling with writing.

Ute Winkler is a German sociologist. Her areas of expertise include Women's Studies, Women and the so-called 'Third World' and Reproductive and Genetic Engineering. She works at the Feminist Health Centre in Frankfurt and was a co-organizer of establishing groups for involuntarily childless women and women seeking information about amniocentesis.

RESOURCES

.

Readers who would like to be put in touch with other women who want to form a women's self-experience group should contact one of the following addresses:

FINRRAGE International
P.O. Box 583
London NW3 1RQ
Great Britain

Feministisches Frauengesundheitszentrum
Hamburgerallee 45
6000 Frankfurt
West Germany

CONCERN
P.O. Box 1347
Parramatta
NSW 2150
Australia

FURTHER READING

.

Arditti, Rita; Klein, Renate Duelli; Minden, Shelley, eds. (1984). *Test-Tube Women. What Future for Motherhood?* London and Boston: Pandora Press. Retortenmuetter. *Frauen in den Labors der Menschenzuechter.* Rowohlt Frauen Aktueil. Reinbek, 1985.

Conseil du statut de la femme (1988). *Sortir la Maternité du Laboratoire.* Gouvernement du Quebec. (French and English Conference Texts).

Corea, Gena (1985). *The Mother Machine. Reproductive Technologies from Artificial Insemination to Artificial Wombs.* Harper & Row, New York; The Women's Press, London (1988).

Corea, Gena et al. (1985). *Man-Made Women. How New Reproductive Technologies Affect Women.* Hutchinson Press, London/Indiana University Press, Bloomington (1987).

Die Gruenen im Bundestag. AK Frauenpolitik & Sozialwissenschaftliche Forschung und Praxis fuer Frauen e.V. Köuln. Hrsg. (1986). *Frauen gegen Gentechnik und Reproduktionstechnik.* Verlag Kölner Volksblatt.

Fetz, Anita; Koechlin, Florianne und Mascarin, Ruth, eds. (1986). *Gene, Frauen und Millionen.* Basel: Rotpunktverlag.

Hansen, Friedrich und Kollek, Regine (1985). *Gen-Technologie. Die Soziale Waffe.* Hamburg: Konkret Literatur Verlag.

Hartmann, Betsy (1987). *Reproductive Rights and Wrongs. The Global Politics of Population Control and Contraceptive Choice.* New York: Harper & Row.

Holmes, Helen B.; Hoskins, Betty and Gross, Michael, eds. (1981). *The Custom-Made Child? – Women-Centred Perspectives.* New Jersey, USA: Humana Press.

Homans, Hilary, ed. (1985). *The Sexual Politics of Reproduction.* Aldershot: Gower Publishing Company.

Kane, Elizabeth (1988). *Birth Mother. The Story of America's First Legal Surrogate Mother.* Harcourt Brace Jovanovich, San Diego.

Kollek, Regine; Tappeser, Beatrix und Altner, Guenter, eds. (1986). *Die ungeklaerten Gefahrenpotentiale der Gentechnologie.* München: J. Schweitzer Verlag.

Lasker, Judith N. and Borg, Susan (1987). *In Search of Parenthood and Coping with High-Tech Conception.* Boston: Beacon Press; London: Pandora Press, 1988.

MacNeil, Maureen et al. (1989). *The Social Dimension of Reproductive Technologies.* London: MacMillan.

Overall, Christine (1987). *Ethics and Human Reproduction. A Feminist Analysis.* London and Sydney: Allen & Unwin.

Pauritsch, Gertrude et al., eds. (1988). *Kinder Machen. Strategien der Kontrolle weiblicher Fruchtbarkeit.* Wiener Frauenverlag.

Reproductive and Genetic Engineering: Journal of International Feminist Analysis. New York: Pergamon Press (1st issue April 1988).

Roth, Claudia, ed. (1987). *Genzeit. Die Industrialisierung von Pflanze, Tier und Mensch. Ermittlungen in der Schweiz.* Zürich: Limmat Verlag.

Scutt, Jocelynne, ed. (1988). *The Baby Machine: Commercialisation of Motherhood.* Melbourne: McCulloch.

Sozialwissenschaftliche Forschung und Praxis für Frauen, eds. (1986). *Frauen zwischen Auslese und Ausmerze. Beiträge zur feministischen Theorie und Praxis, 14.* Köln.

Spallone, Patricia and Steinberg, Deborah Lynn eds. (1987). *Made to Order. The Myth of Reproductive and Genetic Progress.* Oxford and New York: The Athene Series. Pergamon Press.

Stanworth, Michelle, ed. (1987). *Reproductive Technologies: Gender, Motherhood and Medicine.* Cambridge: Polity Press.

Straeter, Ulrike (1988). *Ungewollt Kinderlos – Was kann man Tun und Lassen?* Heidelberg: Verlag für Medizin Dr Ewald Fischer.

Weikert, Aurelia; Riegler, Johanna; Trallori, Lisbeth N. Hrsg. (1987). *Schöne Neue Männerwelt. Beiträge zu Gen – und*

Fortpflanzungstechnologien. Wien: Verlag Gesellschaftskritik.

Zipfel, Gaby. Hg. (1987). *Reproduktionsmedizin. Die Enteignung der weiblichen Natur*. Hamburg: Konkret Literatur Verlag.

INDEX

.

90-532

M

WOMEN'S HEALTH RESOURCE CENTRE
REGIONAL WOMEN'S HEALTH CENTRE
790 BAY STREET 8TH FLOOR
TORONTO ON M5G 1N9
416-351-3716 / 3717